HEARTLANDS

TRAVELS IN THE TIBETAN WORLD

MICHAEL BUCKLEY

SUMMERSDALE

Summersdale Publishers Ltd
46 West Street
Chichester
West Sussex
PO19 1RP
UK
www.summersdale.com

Printed and bound in Great Britain.

ISBN 1 84024 209 4

Maps by Dominic Bradshaw.
Photographs copyright © Michael Buckley 2002

About the Author

Michael Buckley has travelled widely in Tibet, China, Central Asia and the Himalayas. He is author or co-author of eight books about Asian and Himalayan travel, including *Tibet: the Bradt Travel Guide*, and Moon Handbooks' *Vietnam, Cambodia and Laos*. He is author of *Cycling to Xian*, a travel narrative about cycling across China and Tibet, and has contributed stories to *Travelers' Tales Tibet*, *Travelers' Tales India* and *Travelers' Tales Thailand*. Buckley thrives on adventuring in remote places – whether rappelling from the treetops in Costa Rica, trekking through the jungles of Borneo, cave-kayaking in the south of Thailand, or bicycling the Karakoram Highway. He sees travel as transformation – a constant learning experience on the road.

Author's Note

This book is based on a series of trips involving more than twelve months of travel, spread over the period 1989 to 1999. My travels embrace the Tibetan cultural sphere of influence: Himalayan India, Mongolia, Kham and Amdo, occupied Tibet, Nepal and Bhutan – the vast and majestic region of the Tibetan plateau. The three major sections are based more on chronological travels and theme than on geographic areas. I think of the three-part division as serving up a meal: 'Chilling Out in Shangri-La' as an appetiser, 'Hitting the Roof' as the main course, and 'Tales from Tiny Kingdoms' as dessert.

Inspiration, Insights, Thanks

First and foremost, my heartfelt gratitude goes out to a number of Tibetans I met, but who cannot be named here (their identities have also been concealed in the book). Their fearlessness and candour provided the main inspiration for this book.

On-the-road inspiration was provided by fellow travellers: Scott Harrison and D'Arcy Richardson, Thysje Strypens, Terry and James Anstey, Kat Meahl, Gary McCue and Kathy Butler, Pat and Baiba Morrow, and a host of others. Special thanks to fellow conspirators Lesley Thomson, Derek Henson, Jane Garnett, and Gerry.

Some trips written about here would have been tough to impossible to tackle without the intervention of Divine Agents (outfitters and travel agents, that is): Gord and Gail Konantz of Everest Trekking, Vancouver; Tashi and Nancy Sherpa, Kathmandu; and Shelley Guardia of Great Expeditions, Vancouver.

It was with the help of another Divine Agent – the literary kind – that this manuscript found its way into publication: special thanks to Robert Mackwood for seeing this project through its final stages.

Parts of this book have previously appeared in *The Globe & Mail, Outpost Magazine, Escape, Himalaya Magazine, The Georgia Straight* and the anthology *Travelers' Tales India.*

Thus of the whole enormous area which was once the spirited domain of Tibetan culture and religion, stretching from Ladakh in the west to the borders of the Chinese provinces of Szechuan and Yunnan in the east, from the Himalayas in the south to the Mongolian steppes and the vast wastes of northern Tibet, now only Bhutan seems to survive as the one resolute and self-contained representative of a fast-disappearing civilisation.

– Hugh Richardson and David Snellgrove
A Cultural History of Tibet

My main interest is the preservation of Tibetan Buddhist culture and Buddhism. In that level, the national boundary not important. So therefore, from Ladakh up to Arunachal in the Himalayan range, then Tibet, then further north, you see, Mongolia, Inner Mongolia and in Russian Federation republics – Kalmykia, Tuva, Buryatia ... So all these thirteen, fourteen millions follow same religion – Tibetan Buddhism. Of course, you see, in the case of Mongolia, different language, different script, different race or nation, but same culture, same Tibetan Buddhist faith ... Whether people consider me as a leader or anything ... that's not my botheration. My side is simply follower of Buddha Sakyamuni and Buddhist monk.

– HH the Dalai Lama, interviewed by the author
Dharamsala, 1998

Wherein our Narrator visits the ancient Lands of the Tibetan Realm and finds there many strange and wonderful Aspects, including karaoke Bars, giant Phalluses and bizarre Phenomena such as: the wicked Witch healing Oracle, a High Lama encased in a Statue, the Dance of the Day of Judgement, a magical black Hat and other things that fly in the Face of Reason; speaking of which, he also gets an Earful from New Agers in India and survives Interrogation by Chinese Police — for the Tibetan Realm is a political Hot Potato and not a Place for a Writer to venture into lightly . . .

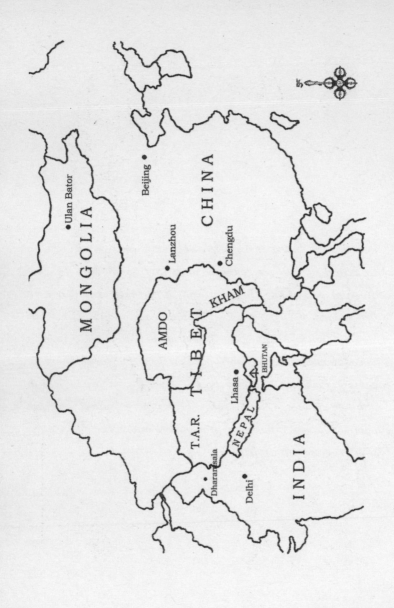

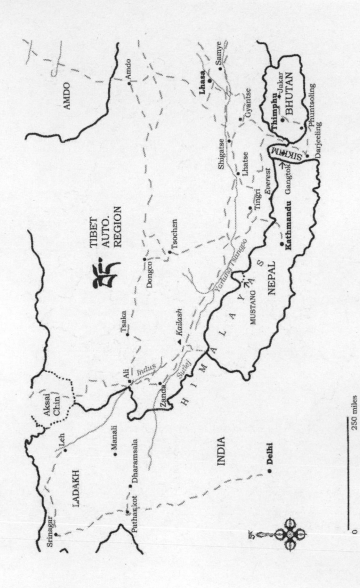

Contents

Introduction

Black Box Experience

Dhondup told me a story about the small village he comes from in eastern Tibet, where he lived before he escaped to Nepal. One day, the village headman gathered everyone together and said that he would show them the whole world in a little black box. The villagers howled with laughter. He was either completely cracked, or maybe, just maybe, he was some kind of magician.

That night, everybody gathered round the little black box, people who'd never heard of Elvis or The Beatles, Kennedy or the Berlin Wall, McDonald's or Pizza Hut. The box crackled into action. The villagers marvelled at what they saw: tall buildings, strange cars, strange women in high heels, acrobats tying their limbs in knots, animals they'd never seen before, orgies of kung fu fighting. This was no longer a little black box; it was Pandora's box, fuelling fantasies, unleashing powerful forces – and demons. The villagers stayed up late, mesmerised by this sorcery.

In fact, they stayed up late all week, glued to the box. Then, suddenly, without warning, the Chinese-made TV set started 'snowing'. It was poorly put together and produced only snow patterns and static – no pictures. Life in the village went back to normal. They'd all seen snow before.

But had they seen the world in a box, as promised? Probably not, according to Dhondup. Not the world as the Tibetans know it. The Tibetan concept of 'world' is both simple and very complex. Complex: to Tibetan Buddhists, the earthly world is an illusion; it is only one of an infinite number of worlds, some of which exist in other dimensions, invisible to most mortals. Simple: in Tibetan lore, the idea of 'world' is limited to the Tibetan plateau. They have no reason to journey beyond it – they only travel for the purposes of trade or pilgrimage; otherwise they stay with their yak herds and barley crops. The Tibetan plateau – the size of Western Europe – already seems vast enough to them.

Russia they've heard of, China they know all too well, India is the source of their Buddhist faith, Nepal and Mongolia they know from trading links, as well as tiny, distant kingdoms like Bhutan and Mustang. The rest of the world is a blur. Tibetan knowledge of cosmology is somewhere back in the pre-Copernican age. Tibetans are essentially flat-earthers with a twist: some believe the world to be triangular or trapezoidal in shape rather than square with four corners.

I can pinpoint the exact date I stumbled across the parallel world of the Tibetans. It was quite a different black box experience. It was a film in a cinema – the night I saw *Lost Horizon*, shown as part of a film festival. This 1930s Hollywood classic was shot in black and white. A group of Westerners crashland in the mysterious Tibetan kingdom of Shangri-La, where knowledge is exalted, where goldmines take care of any cashflow problems, where the rooms are centrally heated, and where the lamas live to well over a hundred years. The main luxury at Shangri-La is time, the slippery gift that often eludes those in the West.

There wasn't a single Tibetan in the cast of *Lost Horizon*, nor a single line of Tibetan dialogue spoken. The director, Frank Capra, shot the whole thing on an enormous sound stage in Hollywood, using Indians from San Diego to play Tibetans. But it was heady stuff all the same. The special effects on the mountain sequences were superb, imparting the terror of avalanches, whiteouts and deep crevasses. I was spellbound by the story, yet was at a loss to explain why it had such a powerful impact. Growing up in Sydney, Australia, where there are no mountains, and nothing remotely resembling a temple, might have accounted for the fascination. Summiting the highest peak in Australia, Kosciusko, is a half-hour stroll.

The word 'Shangri-La' made its debut with the publication of the world's first paperback novel, *Lost Horizon*, in 1933. No sooner had the British author, James Hilton, created Shangri-La than he seems to have lost control of it. He was quickly summoned to Hollywood to assist with the film version, which became a box office blockbuster. Hilton never wrote a sequel to his wildly successful novel, although he left the way open for one, with the lead character still going strong. He died in 1954 in California, not living to see Shangri-La become a synonym for paradise, adopted as the logo of Nepalese trekking agencies, an Asian hotel chain and beach resorts from Mexico to Fiji.

Shangri-La's power lies in its simplicity, serenity and spirituality – values lacking in Western culture. *Lost Horizon* is a metaphor for our times: a land of harmony where the values of civilisation are preserved during times of war and great destruction. In fact, the film was widely circulated among the armed services during the Second World War to boost morale and to bolster hope that such a place existed. The film created a mental map and sparked my interest in this mythical realm.

But Shangri-La, I discovered, was not entirely mythical. There were real places like this, with towering Tibetan monasteries backed by magical landscapes and snowcapped peaks. The inspiration for the legend came from the ancient Tibetan utopian kingdom of Shambhala. And there are Tibetan tales of the hidden valleys or *beyul*, consecrated by a great Tibetan guru. Clues are contained in Tibetan guidebooks on how to find them, but they are very dangerous and difficult to reach. Similar to Shangri-La, the hidden valleys provide retreats for the righteous in times of invasion and persecution of the Buddhist faith, and in periods of world destruction. Twenty-one such valleys are described, each a kind of earthly paradise, scattered through the Himalayas in Tibet, Nepal, Sikkim and Bhutan.

My fascination increased; I wanted to see this terrain with my own eyes. I wanted to make the leap from mythological to geographical, from illusory to real. There was a particular image – a pivotal moment – from the film that stayed with me. It's where the 'visitors' mount a snow-pelted pass buffeted by howling winds, and descend into a quiet green valley, the Valley of the Blue Moon, into Shangri-La. It was incredible how you could cross over from one world to the next as if through some kind of doorway or portal.

Lost Horizon was released in 1937. At the time Tibet was independent: it remained neutral during both world wars, a kind of Switzerland in Asia. In 1950 the Chinese invaded. Since then, art treasures spanning millennia and libraries stocked with ancient Indian classics have been ransacked, monasteries dynamited to rubble, monks and nuns savagely killed, and Tibet's pristine environment has been trashed. The Chinese have systematically plundered Tibet's untouched resources and attempted to wipe out its culture and people. The setting for the mythical Shangri-La itself faces annihilation.

For the longest time, the doors to Tibet remained firmly bolted. Tibet was only accessible to well-heeled group tours. The tariff to visit was extortionate; tour groups were shepherded by their Chinese charges and manoeuvred so they had little contact with Tibetan people. Then, for some inexplicable reason, in the mid-1980s the Chinese abruptly flung open the creaky doors of the high plateau to all and sundry, including backpackers (this was an experimental phase – these later turned out to be revolving doors, prone to sudden closures). I was in there like a shot.

The place defied all expectations. Maybe it was the rarefied air, maybe it was the high-altitude sun, but everything looked so fresh, so different, like seeing with the eyes of a child. The colours practically glowed. I felt like my brain was being emptied and cleansed: Tibet was an encounter with a culture whose belief system ran counter to everything I knew. I was eager to see – and learn – more, to make a personal pilgrimage. After two visits – one bicycling across the plateau – I was a Tibet addict.

I got caught up in the conundrum of Tibet itself. How had the world allowed Tibet to get into such a mess, to slide into such a moral morass? Why wasn't any major power doing anything about the Chinese military who had turned it into the world's largest remaining colony? How could governments turn a blind eye and watch a peace-loving people crushed? Why wasn't the United Nation doing anything about Tibet?

Then, as abruptly as they had opened them, the Chinese closed the doors again on the heels of Tibetan pro-independence rioting in 1987. They beat the living daylights out of the protesting Tibetans while the governments of the world stood back and did nothing. The news headlines ran: CRACKDOWN IN TIBET; TIBET IN TURMOIL; STORM ON LOST HORIZON; CURFEW IN LHASA; TIBET UNDER SIEGE AFTER

RIOT DEATHS. The Chinese ruthlessly crushed any protest, firing on unarmed Tibetans, killing scores and injuring hundreds. The situation deteriorated in the late 1980s: more protests, many more deaths and arrests, more brutality, the imposition of martial law in Lhasa, tanks rumbling through the streets.

Travel to Tibet at the time was out of the question. So instead I went to Ladakh, in northern India. Though politically splintered, the Tibetans share the same culture, religion and language, whether dwelling in northern India, south-west China, Nepal or Bhutan. In Ladakh, I discovered that stepping back four or five centuries was not only easy, it was downright relaxing. Time and space have a completely different feel in Ladakh. Get yourself to a place high in the Himalayan snowcaps with cliff-hanging monasteries, chanting maroon-robed monks and cavorting shaggy yaks and you have the blissful antidote to time-squeezed Western ways. Immerse yourself in a stillness and silence that run deep. A thousand years deep.

I started to spend more time in these slowed-down Tibetan realms. Zoned out in Shangri-La, far from computers, MTV, appointments, calendars, tax returns, mental fatigue and data overload. This is about as far from the digital world – from Nerdistan and Techistan – as you can get: the Tibetans haven't even hurdled the wood-block printing era. They have no word for barcode or computer chip; they've never even seen these things. And yet we can learn a lot from these people. I love the hardy nature of the Tibetans, their self-reliance, their resilience in the face of extreme adversity, their calm demeanour, their ribald sense of humour, and their bizarre beliefs, which seem to be not of this world, but of entirely another.

These elements have kindled my passion for travelling to remote Tibetan lands, and my passion for writing about them, too. You need to be highly motivated to reach these places because the obstacles are formidable. The Tibetan plateau can generate some of the most ferocious and hostile weather conditions in the world: howling wind and biting snow on high-altitude passes. But the greatest hurdles are closed-door politics and stonewalling officialdom. Of course, if you have money coming out your earholes, access is easier. But minus the money, here lies the great challenge and the adventure: how to sneak past the cretins guarding the gates.

My wish-list looked pretty hopeless back in 1989: the kingdom of Mustang in Nepal was firmly closed, Mongolia was bolted shut, travel to the kingdom of Bhutan was severely restricted, and Tibet itself was under martial law. For the exploring spirit in me, the Tibetan badlands provided all the impetus I needed for indulging in outrageous travel – for sating a serious case of wanderlust. I was determined to take on the impossible, to surmount the obstacles, to reach my dream destinations. Travel feeds off dreams; I never let go of those dreams. The Tibetan way of life is fast disappearing; I hope that this book raises awareness on that score, for there is much to learn from their ancient civilisation.

In 1997, exactly 60 years after the release of *Lost Horizon*, Columbia-TriStar released another big-screen effort, *Seven Years in Tibet*, about Austrian adventurer Heinrich Harrer's remarkable wartime escape to Tibet to find sanctuary there. It put quite a different spin on Shangri-La: one man's vision of the last years before Tibet itself was engulfed in war and chaos. A spate of big-screen films on Tibet followed, *Kundun* and *Windhorse* among them. Through them, in the imagination of many, Tibet has become the world's last great battleground between the forces of good and evil – a kind of real life *Star Wars*. But the reality is far more complex; this book delves into the twilight zone between fable and fact …

PART ONE

CHILLING OUT IN SHANGRI-LA

1

LAND OF THE BROKEN MOON

Bicycling the high passes of Ladakh

Out of the window, a dazzling set of snowcaps rising out of the plains: I am mesmerised by the immense domain of ridges and crests, buttresses and glaciers – the Zanskar range. Geography lessons have never been so vivid. After the chaos of boarding at the airport, a civilised breakfast in the clouds, and Leh is only an hour away. *You lucky dog! You did it! You're on your way!* On your way to the cool highlands of Ladakh aboard a 737. And back there in the sweltering heat of Delhi are the poor bastards who didn't get on. Then the plane turns – I glance at my watch. Half an hour gone. Where is Leh? Why is the pilot banking?

'Clouds!' groans Tashi, my fellow passenger. 'Too many clouds!' He slaps his armrest in despair. We are heading back to Delhi. A hailstorm and high winds in Leh make it too dangerous to land. *Son of a bitch – that's torn it!* Back to that awful sweatbath with its oppressive humidity, con men, aggressive hawkers, touts, beggars, horrendous traffic and fumes ... *God, it's back to square one.* No reservation, no flights, nothing. If I can't get a plane into Leh, I'm sunk – the road into Ladakh won't be open for at least a month because heavy snowfalls this year have sealed off Zoji La, the approach pass to the region.

Back in Delhi I wait for the miscellaneous baggage to come off the plane. Down the carousel comes a dog (small, white, terrified) in a cage, a cine-camera tripod (half sticking out of a smashed-in case), a set of golf clubs (where on earth could you play golf in Leh?) and my bike box. Back to square one. But wait – a rumour about a special flight being put on. The disgruntled passengers troop over to the Indian Airlines counter. To our surprise, the clerk announces a special flight the next day. I shove my ticket forward. Three Westerners I met in the queue decide to split a room at the airport hotel.

Tuesday is a repeat of Monday, but earlier, and much worse. The Ladakhis have slept out with their baggage, right at the check-in counter. Sylvia, the French traveller who is getting our tickets validated for us, has her backside fondled. She turns round and clouts the offender. I am carrying on a shouting match with an airline official who refuses to take the bike box, saying it's not allowed as baggage. Or does he want a 100-rupee bill? I finally get him to weigh it – it comes out at 35 pounds, which is below the permitted weight on my ticket. He pushes the box behind him somewhere – maybe it goes on, who knows?

Two hours later, we are flying low over Leh airfield, circling around the snowpeaks. I can see a monastery below – so close I can even see monks on the rooftop. Suddenly the pilot banks sharply and nosedives. The plane hits the tarmac roughly, the overhead bins shake and rattle, a panel at the back of the plane drops off revealing a large array of wiring. For a moment I wonder if we will hurtle onward without brakes and smash into a mountainside, but with a horrendous roar the flaps go up and the plane comes to a jarring halt. The Ladakhis on the plane hoot and clap and holler for all they're worth – we have landed.

In the tiny terminal building at Leh airfield, I find the bike box. The bike appears to be bruised but not broken – it is loaded into a van, commandeered for the run into town. The van ride is free – it's just that the driver, called Tsering, manages the Antelope Guesthouse, and that's where the van ends up. If you still have the energy at this altitude to walk off with your backpack and look for another hotel, good luck. I am shown room 108 – an auspicious number.

★★★★★

I feel quite at home in Leh. I have put the nightmare of Delhi behind me: traded its heat and squalor for the cool silence of Leh. Leh has desert, low housing, a sense of space. At 11,500 feet, the air is brisk and refreshing. The area near my guesthouse holds tiny bread shops, cafés, clothing shops, tailors, small businesses. I feel more at home here than I do at home. I can spend my time the way I want to – riding, hiking, exploring, reading, writing, taking photos. There is another reason for feeling at home here: this place reminds me of Lhasa – the altitude, the desert moonscape, the monasteries (*gompas*), the squat buildings, the people. This is more than coincidence: Leh was once part of western Tibet, and for centuries it looked to Lhasa for its cultural and religious direction.

Leh used to be the meeting point of caravans from India and Central Asia. Merchants from Lhasa, Hotan, Kashgar and Skardu converged with those coming in from Kashmir and Punjab. Cotton and woollen clothes or tea and coral from India were traded for gold and silver from Turkestan, or wool and salt from Tibet. In the late 1930s, problems in Turkestan disrupted trade, and Leh's prosperity rapidly dwindled. In the 1940s most of the other trade routes closed down. The present road route into Leh from Srinagar follows the old caravan route, but for quite different reasons – it is maintained as a military road, and to bring tourists in. The road was constructed in 1962 as the result of Indo-Chinese border disputes; Leh is an Indian military garrison. It was opened to foreigners in 1974, and since then tourism has become the mainstay of the local economy.

I've decided to tackle the road by mountain bike for the hell of it. People tell me that it is too dangerous for a bicycle, that I will be run over by a truck, robbed, mugged, knifed by tribesmen, kidnapped by terrorists, get sick, freeze to death – things like that. There is, to be sure, some danger involved, but I need that intensity. The travel magazines harp on travel as escapism: *Escape into Summer*; *Escape the Crowds*; *The Ultimate Escape*; *Twenty Great Escapes*; *Escape Routes* – but the truth is, you don't escape. You come face to face … with yourself. Travel is the ultimate way of reinventing yourself. Freed from all the advertising, TV, nonsense and trivia that bedevil routine existence, life reprioritises itself.

★★★★★

A curious place, Leh. After all the mysterious images you build up from reading about the place, you find it is full of Indian army patrols, hardware shops, carpet shops, trucks, video rental shops and *Rambo* posters. It has a mosque, a legacy of Kashmiri Muslim invasion, and a cinema that shows terrible films from Bombay. Beneath that veneer lies a much older Leh: bazaar, polo ground, ruined palace. On the main street are old Ladakhi women with winged stovepipe hats, upturned shoes, long cloaks and sheepskins, crouched over piles of radishes and potatoes, fighting off wayward holy cows. Outside the town are terraced farms and apricot trees in blossom. The motorised traffic is Anglo-Indian – left-hand drive Ambassador taxis (copies of 1950s Morris Oxfords), Enfield motorcycles, and Ashok Leyland buses.

Leh's royal palace is a splendid sight. It towers above the town, eight storeys of it; great snowcaps loom in the distance. The palace commands the entire valley, but inside it is an empty shell. In a small chapel, some superb clay statuary and masks attest to its seventeenth-century splendour. The rest is home to flocks of pigeons; crumbling, decayed, beams fallen down, intricate woodwork scattered. Even in decay, this colossal fortress-palace has a definite presence: it resembles Lhasa's Potala Palace, and was built at roughly the same time.

Although originally settled by Tibetans, Ladakh splintered into separate kingdoms around AD 900 – Ladakh, Guge and Burang, Zanskar and Spiti. The kingdoms of Ladakh and Zanskar changed hands numerous times over the centuries, while Guge and Burang were eventually wrestled back by the Tibetans.

King Sengye Namgyal built Leh's palace in the early seventeenth century, as well as the monasteries of Hemis, Stakna and Chemre. He was the most famous of the great warrior kings of Ladakh: he even threatened central Tibet. But by the end of the seventeenth century, Ladakh's power had declined, leaving it vulnerable to Muslim incursions. During the Dogra war of 1836, Leh's palace was besieged and partially destroyed by the Kashmiris. The royal family was exiled to Stok, south of Leh, where their descendants still live. The palace would never again be a royal residence. In 1947, Ladakh was absorbed into the new

Indian state of Jammu and Kashmir; Pakistan and China both seized chunks of Ladakh in subsequent border wars. Although royalty has largely disappeared from Ladakh, neighbouring Zanskar still has two kings. The king of Zanskar lives in Padam, and the king of Zangla controls one castle and four villages.

★★★★★

May 9th: afternoon tea in the garden of the Antelope guesthouse with Sonam, a trekking and mountaineering guide. Sonam is a very fit-looking Ladakhi with blazing eyes, jet black hair and a missing front tooth. The tips of his forefinger and thumb are missing too – lost to frostbite, he says. He has a gift for telling stories. He tells us about all the weirdos he's guided through Ladakh. About an Austrian woman who arrived with her own dogs for a ski-trek at the height of winter. About Shirley MacLaine, who just loved the place – all those monasteries, shrines and extra-terrestrial architectural forms. And she was perfectly at home with the concept of reincarnation, offering lurid sexual vignettes from her own past lives.

Sonam talks about his worst flight: the pilot, co-pilot and the navigator were having an argument and refused to talk to each other with the result that the landing gear was not lowered and the plane landed on its belly. He tells us about the hundred trucks trapped in Zoji La Pass in the autumn of 1986. A truck had stalled, causing a bottleneck. Then it snowed. Drivers and passengers were either frozen to death or killed by avalanches when they attempted to walk out. Only a few souls survived. The official death toll was never released, but may have been three hundred, or maybe a thousand. He tells me that Ladakh is *La-Dakh* – Land of the Passes. It is also called Land of the Broken Moon, perhaps because of its barren landscape.

★★★★★

The flight from Srinagar has brought three zany Brits – Peter, Tracy and Edward – a Swiss couple, and two American women.

Trust the British to find a pub in Leh. It's a grimy place down a back alley, with wooden tables and Ladakhi men huddled around them, smoking. Indian beer and spirits are served, as well as Tibetan home-brewed barley beer, *chang*. On the walls are some risqué posters – well, risqué by Indian standards – pin-ups of female Indian film stars. The circle from the Antelope has widened now: Laura, Peter, Tracy and Edward, and John. Laura, one of the American women, is doing a Master's degree in Hindi; Tracy and Edward are the most unlikely solicitor-barrister combination you'd ever want to meet; John the Scot is traipsing around the world – his last job was opal-mining in Australia. He's had a haircut in Leh: short back and sides, Star Trek-style, and looks just like Mr Spock.

Peter, an astrophysics researcher, entertains us with lurid stories of space launches: how chimpanzees in space got out of control and evacuated everywhere. No wonder he hadn't got his fellowship renewed. Other moonlore: the second man on the moon, Buzz Aldrin, suffered severe post-lunar depression, with alcoholism, a nervous breakdown and divorce, because his wasn't the first footprint. And the moon was developing into a junkyard – discarded tail sections of landing vehicles, moon cars, tools, bags of rubbish and human waste. We have altered the moon in our minds, made it more mundane, says Peter, but the perspective from outer space has forever altered our perceptions, too. Imagine how terrifying, how humbling it must be, to look down from space and see Earth the size of a tennis ball.

★★★★★

I'd been waiting a few days to acclimatise before riding the bicycle. I wheeled the newly assembled bike out of the guesthouse to go for a short spin. A silly grin spread across my face – the impossible now looked possible. I was at the starting point of my route and the bike was still in one piece.

Riding around Leh, it struck me that there were only a few Indian clunkers in town. The locals didn't seem to use bikes. But

I found a small bike shop in the bazaar, and discovered it was just too early in the season for any biking. The locals were unanimous in their verdict about the mountain bike: where could they get their hands on one? They recognised the strength and lightness of the bike, and they were stunned by its uphill performance.

To acclimatise, I biked to temples in the valley, to Shey and Tikse Gompa. There was a Tibetan refugee camp at Chonglongsar where I dropped in on Rinjing, whom I'd met in the bazaar at Leh. Rinjing and his family invited me for lunch. I showed him the tiny *Om Mani Padme Hum* stickers, in Tibetan script, that I'd placed on the wheel rims. *Om Mani Padme Hum* is the sacred mantra attached to prayer wheels in Tibet: the holder accrues merit by spinning the prayer. My wheel rims, therefore, were part of a computerised merit accrual system: as the wheels span around, the computer at the front recorded mileage, which could later be calculated at the number of revolutions. I was proud of this new device for computerised pilgrimage.

'How do you like my mantras?'

'Very interesting,' said Rinjing. 'But take them off.'

'What?'

'They are below the belt. You cannot have this chant below the belt. Mantras are holy and must be in a high place. The monks will throw stones at you if they see this.'

Crestfallen, I removed them all, except for one hidden on the back wheel.

The closest cycling destination was Spituk Gompa, about four miles out of town, near the airport, and downhill all the way. This was the place I'd seen as the plane was landing in Leh. As I gained the rooftop of the *gompa*, there was a horrendous racket when the daily flight circled round the valley, coming in so low as to make any attempt at peaceful study and prayer impossible.

The monks were delighted with the bike – they played with the gears and took it for short spins. They fed me, and showed me a sand mandala that was in progress. It was spread over a large flat area, perhaps five feet in diameter. It was a complicated coloured pattern that the monks had been working on for a week, getting ready for the full moon event of Buddha's birthday. Then, at the end of the festivities, it would be dispersed. Take it or leave it: all is impermanent. The sand mandala is cohesive and beautiful – then scattered to the wind and water. It is a metaphor for the Tibetan world itself: once close-knit and strong, now scattered, fractured, cast to the winds. In the seventh and eighth centuries, Tibetan kings ruled over a huge area, extending from northern India to the frontiers of the Chinese and Turkish empires. The warring Tibetans were a force to be reckoned with in Central Asia. But in the ninth century, internal rivalries and skulduggery led to assassinations and precipitated the break up of the Tibetan Empire into kingdoms and fiefdoms. After this, the Tibetan world was never again unified in a political sense: it was welded together by common beliefs and culture, and by commercial and religious ties to central Tibet. Tibetans are essentially tribal – each to his or her own fiefdom. Ladakh broke away from Lhasa as early as the tenth century; Bhutan waged war with forces from Lhasa in the seventeenth century. And present-day China has its beady eyes on the remnants of greatness: on the kingdoms of Ladakh, Zanskar, Nepal, Sikkim and Bhutan.

*****

The oracle's house at Sabu was unmarked; it looked like any other Ladakhi farmhouse, except that it had two Bruce Lee posters mounted near the gateway. Four of us – Peter, Tracy, Edward and myself – had come by bus from Leh, a one-hour journey. It had taken us a further forty minutes of detouring through fields to reach the right house. We were motioned in. The main room had no windows – the thick, windowless walls provided good insulation in the harsh winters. The only light was provided by a squarish hole cut out of the ceiling where the stove found its vent and incense curled up through the shaft of sunlight. In traditional Ladakhi style, the room was largely bare except for one wall, which was stacked to the ceiling with brass and copper cauldrons, silver plates and goblets, ladles, thermoses and huge teapots. In another section was a magnificent stove with a bright copper sheen and a few pieces of turquoise studded in it.

Squatting on the floor was a family: mother, son, daughter and elderly father. There are many kinds of oracles in the Tibetan tradition of Buddhism. We knew little about the Ayu Lhamo except that she was a healing oracle, reputed to be able to divine and even cure diseases. An older lady entered the room, nodded, gave us a smile and settled down on a cushion to open her bag. The bag contained her ceremonial clothing. Her? She looked an unlikely shaman – a sweet old lady.

We watched spellbound as she underwent a transformation. She arranged some ritual objects around her, then picked up a small drum and started chanting, a chant that was only interrupted when she sucked her breath in. She had her back to us as she put on the oracle's vestments: an apron, a top, a crown. She waved around a small *dorje*, a Tibetan ritual thunderbolt sceptre. The chant went on, long and monotonous, presumably calling upon Bon gods, in the shamanist tradition. Her assistant sprinkled rice about, and spilled libations of *chang* on the floor.

When the Ayu Lhamo finally turned around, she was a completely different person – bright-eyed, wild, powerful – a witch, a woman possessed by a different spirit. Her voice had suddenly altered to a high-pitched cackle with a faster pace. By the time she'd finished this dirge, not only was she in a trance, but we were all in a trance. The oracle took out a silver bowl and a short stick, and passed the *dorje* over the incense burner.

The chanting stopped. She boomed directions at the Ladakhi family, she hissed and shouted, and her eyes flashed. The first patient, an old man, was propelled forward on his knees. He was in such a state of terror that two others had to support his arms and hold him there. The oracle screamed at him and hit him on the head with her stick. She passed the *dorje* over his head. She was holding not a stick, as I'd first thought, but a wooden tube. This she applied to a place near the man's eye, and began sucking on it. She spat into the silver bowl and showed it around; inside was a sickly brown sludge. She had sucked the evil spirits out of him – he must've had an eye condition. The old man looked at the bowl and almost passed out.

Then the son of the family came forward on his knees. He was braver, and needed no assistance. The oracle didn't dwell on preliminaries; she barked some terse directions and the man lifted up his shirt, exposing his stomach. The oracle leaned over and clamped onto his stomach like a leech. She sucked on the exposed flesh, and the man's eyes rolled. And then the oracle let go, and spat into the silver bowl: more brown sludge. The man had a fresh weal on his stomach. Two more cases were treated. The procedure immediately brought to mind the medieval precepts of medicine: using leeches to suck blood out and thus rid the body of poisons and balance the humours of blood, phlegm, choler and melancholy.

I was feeling quite shaken; this shamanism flew in the face of all that I was brought up to believe: that 'doctors' do not rely on evil spirits and magic; that medicine has rational explanations for each malady, and rational cures. The oracle brought back feelings I hadn't experienced since childhood – weird, scary things. Did magic spells and trances really work? Were storybook fables really true? And I was thinking that travel turned you into a child again – everything was fresh and amazing, and I was fumbling with new concepts – it seemed like there was unlimited time to explore.

The oracle and her assistant glanced in our direction. We looked at each other. Did we want any brown sludge removed today? Peter, the maniac, went forward on his knees. He bared his stomach. The young assistant enquired, 'Where ill?' Peter didn't reply, he looked straight at the oracle instead. The Ayu Lhamo passed her *dorje* over his head, then over the incense burner, leaned forward and clamped onto his stomach. Peter grimaced. The oracle finally let go, spat into her bowl, and showed Peter the results. We all craned forward for a glimpse; Peter's prognosis was a lot better – only a trace of brown sludge.

The assistant sounded a ritual bell. The oracle muttered in a hoarse, low voice. She shook, shivered, trembled, and threw handfuls of rice around the room. She was coming out of the trance. And soon she was the sweet old lady she had been when she walked in, smiling, relaxed, giving us handfuls of rice to take with us for good luck. The smiles on the faces of the Ladakhi family were real – the oracle had given them new hope, renewed spirit.

'All right, Peter,' I said, as we left the house. 'Tell us about it.'

'Abso-bloody-lutely not!'

'Oh, come on, tell us. What was wrong with you?'

'No way. She knew what was wrong. She *knew* it.'

'Bet he's got cirrhosis of the liver from all that drinking,' said Tracy.

'No, I'll bet he's got the squits!' said Edward, 'squits' being slang for loose bowels.

Peter declined to reveal any of what had gone through his mind. Maybe nothing.

'Couldn't have been too bad anyway,' Tracy concluded. 'His gunk was a lot cleaner than the old man's.'

'Crikey! Can you imagine if the oracle got a busload of tourists? She'd be there all week sucking out the evil spirits!'

★★★★★

My sojourn in Leh was becoming lengthy. I had stayed past the acclimatisation period I'd given myself, seduced by the simple charm of the place, and by Ladakhi friendliness. Departure was complicated by the fact that no one seemed to know when Zoji La would be clear of snow; some said the end of May, others halfway into June. It would take maybe ten days to get to Zoji La. I had to set a departure date: I chose the twenty-first of May, the day after Buddha's birthday. Then I cycled out to Spituk Gompa to check on the progress of the sand mandala.

In the afternoon I paid a visit to Tashi at the Ecology Centre. I'd met him on the plane. On the wall behind him was a big map of Leh's water supply, showing how polluted it had become from discarded engine oil, batteries, bottles, plastic and packaging.

'Yes, Leh has many problems,' said Tashi. 'Water is only one of them. Our identity is our biggest problem. We have lost our ways. We have become ashamed of our own culture.'

He recounted how after Leh opened to outsiders in 1974, the

place changed rapidly. Prior to 1974, Ladakhis led a simple farming life, labouring through the short growing season, and then retreating into stone or mudbrick houses for a leisurely winter of craft-making, storytelling and religious celebrations. Life was simple, but peaceful and healthy. Since there was no sugar in the traditional diet, Ladakhis had strong teeth; since they had to climb to go anywhere, they were very fit. Imagine what happened when the region opened to tourism: thousands of camera-toting foreigners appeared one season, leading a glamorous, carefree life. They didn't work, but paid ludicrous amounts for souvenirs. The locals were soon falling over themselves for things they never needed before: motorcycles, television sets, blue jeans, sunglasses. The Ladakhis didn't benefit from tourism as although they ran hotels, they ran few of the shops, handled little of the transport, and didn't run any of the restaurants. The Ecology Centre has focused on self-sufficient projects, particularly using abundant solar energy, and on developing pride in Ladakhi tradition. Leh was the last stronghold of the Ladakhis who numbered only 125,000, with perhaps half that number living in the valleys around.

'Now there are no tourists in Leh,' Tashi said, 'but soon, when Zoji La opens, they will come in by the busload. And along with them come many Kashmiris, Bengalis and Punjabis for the tourist trade. It is a bad time for us – the Kashmiris take away our business. We are happier in the winter. There is no food in the winter, but also no outsiders. We Ladakhis speak to each other and are polite for a change.'

★★★★★

The scale of Buddha's birthday celebrations took us all by surprise. Tsering had assured us that it would be a small affair, just a get-together in the main temple in the bazaar. We were astounded to find the entire Ladakhi population of Leh choking the streets around the bazaar: schoolchildren in their uniforms, townspeople dressed in their finest, and many out-of-towners, who stuck out with their elaborate headgear. The town was awash with colour, banners on rooftops, across the street, along the street, on taxi aerials. My eye took in the whirl of colour, not seeing people any more, but abstract patterns.

Forging my way through the milling crowd, I gained the inner courtyard of the temple. A dozen Ladakhi women in full traditional dress – long robes with elaborate silver and gold brocade – were the focus of attention. They were singing in high-pitched tones, and dancing slowly – slowly, I thought, because of the weight of all the jewellery each bore – a heavy necklace of amber and turquoise, and a huge peaked headdress studded with pieces of turquoise.

Abruptly the dance ended, and a scene of great commotion ensued when a procession of monks wound out of the main temple, bearing large yellow cloth-bound objects that I recognised as Tibetan holy books. Tibetan books consist of loose-leaf oblong pages which are set between heavy covers, usually of wood, and then wrapped in yellow or maroon cloth as 'binding'. In temples, the books are not so much read as worshipped; like the statues and paintings, they are objects of veneration.

I scrambled up to a vantage point looking down over the courtyard and could now make out what the commotion was: the monks and other bearers were trying to bring the holy books out of the temple and onto the street, but their path was barred by hundreds of Ladakhis seeking to have the blessing of the books bestowed on them by being tapped lightly on the head with the book. White scarves were placed around the necks of those bearing the books, incense was lit, there were flashes of amber, turquoise, gold trim, fur-lined hats. Those who managed to get close to the holy books murmured and moaned, and a loud chant rose up from the ranks.

Finally the bearers gained the gate of the temple and headed out, followed by the dozen women in traditional dress, then a long trail of Ladakhis. They swung north through the town, and took a wide arc around the back of the palace, around Tsemo Gompa, and back down to the polo ground. For the entire route, locals knelt at the wayside to receive the blessings of the holy

books, but some were beaned on the head a little too
enthusiastically and came away unsteadily. This was all so strange
– the town was completely traditional now – the past had sprung
to life. For once, it was the Ladakhis' town, not that of Indians,
Kashmiris or tourists. Down the back alleys, in the old part, the
illusion was complete. It was like being in the Leh of several
hundred years ago, complete with donkeys, stone dwellings and
women in traditional dress.

Over the course of this celebratory day in Leh I bumped into
every person I'd met during my stay. I saw Tashi from the Ecology
Centre, smartly dressed in traditional robes, officiating at the dais
on the polo ground. I saw the French couple who'd come in on
the same plane – they'd been out trekking. I met Sonam, the
guide, and Rinjing, the refugee. I gave Rinjing a duffel bag that
I'd flown my equipment into Leh with, and he gave me a *khata* (a
white greeting scarf) and some tapes of Ladakhi music.

★★★★★

Evening: Dreamland Restaurant. The usual fare – variations on
potatoes, dhal or rice. An English woman at a nearby table was
driving us spare with her optimism. Serve her up a greasy soup
and she said, 'Great! That's perfect!' Serve her a sickly-looking
custard and she gurgled with delight, 'Oh fabulous! This is just
wonderful!'

'I bet if you served her cockroaches on toast, she'd be in seventh
heaven,' said Peter.

Coming out of Dreamland, we looked up and saw lights in the
Tsemo Gompa and near the rock painting of the large Buddha.
And rising above it the great orb of the moon. John suggested we
climb up and investigate the lights at the Buddha. With the strong
moonlight, this was easily done. John, who'd done a lot of rock
climbing, pronounced the granite to be first rate. We climbed on
up to the Buddha painting. The flares we'd seen were canisters of
kerosene. I turned to look back across the valley. In the distance,
Spituk Gompa blazed with thousands of lights – butter lamps,

candles, lanterns. The *stupa* of Nyemo, straight ahead, was lit up too. And that full moon, burning clear and bright. Peter said he'd never seen a sky like it in all his days of looking at the stars. There was no scattered light at this altitude, he said. In the old town we could hear laughter – the Ladakhis were drinking themselves stupid on *chang*.

Back at the Antelope, Tsering arrived with our evening *chang* order: it was a record six bottles of the stuff and I had to wonder if I would ever get up the next day to start cycling. I hadn't got a *chang* hangover yet, but who knew what the strength of this brew was? It varied with each batch, all of it illegal as far as the Indian administration was concerned. And as we sat there in the moonlit garden, I reflected that it had been my 'misfortune' to arrive in such a fascinating place right at the start of my trip – somewhere I could not tear myself away from.

★★★★★

May the twenty-first dawns clear and bright, and I have no hangover from the *chang*. I've only had five hours' sleep, but I feel fine. I fetch some fresh bread from the bakery, get a last cup of tea from Tsering, handshakes all round from Peter, John, Laura and the crew, and I'm off downhill past the palace, through the main bazaar, then down, down onto the road past the airport. Tied to the handlebars is the scarf from Sonam.

A military aircraft has just arrived, and a Sikh soldier is making his way on foot to his barracks wearing combat fatigues, a khaki turban to match, and carrying a camouflage-patterned suitcase. Two other soldiers are walking hand-in-hand – a startling sight to Western eyes, but a normal expression of friendship in Asia among adults of the same sex. A convoy of twenty or so army trucks overtakes and I pass Spituk Gompa. The sand mandala will be gone now, dispersed after Buddha's birthday, to show the impermanence of all things. I can see the daily flight from Srinagar coming in, sweeping low over the valley, over Spituk Gompa, disturbing the monks at prayer.

Out of Leh, mile after mile of military barracks. At one of these installations a guard dog races out. I do some rapid calculations – speed of dog, ferocity of dog, distance to close the gap to my ankles – and take advantage of a slight downhill to outrun it. And then I leave that valley behind, and another opens up. I drink in the landscape, a world of snowcaps, desert, rocks, and a black strip of tar through the middle. My tyres are humming along and the white scarf on the handlebars is flying. It is majestic, desolate terrain – there's a fantastic sense of space. Shimmering heat rises off the ground; steely ice glistens on the snowpeaks. Nothing out here now: no habitation, no army barracks, no traffic.

Cycling with a full load is an odd feeling. In the last few weeks I've barely done any cycling, just a hundred-odd miles around Leh. Up ahead lie several thousand miles of *terra incognita*. When you set off on a bicycle from Leh, it seems like a long, long way to Kashgar, but I have great confidence in my bicycle. It is brand new, so I don't expect any mechanical problems for the first few thousand miles. It is a red mountain bike, not top of the line, but I've had some of the components changed for the trip – stronger headset, better pedals. And I have expensive racks, made of hand-welded chromoly, with each rear pannier held in place by five strong clips. No camping gear, very little food – I want to travel as light as possible.

One valley opens into another, and more surprises – purples and greens in the rock formations of the hills. That high-altitude light is like no other; it has a supernatural glow. When you go scubadiving, you have to make adjustments as your depth perception is different, and you become acutely aware of your breathing. Going to altitude demands physical changes too; your body must adjust to the supreme dryness in the air, to the shortness of breath. And visual acuity seems to be somehow sharpened: you see with new eyes.

Road signs warn drivers to slow down and, to reinforce the message, there is the odd plaque to commemorate the dead. The road runs along a sheer slope, scree above, scree below, scree held in place with wire meshing.

I cycle past Basgo, a Tibetan-style village with a ruined *gompa* high on a ridge. Ladakhis are ploughing the fields with yaks, and their rhythmic work song echoes across the valley. There is a stiff climb after Basgo, but after that a long downhill into Saspol, an oasis with deep green fields. From here, a three-mile detour on a dirt road that deadends at the village of Alchi.

The monastery at Alchi is about a thousand years old, and looks it. Decrepit, worn down *stupas* dot the fields. Few visitors stay as all that Alchi holds, monastery-wise, can be seen in an hour or so. It has an air of fallen grandeur, of stately old age – musty, worn, faded. Everything seems old: the houses, the people, the fields. Gnarled old apricot trees stand in the gardens. Tending the fields are women in Ladakhi top hats, wearing full-length robes with pieces of fur attached to the backs, like goblins from a fairytale.

I decide to hold off on visiting the monastery till the morning. Back at the guesthouse, I find I have company. Sitting on the veranda are two Frenchmen who look like they've been out in the sun too long – severely chapped lips, peeling ears, cracked hands, and noses that shine like red lightbulbs. This despite the fact that one of them is wearing a Foreign Legion-style cap. They hiked across Zoji La ten days before. They mention it took several days to cross, and that they saw the body of a man who'd frozen to death in the snow. They talk about the danger of avalanche. I ask about food. Dhal, potatoes and rice all the way, they say, until the pass opens.

I drop into the local teahouse across the road, wolf down a few packets of noodles and two packs of biscuits, then wash that down with tea, and get a shot of rum that is being passed around. This is Naval XXX Rum, marked 'For Defence Services Only', though none of the gentlemen in the teahouse seem remotely connected with the defence services. I stagger back to the guesthouse, fumble with a padlock in the dark, and collapse on the lumpy mattress – the cycling and lack of sleep have caught up with me.

The Frenchmen have overlooked a few things in the food line. The owner of the hotel has eggs and *tsampa* (barley flour). I get myself invited to his home for breakfast. It's a large house, two storeys in traditional Ladakhi style. The main dining and kitchen area on the upper floor is illuminated by a shaft of light from a hole in the roof, where the stovepipe and smoke make their exit. The room has four large pillars of wood, and one entire wall is lined with thermoses, brass and copper cauldrons, and giant teapots. There is a stove decorated in brass, a butter churn, a stack of yak dung and wood for fuel. I eat breakfast on a low table – home-made bread and jam, an egg, and a little *tsampa* – guarded by a snot-nosed child with a laser gun.

After breakfast, I find the wizened old lama who has the keys to Alchi Gompa. He's dressed in tattered brown and orange robes, and his Tibetan boots are worn to shreds. There are five chapels, some in their original state, some retouched. In one chapel thousands of painted miniature Buddhas line the walls; in another, elaborate mandalas can be made out with the help of a torch. Another holds a lifelike portrait of Rinchen Tsangbo, the founder of the monastery in the eleventh century. People must've been a lot smaller then – the scale of everything is tiny – and I keep banging my head on the low doorways. It is hard to believe that something built almost a thousand years ago is still standing, still being renovated. In the courtyard a work team, mostly of Ladakhi women, is busy removing baskets of earth.

★★★★★

I leave Alchi at 6 a.m. and cycle to a place called Uletokpo, which has a small lodge for travellers where I can leave the bike while I hike off towards Rizong Monastery. On the way in I pass an orchard where two woodcutters are operating a huge handsaw to slice up a treetrunk. They work in time to a lilting song with counterpoint harmony – back and forth, question and answer – an entrancing refrain.

Rizong is a fantastic sight: an entire monastery constructed in levels on a sheer rock face. The name means 'mountain fortress', and it is the 'newest' Geluk monastery in Ladakh, built 150 years ago. After seeing the prayer flags on the topmost crest, I wander down to the *gompa* again and find a group of novice monks sitting cross-legged with their tutor, taking lessons outdoors. They are a ragged bunch, ranging from eight to twelve years old. They're studying from an English textbook, and the tutor gestures that I should take over the teaching for a period. I quickly get bored with the textbook, so I decide to teach parts of the body, a more concrete exercise. We chorus the words for various parts of the body. I get them to point to the relevant parts as they are spoken. So when I say 'Ears!' they jam index fingers into both ears and shout 'Ears!' When I say 'Eyes!', likewise with those. But their favourite is 'Nose!' because they can jam index fingers up their runny nostrils.

The monk-tutor has a purple cowl over his shaven head to stave off the harsh sun, and is wearing sunglasses. He has a row of crooked teeth, a stick and a mean disposition. I get all the urchins to stand up for a review of body parts, vaguely aware that the monk has moved in close behind them. 'Ears!' I shout. Four of them point to their ears, two point to their feet, and two more – undecided – look at the others to work out which answer is correct. The monk whacks the nearest boy on the ear; the boy lets out a great howl of protest. Then he cuffs another boy on the head – hard. That's what you get for the wrong answer.

Trying to change tack, I select the star pupil, who does faultless matching of body parts. Not so the next poor ruffian, who has trouble matching any of them, and is alternately cuffed on the head or whacked on the ear for each answer. 'Eyes!' I say. He points to his mouth. Whack! 'Nose!' I say, certain that he'll remember the association of two fingers up runny nostrils. The child looks around nervously, and then holds up two fingers to his ears. The monk smacks him squarely over the back of the head. 'OK! Everybody sit down!' I shout, trying to defuse the situation. 'Pick up your books!' I turn to the monk, 'That's enough for today – you take over.' And he does.

★★★★★

How did they make this road? Parts of it have been blasted out of sheer rock, with precipitous drops into the roaring Indus River below. A bus comes crawling towards me, so overloaded that it has passengers stuffed down the aisles and hanging off the back end. On the bike, I feel like I have unlimited freedom in comparison. After following the Indus – known as the Lion River – for the afternoon, I make it to Khalsi by dusk, a truck-stop town lined with – can it be true? – canopied restaurants. I sit down expectantly at one of these places and asked for a menu. 'Dhal, potatoes and rice,' recites the cook. No other items on the menu till Zoji La opens.

There is nothing polite about road signs on the Leh to Srinagar road: they are directed at Indian drivers fond of taking hairpin bends and blind corners at full throttle. Beacon, the paramilitary organisation that constructed and maintains this highway, has erected bright yellow concrete markers along the route, or painted signs into rock walls. Signs that range from the cryptic – IF MARRIED, DIVORCE SPEED – to exhortations like: GO MAN GO – BUT GO SLOW. A bit below the belt is BE GENTLE ON MY CURVES, later reinforced by DARLING I WANT YOU – BUT NOT SO FAST. And, to really tug the heartstrings, PAPA GO SLOW – ORPHANAGE NO NO. But the strangest one offers this stark warning: DEATH LAYS ITS ICY HANDS ON SPEED KINGS. Imagine road signs like this along an interstate highway in Nevada! Because Zoji La is still closed, I don't have to deal with manic Indian truck drivers, a definite blessing, judging from the signs. In a day, I might only see three or four vehicles. When the pass opens, it will be bumper-to-bumper trucks, spewing exhaust fumes.

On the approach to Lamayuru there is a long uphill stretch called the Hangroo Loops. It is also nicknamed the Jalabi Bends by truck drivers, *jalabi* being a kind of Indian sweetmeat with orange twirls. A laborious climb up these coiled zigzag roads, with rock bands of alternating green and purple shale. Near the crest I come across some traders with donkeys, having a tea break. They motion me over to their campfire and foist Ladakhi tea on me, a horribly salty, pinkish concoction that I knock back out of politeness. I give them some chocolate. They examine the bike; I examine their gear; we sit around the fire. These encounters are strange and almost wordless, but somehow still meaningful.

★★★★★

The road continues through a bizarre moonscape of yellowish clay and pitted rocks. Rounding a bend I catch sight of Lamayuru Monastery, dramatically lit by the afternoon sun. It's an impossible structure fused to a rocky outcrop, with dark, brooding hills behind it. It seems to have come off the pages of a book about mythical places; even in its advanced state of decay it exudes an air of majesty and splendour. Lamayuru is set down a valley: monastery at the top, village below, a stream and barley fields at the bottom. The village is small, perhaps five hundred souls, and has only a rough jeep road in.

I ride the bike down a dirt track to the monastery. Travellers are allowed to stay in a wing of the *gompa*. Chuntsog, the monk in charge, is a wheeler-dealer. He runs a small shop, which has the best stock I've seen so far; he has Indian peanut butter, chapattis, dried apricots, biscuits, garlic, tea. The monk immediately takes a fancy to my pile sweater, a bright monastic red, and enquires about trading food for it.

'You dhal? You ricing? You potato? How much you jacket? How much shopping you jacket? You biscuit? You tea?' Chuntsog speaks a variety of English that conveniently eliminates all verbs. I resist the attempts to buy the sweater and sip tea while he cooks up some dhal.

Two other travellers come in for food. Stephanie is from England, and her boyfriend, Wally, is from Portugal. They look like throwbacks to the 1970s. Stephanie has a hippy headband; Wally sports five earrings in each ear. They rate all their travel destinations in terms of hashish – how available it is, the quality, the price, and whether smoking it is tolerated or not.

'Ah, Singapore, freak me off!' cries Wally. '*Incroyable* the *policia* there. *Quand* I arrive they search me everywhere. *Everywhere*. Freak me off!' He takes a toke on a hash-lined cigarette. 'Kathmandu was the best place – smoking in the restaurants, *ma* the laws they change. Even in India they change the laws. Goa was the place, lots of crazy people. Carazey! And then the police arrest me in India. Shake me over, you know. *Bastardos!* So we go up to Tibet. Lhasa was the greatest, lots of good hashish there, *ma* then the riots, they close out the place. *Ma* now Kashgar is the best. Number one hash. Nobody stop you to smoke. And plants growing all around in that part of China – in Xinjiang, Gansu, Qinghai, Yunnan.'

'We *loved* the hash parties in Lhasa,' coos Stephanie. 'It's such a pity to have closed it all down.' Stephanie somehow had her air ticket from Los Angeles to Hong Kong wrongly validated for a stop in Honolulu. 'That threw out all my plans,' she says with a sly smile, 'but you know, Hawaii has some very high-quality grass.'

'You biscuit? You tea?' asks the monk.

'Yes, both thanks.'

Hoping to change the subject, I enquire about Zoji La. They crossed the pass several days ago.

'Ah yes, we met with one dead man there,' says Wally. 'He was lying on the snow, very stiff. Poor bastard.'

'It was fucking freezing!' pipes in Stephanie. I glance at her gear.

'Were you wearing those?' I ask, pointing at her sandals.

'Yes, but with socks,' she says.

God spare us – no wonder it was freezing. And they crossed at night, by the light of the full moon. That way, claims Wally, there was less chance of an avalanche.

'How did you get to the pass?'

'Oh, with some Indian soldiers in a jeep,' says Stephanie. 'They were all sex-starved or something – kept asking me about kissing. Wanted to know how I kissed, and whether I liked kissing and things like that.'

'Freak me off!' cuts in Wally.

As I leave, they are arguing furiously with the monk over the seven rupees for the dhal. I'm glad I'm travelling in the opposite direction. I step outside and find it is snowing, and I curse and curse. The fresh snow has thrown all my calculations about crossing the pass into doubt again.

★★★★★

Lamayuru is a dramatic cliff-hanger, harking back to the seventeenth century. Chuntsog offers to be my guide. He unlocks a series of doors leading to the main prayer hall, and shows me the dusty Tibetan sacred texts on the shelves.

Back at the guesthouse Chuntsog serves up tea. Sipping the tea, it crystallises why I am so mesmerised by Tibetan culture. Travelling back in time is not only easy, it's very *relaxing*. We're not talking about going back in time just a few centuries here, we're talking about deep time, a link that goes back possibly twenty centuries, preserving traditions from ancient India.

It's so deep-seated, so basic, that it calms me. I even have a name for this phenomenon: I have christened it 'Chilling out in Shangri-La' because Shangri-La has an ethereal landscape crowned with a Tibetan monastery, just like this one. And like those who learned from the wise lamas of Shangri-La in *Lost Horizon*, there's a lot I can learn from the people of Lamayuru.

Take time, for instance. Nobody is in a hurry in Lamayuru because there are no appointments to keep, except for getting the harvest in. The Tibetans believe time is cyclical; it swings through incarnations, so if you miss out the first time round, there will be more chances – you might even catch up with it in the next incarnation.

★★★★★

Back on my bike. From Lamayuru there's some very tough climbing. I reach the top of Fotu La, the highest pass along this road at almost 13,500 feet, marked by some frayed prayer flags. But my legs aren't tired. I feel high. I feel like riding and riding. A rhythm has been set up that I can't break now – nothing can stop me except a sunset. And so I bound along, headed for the next pass. After all the complications of getting to Ladakh, this part is remarkably simple: a bicycle, a ribbon of road, and crisp mountain air. I move along in a kind of trance with a cadence that seems effortless. Rather than trying to conquer a pass, I find myself somehow integrated with the landscape.

It occurs to me that if a state of meditation can be achieved by concentrating on a single action such as breathing, or on the rise and fall of the stomach, then any repetitive action can induce a similar calming of the heart. So if there is walking meditation (that concentrates on the act of walking), there must also be jogging meditation (focusing on footfalls), snorkel meditation (concentration on breathing sounds), ski meditation (homing in on the sounds of skis scraping the snow), and bicycle meditation (my foot is going down, the chain is going around, the other foot is coming up, the chain is going around …).

And so I whip through to the next pass, Namika La. Then I put on my downhill gear (foxfur hat, silk scarf) ready for a glorious six miles of switchbacks down into the green, green valley of Mulbek.

Not much in the way of lodgings in Mulbek. Finally I find a family with a spare room. The owner says it is ten rupees. The room turns out to be completely bare.

'There's no bed.'

'Fifteen rupees with a bed,' says the owner.

'What? A room includes a bed. Ten rupees with a bed.'

'As you like. I will get the bed.'

'And a lamp while you're at it. Where's the toilet?'

'It is out there,' he says, pointing through the door.

'Where?'

'Everywhere,' he says with a flourish of his hand.

Mulbek is a very small place, and I am an instant celebrity. Across the street is a 30-foot-high Buddha sculpted into a granite rock face with a tiny monastery at its base. The monks take turns riding my bike. I am given tea. A townsman takes me off to his house for dinner, a two-storey place with animals below and living quarters on the main floor. His family and neighbours crowd into a courtyard to get their photos taken, and I promise to send some copies. One duo especially catches my eye: a grandmother cradling a child. The child has smooth, pinkish skin; the grandmother is dark and leathery, and when she smiles, a thousand wrinkles crease her face and rows of stumps appear instead of teeth.

★★★★★

At Kargil you cross a cultural divide from Buddhism to Islam. It's only a matter of twenty-five miles from Mulbek, but there is a very different kind of energy here. 'Salaam aleikum' is the new greeting. The town has several mosques and a heavy military presence because Kargil sits right near the border with Pakistan. My map shows an old trading route that cuts across from Kargil to Skardu, but it has not been used since 1948, when Pakistan was partitioned from India. It is a short distance directly through the mountains to Skardu, one of my key destinations, but I have to cycle on a huge loop right through the Indian plains and the Punjab to get there.

I left Dras early in the morning after tea and biscuits, and climbed steadily up to 11,300 feet into a snow- and icebound area. My goal was to get as close as I could to Zoji La, which meant a stop at Gumri army post. Gumri was a quagmire of slush and dirty snow; petrol barrels were embedded in the muck, and hundreds of empty tins were scattered around, with flies and crows picking at them. Obviously no rubbish collection here – the detritus of the years just piled up in the snow.

I saluted the platoon commander. He was decked out in a down parka, with heavy snow-goggles perched on his head.

'You're near Zoji La now,' he said.

'Can I stay here tonight?'

'No need. It's only a few hours over the pass.'

'It's dangerous in the afternoon – avalanches.'

'Soon night will come. It's better to cross at night.'

What, and freeze my bollocks off? Not bloody likely! I'll be damned if I'm going over at night – after I've come all this way, I want to see the pass.

'I want to cross early in the morning – at sunrise.'

'We have no space for you here.'

'All right then, I'll sleep in the snow.'

Finally he relented, and I was shown a shed littered with empty rum and whisky bottles.

There were a dozen men at Gumri, locked in for the winter. It was an isolated posting. Behind the army huts stood Gumri Glacier, shaped like a gigantic *stupa*. There was about two miles of snow blockage on the road through Zoji La. Bulldozers were working it from both ends so it would be open in four or five days.

I got some hot water and added a packet of noodles. The hot food lifted my spirits. It had been a rough day. I was glad I'd found refuge here because I didn't have the energy to carry on.

At sundown the road crews returned. They had blackened faces, and the blackest clothing I'd ever seen. I doubt if any of them had washed their clothes since the date of acquisition. As for themselves, well, that was hard to tell … it was probably too cold in this region for cleaning up. It all reminded me of a grimy fairytale: the soot men, back from their grimy stint on the road, going into grimy rooms full of soot from stoves, smoking grimy cigarettes, sleeping in grimy beds in grimy buildings covered in grimy snow. Spattered in mud up to the knees, I must've looked immaculately clean to the grimy men. At least I had a few colours to show – red and blue. All their stuff was either camouflage khaki, or diesel-fume black.

In the shed, I slept with every stitch of clothing on, my head in a foxfur hat, body in a sub-zero sleeping bag, and all of this inside a bivvy sack – and I was still freezing.

I had no idea how I was going to cross Zoji La with a bike. All I knew was that I had to start off at dawn, when everything was still frozen, so there was less chance of an avalanche. I just hoped the crossing didn't involve any climbing. I tied down the flaps on my hat so my ears were covered, and set off. The track from the army base turned into a roadway with a layer of solid ice and walls of frozen snow on either side. Great! I got on the bike and started wheeling off – and promptly went for a six on the ice, banging my elbow. I got up slowly. This was not going to work.

Then I saw a group of horses trudging along in the distance. They were up on the snow – naturally the horses couldn't get any grip on the road of ice. The horsemen spotted me and pulled me onto the snowbank. The horse track went away from the road, cutting a wide arc around it, across a snow-filled basin. I trudged along the trail. The landscape was exuberant and I stopped to take pictures as the sun came out with blinding force as it reflected off the snow. This was more than chilling out; it was a trip to the freezer. In the distance a caravan of packhorses was dwarfed by a massive peak of snow, ice and rock. Zoji La was stunning yet dangerous. One half of me wanted to stay and look longer, bewitched by this icy domain, but the other half told me to hurry on before the sun climbed higher and loosened the snow.

The packhorses were bringing sacks of food across this bridge of snow to trucks waiting near Gumri. As they went they dropped vegetables here and there, so I could tell if I was on the right track by following the odd tomato, carrot or pea-pod in the snow. And horse droppings. I could only hope I wouldn't fall into a crevasse or a sinkhole. The occasional rough burial site, marked by a pile of clothes, speeded me along my way. By late morning I was over the worst of it, and an Indian traveller helped me to climb over the last bank of snow back onto the roadway.

Around a bend I left the desert plateau of Ladakh behind me. Just like that. The transition was abrupt, complete and most bizarre. An exhilarating set of hairpin bends took me down into the Vale of Kashmir. It was as if the gods had spilled green paint over the landscape: spruce and pine trees, lush meadows, alpine vistas, cool breezes. The precarious road I was travelling on had been blasted out of a mountainside. I raced down the switchbacks – down, down, down to the alpine resort of Sonamarg. From Sonamarg, it was fifty miles of glorious downhill to Srinagar, the capital of Kashmir.

2

MEETING GREAT OCEAN

A chat with the Dalai Lama

On the map of Srinagar, I had scribbled some notes: *houseboats, bombs, ice cream, Glocken.* I was to experience all of those things. Srinagar, being ten degrees cooler than places like Delhi, has long been a summer retreat; however, there is no respite from the greed of Kashmiri merchants. They buzz around, droning the same old spiel: *My friend, I have houseboat, you come see. Cheap. You want a carpet? I have excellent carpet. Have tea at my shop. No need to buy, just look.*

At the Glocken Bakery I had a temporary cultural relapse, went berserk, and devoured four apple pies in a row. A traveller I met at the Glocken showed me one of the newest sights of Srinagar: around the corner, along the Bund, was a urinal that had just been blown up. A Kashmiri separatist group had picked this harmless target as a warning, setting off a bomb after midnight when no one was around. The root of all the violence in Srinagar was the inclusion of Kashmir, a Muslim-majority state, in newly independent India in 1947; the inhabitants identified more with Islamic Pakistan. Violence had escalated over the last few years as separatists had started to use superior weapons in their confrontations with the Hindu police who patrolled the area. The manager of the houseboat I stayed on told me there was no trouble in Kashmir. When pressed – when I told him about the urinal on the Bund – he said, 'Well, we are having a few bombs, but only *small* bombs.' A cycle-tour through the dusty, squalid, old town sector revealed a different story: soldiers in full riot gear with shields, Sten guns and .303s. I passed a heavily sandbagged police station that had a blue paddywagon and a fire engine outside with steel mesh across the windows.

Srinagar was like a powder keg, ready to go up at any second. I got out quickly, headed for the next destination, Dharamsala, seat of the Tibetan government in exile. In early June I cycled through the foothills of north-west India, through pinewood forests. I hitched a ride on the open back of a truck for a hair-raising ride through Jawahar Tunnel, which bored two miles through a mountainside. Then I carried on cycling past the hill resorts of Patnitop and Batote, and dropped down to stony plains with cactus shrubs. I stopped at small lodges for the night, or got myself invited in as a guest at Public Works Department buildings, which had been set up for travelling VIPs and engineers. The weather see-sawed from thunderstorm cool to searing hot. When the sun came out, the road turned to hot, sticky tar. Roadworkers with black umbrellas and watering cans full of pitch were mending holes one by one in the awful heat. What a hellish job!

My diet consisted mainly of fresh mangoes – the only food available that wasn't booby-trapped with chillies. 'Only a little chilli,' the man at a roadside stand reassured me, motioning to cauldrons of food. *Oh yeah? Tell me about it – the last dish just about blew my head off.* Stopping in the shade to peel a mango, I looked up to see the doleful eyes of a huge Brahmin bull staring at me. So I surrendered the skins, and the bull promptly vacuumed them off the highway.

Travel is a kind of sensory deprivation. There's always something you crave – cheese, chocolate, or, on the Indian plains, water. It's not ordinary tapwater you crave, but a glass of sparkling, clear, cold mineral water from the French Alps with a slice of lime. In north-west India the choice was between bad colas or mango drinks. I say bad colas because most had carcinogenic additives. Thums-Up Cola – which tasted horrible – definitely warranted a name change to Thums-Down. Some fizzy drinks were rumoured to provide effective birth-control when used as a douche. The mighty Coke had withdrawn from India – the Indian government booted the company out because it would not reveal its ingredients – but the bottles were still around, relabelled Campa Cola or Gold Spot (Coke was later allowed back into India, to continue its terrestrial battles with Pepsi).

I couldn't stomach the Indian colas, so I'd taken to mixing mango drinks with tonic water. I'd order ten mango drinks at a roadside stand, plus tonic water and, for theatrical effect, open all of them. Suspense: a great crowd gathered, gape-mouthed. I consumed two on the spot, and poured the contents of four in one water bottle and four in another.

Upon spotting a bicycling foreigner, local reaction ran the gamut from amazement to indifference. And there was another reaction: pity. Or maybe I mistook that for pity. There was invariably one question in these parts that foxed me: *Are you alone?*

How I hated that question. Depending on how the question was intoned, and which way the questioner's eyes were shifting (back past me to determine if there was another cyclist on the horizon), the question could've meant: *Are you alone so I can mug you?* or maybe it meant: *Are you alone, you poor sod, with nobody to look after you? Out here in the wilderness?* I got the idea that Indians rarely travelled alone. Here's how the conversation might proceed, with me deliberately being cryptic and cagey in case mugging *was* the ulterior motive of the questioner.

'Are you alone?'

'A man with a bicycle is never alone,' I would answer. 'The bicycle is my good friend.'

'No, I mean is there anyone with you?'

'We are all alone, if that's what you mean; it is our natural condition.'

'But are you alone right now?'

'That's a philosophical distinction. I could be in a crowd and yet still be alone ...'

*****

Three days of riding from Srinagar brought me close to Dharamsala, a former British hill station. When they say hill station they mean it: there was a road winding a dozen miles uphill into McLeod Ganj, the seat of the Dalai Lama. Halfway up, at lower Dharamsala, I staggered into the post office to catch my breath and to check poste restante.

There were three pieces of mail waiting for me, one from

Canada, one from France and one from an unrecognised UK address. Curiosity got the better of me – I went straight for the UK envelope. The letter was from a woman called Jane and my eye centred on some graphic drawings of the male appendages and her fond descriptions of them, referring to a particular erection as 'Rodders' and how much she was missing old Rodders and how wonderful it would be to have old Rodders in her hot little hands – and then it suddenly occurred to me that this letter was not in fact addressed to me. I glanced back at the envelope, and found it was addressed to Michael Buckler – the handwritten *r* resembled a *y*. I sealed the letter shut again with glue from the post office counter and wrote 'INSPECTED BY INDIAN CUSTOMS' across the back in big letters, to explain why the letter had been violated. *Phew!*

The next letter was just as obscene, in its own way. It was about food: 'Wonderful cheese: Camembert, Brie, Rocquefort, all on crusty bread with red wine. Delicious pastries: blueberry flan, clafouti, éclairs, pain aux raisins … Fresh fruit – very sweet this year, melons, cherries, strawberries, apricots … French cooking: stewed rabbit, coq au vin, boeuf carottes, biftek et saucisson. Ha! Now tell me about the mountain views!' It was signed, 'From a fat friend'.

My stomach gurgled in protest. I stuffed the letter back into the envelope and moved on to the letter from Bicycle Bob. I'd left this letter till last, because somehow I knew that Bob wasn't going to make it to Dharamsala. We had planned to do this trip together, but he'd called off the Leh section of the trip because he'd said he needed time to sort out some problems, and he promised to meet me in Dharamsala. The first line of the letter confirmed my suspicions. Bicycle Bob hadn't got it together. I cursed him out loud, but at the same time I thanked him for getting me over here, for getting me started.

I got back on the bike to tackle the switchbacks up to McLeod Ganj. In the distance came the eerie sound of bagpipes. What was this? The ghosts of a Scottish regiment? No – it was another Indian army barracks, and the music issued from a doleful reed instrument. I cycled past the Church of St John with its gravestones from a century ago, from the days of the British Raj, when Dharamsala was a summer sanctuary for British officers suffering from the intense heat of the plains.

*****

The first thing that caught my attention in McLeod Ganj were the covers of news magazines, prominently displayed in a shop window. They were about a bloodbath in Beijing: the Tiananmen Massacre. When you've been out of sync with world news, something like this hits you right between the eyes. I purchased *Time* magazine, and leafed through the pages in a state of utter disbelief as the bloody saga unfolded.

McLeod Ganj was a very odd place, perhaps because I'd seen Lhasa first. Here was a town quite capably run by Tibetans – Tibetan merchants, Tibetan doctors, Tibetan schools, Tibetan flags, Tibetan administration – in complete contrast to Lhasa, where Tibetans ran very little of anything; the Chinese ran it all. McLeod Ganj was a small town of perhaps five thousand Tibetans and a few thousand Indians. Simple rows of wooden structures – restaurants, bookshops, artefact shops – formed the two tiny thoroughfares of McLeod Ganj; other dwellings were scattered over pine-forested mountain slopes.

Wandering around, I was drawn to a crowd of Tibetans sitting cross-legged inside the courtyard of a small central temple. Their rapt attention was focused on a man with half a dozen scroll paintings, waving his arms around. The man was a storyteller; in all my months in Tibet, I'd seen nothing like this. I saw many things in McLeod Ganj that were new to me, among them, fire *pujas* – offerings of fire to deities in full-scale temple ceremonies. I saw Tibetan children with textbooks showing yaks, snow lions and the Potala Palace in Lhasa, but they had never set foot in Tibet.

I went to visit Bhuchung, an official in the Tibetan exile administration, and was surprised to learn that my request for an interview with the Dalai Lama was being processed. I had initiated this request three months previously on the strength of having written the first English guidebook to modern Tibet, but I had not expected to get this far. In fact, I was surprised that the Dalai Lama was actually in town; he spent half the year abroad. I was elated to be granted an interview, but at the same time I was in a panic because I had no questions ready. But I had a week to work on them, and I had access to the library in Gangchen.

The Tibetan exile administration consisted of a handful of three-storey buildings and a temple. The Indian government had told the Tibetans 'no political activities', but Bhuchung laughed when I mentioned this and swept his hand around. 'This,' he said, 'is all politics. Our presence here is political. We do not have Indian passports. We have identity cards that show we are Tibetan refugees. Even some people who have been here for thirty years will not take an Indian passport. We have young people who were born in India, who have never seen Tibet – but they are Tibetan.'

At the information office in Gangchen there was a display of photos: monks being clubbed by Chinese soldiers on the rooftop of the Jokhang, Tibet's holiest temple; Lhasa in flames; Chinese security police with AK-47 assault rifles versus rock-throwing demonstrators. Above the photos hung a large Tibetan flag – snow lions, snowy mountains, burning jewels, the rays of the rising sun. To display this flag in Lhasa was to invite a bullet through the head.

★★★★★

Along the main street of McLeod Ganj, I met a Tibetan teacher and his son. His son was four and dressed in yellow robes; he was an incarnate lama. The teacher, Chosang, invited me out to his home at the Tibetan Children's Village, so I tagged along, intrigued by the little lama.

'Who is he a reincarnation of?' I asked.

'He is a reincarnate of Tsongkhor Rinpoche, a lama from Kokonor in Amdo. This lama fled Tibet and went to Darjeeling. On his deathbed he told his attendant to build a house, because he would return. When my son was discovered to be the true reincarnation, the attendant came to the investiture.'

'Where did the investiture take place?'

'Here in Dharamsala. The Dalai Lama is the only one who can officially recognise a reincarnate candidate.'

We walked along a forested trail winding through the hills towards the Tibetan Children's Village, a boarding school for orphans, known as the TCV. The little lama behaved like any other Tibetan child – he thought it was a huge joke when he blew his nose in a corner of his father's T-shirt. But he was wearing yellow robes and his head was shaven, which made him stand out.

'Do you yourself believe he is the Tsongkhor Rinpoche?'

'Yes,' said Chosang. 'When the Tsongkhor Rinpoche's attendant arrived from Darjeeling, my son rushed over to him and asked him, "Where is my suitcase?" We didn't even know the attendant was bringing it, but he had a suitcase of the rinpoche's personal effects – clothing, books and so on.'

'To hand over to the reincarnate?'

'Yes. The idea, you see, is that the reincarnate will need his old possessions.'

We arrived at Chosang's house. His family lived in two rooms. One was a tiny kitchen, the other a living space for himself, his wife and three children. He offered me tea and chased flies around the room. He caught them in his hand and let them go through the window – a Buddhist cannot kill even a fly. He proudly showed me a *tanka* (a Tibetan cloth painting) from the little lama's investiture, and photos of the Dalai Lama conferring his new status on him. And then photographs of the old Tsongkhor Rinpoche in Darjeeling. He had a book with a biography of the rinpoche. In one corner was the suitcase from Darjeeling, with the deceased rinpoche's personal effects in it.

'Then are you treating him as the rinpoche, or as an ordinary child?' I asked.

'I have a new respect for him. It is hard for me. I have to punish him sometimes, but I do not want to hit a rinpoche. We cannot treat him as a normal child. We will keep him clean, and away from other children. Now he has been recognised, he will dress differently from my other children. He will have a different education; he will go to south India, to Mysore. I must make an offering for his education – twenty thousand rupees. I must save hard for this. He will take religious vows. First, he will take five vows, then thirty-six vows, and after the age of twenty, he will take two hundred and fifty vows.'

'What if he decides not to be a rinpoche? What if he rebels?'

Chosang looked surprised. 'Our religion is so strong that this simply does not happen,' he said. The little lama was doing somersaults, playing with a toy car; he had a boundless amount of energy. Whether or not he was the reincarnation of the Tsongkhor Rinpoche, he would undoubtedly turn out to be competent for the post for which he was destined: a religious leader of a monastery. How could he fail? Out of possibly seven hundred candidates whose birthdates were right (born two years after the death of the rinpoche), he had been chosen, and he was chosen for showing psychic signs of a previous life. That would have to be a special child, whether a reincarnate or not, and then he would receive the finest monastic education available for the next twenty or thirty years.

There was another young lama in town, a celebrity already, at age four. I saw him playing in the courtyard of a meditation retreat centre, a fair-haired boy by the name of Osel Torres, which is not a Tibetan name, because Osel is not Tibetan. He is Spanish. His parents were devoted followers of renowned teacher Lama Thubten Yeshe: fair-haired Osel is the first Western incarnate to be recognised by the Dalai Lama. Since globetrotting Lama Yeshe was one of the biggest transmitters of Tibetan Buddhism in the West, it was reasoned his incarnate was Western also. The process of finding incarnate lamas has become much more complicated because of interference in being allowed to locate them within Tibet. And if they are located within Tibet, how can the Tibetans get them out? The Dalai Lama himself has said that his rebirth will most certainly be found in exile, not in occupied Tibet.

★★★★★

A musky odour – a mix of herbal remedies and spices – permeated the offices and hallways of the Astro-Medical Institute in Gangchen Kyishong, a few miles from McLeod Ganj. I flashed a letter of introduction and was given a tour of the facilities by a woman called Dolma. We strolled through a section where pills were made. There were bins filled with crushed herbs, roots and other ingredients. There were large grinding and sifting machines; on the roof of this part, pellets were laid out on mesh beds to dry in the sun.

The Astro-Medical Institute is the largest supplier of Tibetan medicine in the world, with a staff of two hundred, as well as twenty doctors. There were thirty branches of the institute in India, Dolma informed me. Tibetan medicine, almost eradicated as being 'feudal superstition' under the Chinese in Tibet, has survived here. Some drugs were only manufactured through the knowledge of Dr Tenzin Choedrak, the Dalai Lama's personal physician who managed to get out of Tibet in 1980 after enduring years in prison.

There is no surgery in Tibetan medicine; for that, the patient must see a Western doctor. In Tibetan medicine, herbal and natural remedies are employed to counter disease and improve the health. All diagnosis is done through feeling the pulse or by examining the patient's urine.

I was shown through a small museum attached to the research section. All kinds of potions, extracts, medicinal plants and dried animal parts were displayed in jars or on plates under glass cases: deer bile, rhino horn, alligator skin. The labels were in Tibetan, but I got a translation of this bizarre pharmacopoeia. Musk-deer parts were used for treating lung disorders, armadillo parts for nervous disorders, mountain sheep horn for infectious disorders, and ground antelope horn facilitated childbirth. All this immediately reminded me of the Chinese remedies that have greatly contributed to the extinction of rare species: the demand for tiger penis, rhino horn and bear gall bladder. Didn't this run contrary to the Buddhist abhorrence of killing any life form?

'What are those?' I asked Dolma, pointing to some small wrapped items placed on polished oystershells.

'Precious pills. They are a general tonic. If you're healthy you can take one. If you're sick, you must take a particular precious pill only at an auspicious date, and you must recite a mantra for the Medicine Buddha. The precious pills are in powder form, and are wrapped in silk cloth.'

'What are the ingredients?'

'They change from year to year. Sometimes amber, pearl – that's good for brain haemorrhage; lapis lazuli for leprosy, itching or skin disorders; turquoise for fever of the liver. The base of the precious pills is a mixture of mercury, silver and iron.'

'Mercury?' I gasped in disbelief, thinking that a thermometer dose of mercury was enough to kill a man.

'Detoxified mercury.'

'What kind of research is going on now?'

'For the past few years we have been working on hypertension, since a lot of Tibetans suffer from high blood pressure. And we understand this is a big problem in the West too. You see, we are trying to put traditional medicines to work on modern problems.'

'You mean cancer?'

'We have had some success with cancer. We even tried to develop some medicine for AIDS.'

'A potion for AIDS?'

'A pill. But bad karma surrounded this pill. Three doctors died from accidents while involved in this research. There were other mysterious accidents. And the pill took a long time to prepare in a batch – over four months. So the project was halted.'

She indicated the section where astrology was taught and where amulets were made.

'The astrologists make predictions. Two have come true this year. They predicted a dark year for Tibetans, with the death of a high lama. We were all very worried about this prediction because it might have indicated the Dalai Lama. Then in January the Panchen Lama died. He was young still. You can read the other predictions. They predicted internal strife in China, followed by a shortage of rainfall. That could only refer to the Tiananmen Massacre.'

We walked over to the chapel for the Medicine Buddha. Lining the walls were *tankas* featuring anatomical details; there was a large one of a Medicine Buddha mandala. The focus of the chapel was a *tanka* of the Medicine Buddha, with an altar and butter lamps. Tibetan medicine, as with all else in Tibetan lore, required astrological consultation and depended on auspicious days. I wondered if the day appointed for my interview with the Dalai Lama was auspicious, or whether it was one of those dark days when he would hedge all questions.

I'd been working on the questions all week. It's hard to come up with material that the Dalai Lama has not been asked about before. Tenzin Tethong, the Dalai Lama's private secretary, screens out questions at a pre-interview meeting. *Don't ask him if he's the last Dalai Lama; don't ask questions about his daily routine.* I've been talking to lots of people in Dharamsala: talking to Jamyang Norbu, author of a book about the Tibetan resistance; talking to Lhasang Tsering, president of the Youth Congress, who advocates violent action and sabotage against the Chinese in Tibet; talking to Jetsun Pema, the Dalai Lama's sister, who runs the Tibetan Children's Villages. Jetsun Pema was with the fact-finding delegations that toured Tibet in the early 1980s. She gave a very emotional description of that time – how people were clawing at their bus, how the Chinese could not prevent people from reaching them, how shocked the Chinese were that great fervour for the Dalai Lama clearly existed after years of brainwashing by cadres.

★★★★★

The big day arrives. I double check all my gear. The camera is loaded, the micro-cassette recorder has fresh batteries, I have my fifty questions in hand. I am sitting in an ante-room of the Dalai Lama's Audience Hall. I am a nervous wreck. In old Tibet, protocol decreed that a layman was not allowed to hear the voice of the Dalai Lama or look at him, and now I've got half an hour of interview lined up. Tenzin Tethong appears in his best grey robes. He tells me to follow him.

We move out onto a porch and round to the room where the Dalai Lama is standing. Then comes one of those moments that seems to last an eternity: I don't know what to do. I had rehearsed what I would say to get things going, but I hadn't thought about handshakes. Tenzin never said anything about the protocol at this point. I freeze. Am I supposed to shake hands with the Living Buddha? Should I bow? Or should I throw myself on the ground and grovel on the carpet? Advanced panic sets in, but then the Dalai Lama extends his hand, and that settles that – we shake hands. It's a strong, firm grip and it seems to send heat through my person. Or is it that my body temperature is several hundred degrees and my knees are shaking and my throat is completely dry? I babble something about it being *a great honour to meet you, Your Honour – I mean, Your Holiness ...*

'Dalai' is an honorific title that translates roughly from Mongolian as 'Great Ocean' or 'Ocean of Wisdom'; other titles include 'Precious Jewel', 'Bodhisattva of Compassion' and 'Holder of the White Lotus'. The man in the maroon robes is taller than I expected. His voice is much deeper and richer than I expected too. There is a definite presence – the piercing gaze of an almost other-worldly being looking at me through horn-rimmed glasses. But what immediately strikes me is the size of the Dalai Lama's head. It seems to be quite large, emphasised, perhaps, by the fact that it is shaven. But even allowing for this, it is big. And he is stooping slightly, making his head seem too heavy for his body. I immediately think of the Bodhisattva Chenrezig, who undertook the deliverance of all beings from suffering: when he realised the magnitude of his task, his head exploded, and ten more heads arose from the original one.

We sit down. I hand my camera to Tenzin Tethong and set up the tape recorder. I hand the minuscule microphone to the Dalai Lama. He picks it up and examines it – I recall his intrigue with gadgets. Maybe this will break the ice.

The Dalai Lama has done a very surprising thing; he is sitting almost right next to me. Here is a man who is interviewed hundreds of times a year, who is surrounded by crowds wherever he goes. You'd think he'd want to keep a personal space, but he makes no attempt to do that. His action indicates a warmth, a concern for newcomers. He is looking at me with quizzical high-arched eyebrows, very much like a jovial uncle at a family reunion. I stumble through the first couple of questions. He answers briefly and goes silent, and I mistake this for the end of the answer. But when I'm about to ask the next question, he continues. He takes a while to focus on the question and to get his reply back into English. There is no rush to answer.

'Your Holiness, years of negotiations with the Chinese have come to nothing. What hope is there in negotiations?'

The Dalai Lama shoots a piercing gaze at me, raises quizzical eyebrows, and turns the question over for a while, lost in thought. 'It is the only way. What else can we do? The Chinese have – how to say? – all the cards. The only other thing is give up. To give up is foolish. The world is changing, and many Communist countries changing in a positive direction – and Chinese case also I think you see ...'

He talks about the Chinese hardline leadership, how it has remained unchanged since the 1950s, that behind their smiles and their promises of modernisation their real nature has remained unchanged. But the Chinese people have changed: this brings us to Tiananmen.

'When you see the Chinese hardliners have such a determination, a will, to crush their own people, and students – supposed to be the future of China – to attack hundreds of thousands of students – that is something strange.'

Here he pauses to ask Tenzin Tethong, who speaks fluent English, for a translation of what he is trying to express.

'His Holiness says it is like breaking the seat you're sitting on – self-destructive.'

'So I'm really wondering,' continues the Dalai Lama, 'what kind of logic do they have? What is their logic?'

His deep singsong voice is tinged with desperation: this is Tibet's darkest hour. He points to a huge relief map of Tibet on the wall behind us. If nothing is done within the next ten to twenty years, he says, Tibet will disappear. Engulfed by Chinese settlers, the Tibetan people will disappear, the forests and wildlife will be gone.

'You have suffered many setbacks. There is a new crackdown

in Lhasa – martial law, mass arrests, torture and imprisonment – this has been going on for thirty, forty years. The Chinese have devastated Tibet's fragile ecology. What is it that keeps you going? What keeps the Tibetan people going?'

'A belief in the rights that we have,' he replies without hesitation. It is a very precise answer – the whole Tibetan struggle in a nutshell. Decades of oppression have failed to intimidate them. The Dalai Lama says that Mao Zedong's dictum that 'power comes from the barrel of a gun' is counter-productive, and the use of force is short-sighted. The Tibetan struggle is very different because there is no ideology in it: the Tibetans are simply fighting against the forcible and illegal occupation of their country, fighting for the right to govern themselves and determine their own future.

It is said that the Dalai Lama never gives the same answer to a question he's heard before: he treats each question as brand new, although his patience is short when the answers are all too obvious. Once or twice he snaps at me impatiently for asking an all-too-obvious question, and he gives a short, curt answer. But most of the questions he receives thoughtfully, and turns over in silence for a while before formulating his reply.

I ask him about the institution of the Dalai Lama, about democratic reforms in the Tibetan government in exile, about the environment in Tibet, about his five-point peace plan for Tibet, about martial law in Lhasa, about Buddhism. Though Tibet itself may be suffering destruction, he says, Tibetan Buddhism is not at an end – prophecies make this clear. In fact, Tibetans have been very successful at spreading Tibetan Buddhism on a world stage (there are over five hundred Tibetan Buddhist centres around the world today). But how, I ask, can the ancient practice of Tibetan Buddhism be in tune with the Western world of science and technology? He responds after some thought: 'In Buddhism, especially Mahayana Buddhism, you see, emphasis is on your own investigation, and experiment is more important than just faith. And Buddha himself, you see, made very clear for his followers they should take investigation and through that way find some facts and then accept, and should not rely purely on scriptures. So that way of approach is quite similar to scientists –

sceptical, and carry out experiment and investigation. Once you find something, then accept.'

He asks me some questions about my travels in Tibet, about dealing with the Chinese ... I glance nervously at Tenzin Tethong because we're running over the allotted time. But he doesn't interfere, so I carry on.

As a counterpoint to his serious rhetoric, the Dalai Lama has a down-to-earth, hearty nature, and a great sense of humour. When I ask about the happiest period of his life, he breaks into a mischievous chuckle, and says it was when he was around ten to fifteen years old. He was living in the Potala Palace in Lhasa, and spent his summers at the Norbulingka Palace. The only important worry was his lessons, and he delighted in playing practical jokes. There were only four cars in pre-1950 Lhasa, rarely used for lack of fuel. Out of curiosity, he took one for a spin at the Norbulingka – and promptly crashed into a tree.

'Were you a good student?'

'No, I think bad student – I think lazy, very lazy. But I have much respect for my teachers, and generally speaking, in most subjects, learned easily.'

'Where did you learn your English?'

'Ah! That's the weakest subject!' he chuckles. 'It's never improved. I think I started in 1946, 1947. First I learned through books, the dictionary, the alphabet, and then two Tibetan officials helped me, then on one occasion Heinrich Harrer. Then in Mussoorie, one Indian teacher for a few months – I avoided him as best I could.'

He laughs loudly. He is self-taught in English: this remarkable fact explains the poignant silences while he deliberates his answers. It must be extremely frustrating for such an articulate person to try and express abstract philosophy in a foreign language. One peculiar advantage in all this – his accent, intonation and patchy English force the listener to deliberate on every word, to fill in the missing words, to think about the message carefully.

'What has been the most difficult period of your life?'

'Nineteen fifty-nine,' he answers, without hesitation, and goes on, 'that was the most difficult period – in Lhasa, then Mussoorie.

You see, we didn't know what was going to happen, and many Tibetans – you see, seventy thousand Tibetans – follow after me. And how to settle? What to do? And also, you see, the Tibetan question. How to keep the Tibetan question going, how to fight? And we don't know how to deal with the Indian Government. And then, you see, time goes, these things become clearer, clearer, clearer ... In some ways, having lost our country has led to regeneration. As for myself, I was just a Buddhist monk again – no need to worry about institutions or formalities, things like that – just express myself as a simple monk. Personally, I think I gained many positive experiences. Generally speaking, I think we Tibetans are quite happy people – and my case, hardly much worry – try our best to succeed ... The main point is, you see, one's motivation in daily practice. Try to improve or try to develop proper, sincere motivation. With that motivation ... some good results come, so very helpful, you see, to keep peace of mind daily.'

Incredibly, despite the devastation and upheaval, the Dalai Lama can see positive sides to losing his entire world and having to start all over again. The cassette player clicks: the end of the tape. I present a copy of a guidebook I wrote on Tibet. He gives me a *khata* and a Tibetan silver coin. We go over to the garden, have some pictures taken. He hams it up for the camera, grips my hand again – that strong, firm grip – and then the Living Buddha waves goodbye with a radiant smile.

Tenzin shows me out and asks if I need anything else. Yes, I'd like to get some blessing strings, blessed by the Dalai Lama. These red strings are supposed to have special powers and since it's risky to take Dalai Lama pictures into China, they are a much better 'gift' for me to be carrying there.

★★★★★

Wandering back to McLeod Ganj, I feel like I'm floating on air – a lightness of step that comes from meeting your idol. The Dalai Lama is a source of great inspiration not only to millions of Tibetans, but to many Westerners like myself. Here's a man working against impossible odds with quiet determination and energy, a man selflessly devoted to the cause of world peace and harmony.

His life has undergone fantastic twists and turns, the stuff that legends are made of. He was born on 6 July 1935 in a cow shed in Amdo Province, of a very poor Tibetan family. At age two he was recognised by disguised lamas as the reincarnation of the thirteenth Dalai Lama: he was born on the exact day his predecessor died; he displayed predicted physical features; he correctly identified objects belonging to his predecessor. The lamas informed the parents that the child was a high lama, and a caravan was arranged to take the family to Lhasa. Upon arrival, to the utter astonishment of his parents, the child was proclaimed spiritual leader of four million Tibetans. The family was informed they would be moving to new quarters – into the thousand-room Potala Palace.

When the Dalai Lama was fifteen the Chinese invaded Tibet. Still in his teens, he was given a crash course in statesmanship; at age eighteen, he was in Beijing negotiating with Mao Zedong and Zhou Enlai. In 1959 when he was twenty-three, he took final exams for the highest degree attainable in Tibet, Master of Metaphysics. Shortly after he escaped Tibet, going into exile in India, losing his entire country and his people. At Mussoorie, India, he issued a statement condemning the Chinese: he was just a Tibetan refugee – no passport, no country, no status.

Since then, the Tibetans in exile have fought back: fought to establish themselves in a host country, India, that did not recognise their goals or rights and deliberately kept the Tibetan community scattered. The largest group of refugees is in southern India. Tibetans in exile have established a strong community with their own government, schools and identity. And fought to keep the Tibetan issue alive in a world that largely forgot about them.

★★★★★

At Café Shambhala in McLeod Ganj I bump into Nick. It has been three years since I saw him last in Lhasa. Nick is from England, but is more at home in India. A fervent student of

Buddhism for many years, he has now branched into Zen and 'energy approaches': qigong and reflexology. We talk for a couple of hours; it is easy to linger in the cafés of McLeod Ganj over apricot, plum or peach pies, chocolate cake or banana bread. Nick is helping a Western woman set up a five-year retreat in a cave, bear- and waterproofing the place. Lots of hermits and yogis are walled up in caves around the back of Dharamsala. They let their hair and fingernails grow, and some don't see the light of day for years on end.

Yes, strange things abound in Dharamsala. Nick takes me off to a site above Tushita Retreat Centre, to a colonial house that now serves as a small temple. What am I looking at? I'm looking at a statue of a figure in the lotus position, with hands in the gesture of giving teachings, and a wide grin on the serene face. The statue looks like a laughing Buddha. But there is something very peculiar about this statue. Nick draws my attention to the inscription near the base. The real body of a lama has been enshrined within the sculpture. We are looking at the embalmed body of Ling Rinpoche, the Dalai Lama's senior tutor, and ninety-seventh throneholder of Je Tsongkhapa. He passed away in this house in 1983 at the age of eighty-one after being in a meditative posture for two weeks. The Dalai Lama decreed his body should be preserved according to ancient Tibetan methods (although an American was called in).

'You see that boy over there?' Nick indicates a child no more than five years old. 'He has been selected as the reincarnation of Ling Rinpoche. The old attendant of the lama now serves the young boy, and the rinpoche's old friends drop by for a chat with the boy, or to get a blessing. For these important positions, the reincarnations must now be found outside of Tibet because the Chinese have halted the selection process within Tibet.'

'What about the Panchen Lama?'

'Ah, yes. A very interesting case. With his death, the Chinese are in a very embarrassing position because they must accept the idea of reincarnation and sanction the search for a new candidate. And a candidate can only be recognised by the Dalai Lama, otherwise no Tibetan will accept the choice. But something else came up as well. The Panchen Lama was married to a Chinese woman and had a daughter. While he was alive, his wife pretended to be his personal secretary to preserve the Panchen Lama's spiritual standing among Tibetans, since no Panchen lineage holders have married. But when he died, the Chinese tried to bar his wife from memorial ceremonies, and she was furious, so she spoke out.'

We walk off to a meditation centre where Westerners undergo intensive courses and retreats, led by Tibetan lamas and by Western monks. Westerners with shaven heads and bright blue eyes, wearing robes, chanting and prostrating look as unnatural to me as would a Tibetan herder in the Himalayas wearing a pinstripe suit and talking with a BBC accent.

'You are staying for Saka Dawa, aren't you?'

'Pardon?'

'Saka Dawa – Buddha's birth, enlightenment and death.'

'But they already celebrated his birthday in Ladakh a month ago.'

'Ah, yes, but I think they moved it forward in Ladakh to get around the tourists. On the Tibetan calendar it's June this year.'

Nick fishes out a pocket-sized Tibetan calendar. Getting your hands on a Tibetan calendar is difficult. The Tibetan New Year, Losar, starts in late February or March, but the calendar for the next year is not issued until after Losar because it would be greatly inauspicious to issue one before the old year has finished.

'The Tibetans don't really care about time much,' Nick informs me. 'But they need a calendar to find out which days are auspicious and which aren't. It's like their sense of space – in old Tibet they had no idea what was outside the plateau.'

The entire year on the Tibetan calendar is designated with auspicious and inauspicious days, but the days change from year to year because the astrologers use a lunar calendar with thirteen months. At least half of the days of the year are inauspicious. Robert Ford, a Briton who set up radio links for the Tibetan government in the late 1940s, tells of his departure from Lhasa to Chamdo being delayed until he could set out on an exceptionally auspicious date. Ford could never find out which were the auspicious days and which weren't: he had thirteen pay days a year, but these were irregular because he could not be paid on an inauspicious date. The Tibetan concept of time is also different; it is cyclical. In a 60-year cycle, years are designated by five elements linked with twelve animals.

★★★★★

Lit by the full moon, the road is eerily alive, both sides jammed with squatting beggars. They've come from all over India to McLeod Ganj in time for Saka Dawa. At four in the morning, I meet Nick and we make our way up to the main temple. The moon is burning so brightly that I can make out the beggars quite clearly. Tibetan worshippers file in, chanting and handing out bags of change to the beggars.

'Because Saka Dawa is the most auspicious date on the calendar,' says Nick, 'any positive action will be multiplied ten million times, it is believed. And any negative action will also be multiplied ten million times.'

'Yes, I can see it's an auspicious date on the beggars' calendar, too.'

'They come in from as far away as Calcutta for this one. A lot aren't even beggars. They have portable TVs that they watch in the woods.'

The beggars are arguing, chatting, cooking, listening to transistor radios. It's a peculiar mix: the hardcore beggars (blind, missing a nose, a leg, or an arm) who've come by the busload from Bihar or Mysore; matronly women from Rajasthan dressed in silken finery and dripping jewellery; women with babies clinging to them; and sadhus (holy men), foreheads plastered in white, a red dot between the eyes, dressed in ochre, some shouldering monkeys.

'This is nothing,' says Nick. 'In Bodhgaya, when the Dalai Lama gave a Kalachakra initiation, there were more than ten thousand beggars – lepers on trolleys, the whole bit.'

It is said that Buddha attained enlightenment on the day of the full moon, just before dawn: the first thing he saw upon opening his eyes was the morning star on the horizon. The moon, Buddha said, is an illusion. We see the new moon and the various phases, but the moon itself does not change.

The break of dawn is dramatic: chanting Tibetans doing circuits of the temple, monks filing in from their residences, lights flickering in the valley, beggars clamouring for change, dogs barking and, hanging above it all at an impossible size, the moon.

At six o'clock the Dalai Lama comes out of his residence and strides across to the main temple to conduct a private ceremony for a large group of monks – a sea of maroon robes and crested yellow hats. The Dalai Lama sits cross-legged at the front of the temple to lead chanting and prayers with his rich, booming baritone. The Tibetans shuffle past the temple doors, trying to get a glimpse of their leader. At the back of the temple is a table with thousands of butter lamps. I watch a Tibetan man and his daughter: he holds her hand as she peeps over the table to place a butter lamp on it. Her eyes are wide as she looks at the galaxy of flickering lamps. This is where the last flame of Tibet is kept burning.

Something resonates here. As I look at the flickering flame and the wide-eyed child, something resonates: the nucleus of an idea. I want to see as much as I can of the Tibetan world before the flame is snuffed out, to get cracking before it all disappears. Because according to the Dalai Lama, it's on the brink – and he should know.

★★★★★

I tie a red blessing string onto the handlebars and put the Tibetan coin from the Dalai Lama in my wallet: I need every talisman I can lay my hands on to make it alive through the Indian traffic. I saddle up and, with a last look back at McLeod Ganj, take off at full throttle through the forests, past bands of rhesus monkeys, surprised Indians, delighted schoolchildren, through Kotwali Bazaar, flashing through the foothills on the long drop towards

Pathankot and onward into Punjab. Then on into Pakistan, hitting the Karakoram Highway, bound for Kashgar.

*****

How The Throwing Of Flour In The Air
Came To Be Banned In Lhasa

In October 1989 the Dalai Lama was awarded the Nobel Peace Prize. The Nobel award and Tiananmen were inextricably linked: a special message to China from the world community. China vigorously protested the award, even threatening to cut off diplomatic relations with Norway, which bestowed the honour. Score one for the Tibetans: the tide of opinion was turning their way. The Dalai Lama was suddenly respectable at an international level.

When Tiananmen happened, the world was learning that the Chinese regime was indeed as brutal and repressive as the Tibetans had always claimed. The world got another shock when it was realised that the Chinese authorities manipulate the media to extremes. Not a single person died at Tiananmen, according to the Chinese, and what people saw on TV screens was fabricated in Hollywood (that story was later changed: they said that soldiers opened fire with real bullets because there was a shortage of tear gas and rubber bullets, and because 'thugs' tried to beat up the People's Liberation Army).

In Tibet things became more repressive. Consider this modern parable about the throwing of flour. Unable to celebrate the peace prize award openly in Tibet, Tibetans took to gathering at picnic spots and sacred sites to mark the occasion by simply throwing barley flour (tsampa) in the air. It seemed harmless enough, but the Chinese got wind of it and the practice was banned in Lhasa in December 1989. Tsampa, however, is the staple food of Tibet – it's like banning the throwing of rice in China. How can it be policed? Can you imagine a case where a man is found guilty of throwing flour in the air and confesses, under questioning, that he was celebrating the award of the Nobel Peace Prize?

The Dalai Lama's birthday falls on 6 July. Celebrations of that date were also banned in Tibet. The modern Tibetan calendar is now studded with underground memorial dates. March 10th commemorates the 1959 Lhasa Uprising; September 27th the start of the 1987 Lhasa riots; December 10th is 'celebrated' as International Human Rights Day, which sparked a protest in Lhasa in 1988.

But it was what happened early in 1989 that was to rock the Tibetan world. On 28 January the tenth Panchen Lama died of a heart attack in Shigatse. The Dalai Lama and the Panchen Lama are like the sun and the moon of the Tibetan world, the two highest incarnates. The search for the Panchen Lama's reincarnate would have to take place soon. But who would find him and where? Would he be found in occupied Tibet? These were highly sensitive issues, especially in the light of the Nobel Peace Prize award, which had resulted in a vicious backlash against the Dalai Lama by the Chinese …

3

AT THE EDGE OF TIBET

Through Mongolia and Amdo

In mid-winter, back home in Vancouver, my world started falling apart. A long-term relationship collapsed with a heavy thud, and it was dark, cold and raining. Everybody getting on everybody's nerves and at each other's throats because they either didn't get enough sunlight, or enough sex, or worse, none of both. I had a bad case of the blues, and only good travelling could cure that.

It was as though I'd entered one of the lower hells, you know, Hell Number 15: the land of random dating. Candidate One: a shapely Chinese magician who flicked cards across the lounge to practise and who could break a balloon with a (sharpened) card at twenty paces. She loved chillies, and once took me to an expensive restaurant where we devoured a whole lobster with our hands. When it came to mating, she did her magic act and disappeared.

Then along came someone who looked promising. *Yes, how about her?* She looked great; she seemed very interesting. I asked her out. Mid-way through dinner in a fancy restaurant, I felt a great drowsiness come over me; this woman's chatter about inane things was sending me to sleep. No common ground. I was feeling out for it, but found a void. We got on to music.

'I hate jazz,' she said. 'Doesn't make any sense, it's a whole lot of useless sounds.' I almost choked. We got on to the subject of books; she looked at me and said, 'I don't read books.'

I got up, as if to go to the gents, paid the bill and left. *She doesn't read books!*

Meanwhile, on the subject of books, I was dealing with four publishers, trying to get something to get me out of town – *anything* to get me out of town. I contacted an American guidebook publisher and suggested a few regions to write about. The response was negative, but how about Australia? Or Hong Kong? Or Florida? Boring, I thought, so I chased another publisher. No, they didn't think that India would fly, but Madagascar needed updating, or how about Brazil? And so on: guidebook publishers carving up the planet and parcelling it out piece by piece to various writers, like gifts from the Roman emperor to his best cohorts.

I vacillated wildly from book to book trying to get ideas on these places – just how bad were they? One minute I'd be down at the library looking for the goods on Madagascar, the next I'd go to a travel bookshop to see what was on the shelves for Florida or Hong Kong or ... I felt like a human yo-yo bounced from one end of the planet to the other, not knowing where I would end up or, worse still, why.

And I was getting restless. Strange snippets of news surfaced about distant acquaintances: *X died from cancer – yes, and so young too. Happened so quickly. What happened to Y? Didn't you hear? Killed in a car accident* ... And then there was the tragic and bizarre case of Z, who indignantly tried to get his money back from a faulty vending machine, which fell over and squashed him. I think one of the main reasons I travel is that the prospect of *not* being able to travel is unbearable. What if I had an accident and couldn't get about any more?

In late January an old travel buddy, Scott, called from California. Scott was a glutton for travel to remote places, a robust outdoorsman who was quite in his element in a tent and a sleeping bag, preferably with a howling snowstorm raging outside. He sounded excited as he relayed the news. Mongolia had opened up for the first time since the 1920s. He and a London-based friend, Peter, were thinking about a trip. How about coming along? *Mongolia!* My ears pricked up. *Mongolia?* Somewhere in the back of my head a picture popped up: a Russian turboprop aircraft flying over windswept grasslands filled with camels, horses and yaks. I said I'd think about it. Scott hung up.

Back to the drawing board. *Madagascar? Australia? Hong Kong?* I weighed them up, mulled them over, but they didn't seize my imagination. But Mongolia – that did. Remote, raw, fresh, mysterious, different; the stuff of travel. Mongolia was newly independent, shaking itself free of Russia; the practices of Tibetan Buddhism were being revived. Mongolia dominated the drawing board ...

At Chinese New Year, the beginning of February, I got two fortune cookies in a Chinese restaurant. The first said: 'You will soon receive very special attention' – a cryptic message that I didn't take much notice of. But the second fortune cookie threw me off balance. It simply said: 'Listen to your intuition this month'. At that instant I knew exactly what I had to do: I had been half-hearted about everything except Mongolia. I hadn't listened to my own heart. My travel intuition had been saying 'Mongolia! Mongolia!' – the word spelled adventure. But I had rejected the place because it was not attached to any project. So that's when I said *Fuck it! I'm going to Mongolia!*

So I called up Scott: OK, you're on – how do we get there? On the TransMongolian Express, of course. Meet in Munich, train to Budapest, pick up Mongolian visas there. When? Well, April's too cold – what about May? May in Mongolia. It had a certain ring to it. I felt 300 per cent better – this trip was on the rails. Things were falling into place. My blues disappeared. All was projecting in a forward direction; things were moving along nicely. I arranged to pack in my job for a year: a burn-out leave. A one-way air ticket to Munich sealed my fate. The ticket was non-refundable, non-transferable. I had reached the point of no return. I was going out there – to Mongolia.

★★★★★

There was only one catch: the other fortune cookie, the one about receiving special attention. A few days after I committed myself to Mongolia I met a phenomenal woman. She was madonna, witch, bitch, enchantress, siren, Venus and vixen all rolled into one. Maybe she had supernatural powers and supernatural timing. Maybe she came from outer space. She struck like a bombshell. She had a great sense of humour. She had a malicious tongue. She was sharp. She was sexy. I was still trying to figure out which planet she was from when she phoned me up and said she was calling from heaven. I asked her how come she was still on the phone if she was in heaven, and she said it was a cordless remote, and she always carried it with her, into the bath, or up to heaven. Yes, this one was made in heaven – a heavenly body, in tight orbit around me.

She wasn't the kind of woman who reads all those magazines on sizing men up; no, she wasn't a magazine clone. She didn't check me out – she *sounded* me out. It was as though she'd been let loose in the kingdom of my heart and was indulging in some major renovations, ripping down walls at will, flinging around pipes and plumbing, replacing the nerves and electrical circuits, and not the least fazed by any obstacles. Until, that is, she got to Mongolia.

'You're *what*?' she gasped in disbelief. 'You're going *where*?'

Jesus, I must be going bonkers. What did she call it? That euphemism for the insane – yes, reality-challenged. I was reality-challenged. My realities had shifted up and down with the speed of a freight train over the last two months.

I'm stuck on the horns of a dilemma: do I traipse off to the barren highlands of Mongolia and freeze my arse off or do I stay here entangled with this warm woman? Well, life could be worse … but the choices tore me up. I didn't know if I was coming or going. One minute I was wandering through her islands, charting her waters, testing her weaknesses; the next I was poring over maps of landlocked Mongolia.

So I went to a café, sat down with the morning paper, and consulted my horoscope. I'm Gemini – sign of the twins, the double, the two, the dilemma, terminal indecision, the man with two brains. And what a deadly verdict the morning paper delivered: *The green light is on for travel projects involving writing or legalities; you've been delayed so long it may be hard to believe it's really your time.* I got the first part right away – that meant Mongolia – but it only struck me later in the afternoon that the second part of the horoscope wasn't about writing or a green light. I'd had no long waiting period for Mongolia or anything like that; it was a spur-of-the-moment thing. And I'd had my glutton's share of travelling over the years. No, the last part didn't refer to travel: it referred to the woman from the other planet. So the horoscope got me no closer to a decision – it was back to a 50-50 split again.

The ides of March: stab me in the back. In the end, she resolved the dilemma herself. She asked how she could possibly get to know me when I was about to disappear into Mongolia. She said that because of Mongolia she'd rushed into things, and now she was having second thoughts. If I was away five, six, nine months, I might well meet someone else, she said, a pretty woman from Georgia, or a blushing Mongolian shepherdess – who knows? Or she might meet someone else. No, it was too long; she couldn't wait, she couldn't stand the uncertainty. She wrote the whole thing off as a fling.

Down on my luck again I sunk into great despondency. More rejections followed: manuscripts rejected, an old friend left town. And my car registration was running out. It was all pointing to one thing: I had to get out.

★★★★★

The only person I knew of who'd been to Mongolia first-hand was a filmmaker who had done a documentary about dragon bones. These were actually dinosaur bones, which are well preserved in Mongolia's arid climate. In fact, eggs have been discovered with half-hatched dinosaurs, as well as unhatched eggs. Holy Christ! What if some did hatch after being dug out of some glacier? So my preconceptions of Mongolia were somewhat warped by this piece of science fiction. There was a certain surrealism about the place: half-hatched dinosaurs suspended over a desert landscape. And plague. The Black Death had originally travelled from Mongolia to Europe. The plague bacillus was still found in fieldmice there. I made a mental note: do not get bitten by a fieldmouse in Mongolia.

I was scrambling, trying to track down books on a list from the Mongolian Society, and feverishly trying to assemble gear for the trip. Scott phoned again – Munich was proceeding. His friend, Peter, had been located in London and was amenable to meeting in Munich. Peter's brother Steve had been talked into the trip. That would make four of us, which was a good number for splitting expenses on hired transport. Scott was working on Russian visas via an agency in New York.

'Got some complications,' I told him. 'Fallen heavily for a woman.'

'Yeah, me too,' said Scott. 'This woman, she's going out with my best friend and –'

'You're coming between them –'

'Well, it's just that the chemistry is there and ... You know, I think the mention of Mongolia is an aphrodisiac – it brought us real close real fast. I've got a few other problems – some job offers, starting to look very nice. But that means I cut my time a bit short in Mongolia to take the job. But you know I wouldn't miss Mongolia for anything.'

Mongolia brought them together!

'How come for you and her Mongolia is an aphrodisiac, and for my paramour it's a total turn-off?'

'Sorry, buddy, don't know how it all works. Women are mysterious.'

★★★★★

Duffle bags are loaded with camping gear, freeze-dried food and film. New passport, new bags, new jacket: this has all the frisson of a first date. First stop, Munich. Here, our 'crew' meets for the first time: myself, Scott, Peter and Steve. We shuffle documents around, compare notes, divide up cash US dollars. The trip starts to gain momentum. We're on our way, riding the rails to Budapest. Here, a pause to indulge in more visa shopping, this time the Mongolian visa. With the Russian visa in hand, we can tackle the next country. To increase our chances in the visa lottery, we have armed ourselves with a letter of introduction from a (bogus) New York society about our mission to collect information on Mongolia: the letter waxes lyrical about promoting friendship between the American people and the Mongolians. We had it rendered into Russian script, but couldn't find anybody capable of transcribing it into Mongolian, though most Mongolians knew some Russian.

Luckily, the consul was out and only his assistant was there.

'But this is not an invitation from someone in Mongolia,' said the assistant, eyeing the letter.

'That is true, but it is an invitation all the same,' I told him. 'And we already have our Russian visas.'

He was perplexed. We pressed the case, pushed the envelope. He went inside and stamped the passports. We waited till we were out of earshot to let loose victory yelps and yodels.

We stayed in a medieval castle converted into a hotel. In the morning, I was awoken by what sounded like lots of cooing and lovemaking, echoing in all directions. This turned out to be pigeons nestled in the thick turrets of the castle walls.

★★★★★

Red Square, Moscow: for the first time on this trip, I feel like I'm in a foreign place. Munich has beerhalls, Budapest has medieval fortresses, but Red Square has an *aura* about it. A weird aura, to be sure. To one side of the vast paved square is St Basil's Cathedral, with its eye-popping fantasy spires; on the other side is GUM Department Store, the largest in Moscow, with lots of bare shelves, or long queues if there is anything on the shelves. Down the way from Spassky Tower at the Kremlin is Lenin's mausoleum, with his embalmed body displayed inside. The body is just another tourist attraction these days, with the Russians busy pulling down Lenin statues all over the country and changing all the 1920s revolutionary place names.

This altering of names makes navigation in Moscow's Metro a challenge since my map doesn't match the names on the platforms. But I like getting lost in the Metro – the real wonders of Moscow are under Red Square. In the Metro you can, for a few cents, explore a fascinating underground realm – stations decorated with chandeliers, art nouveau stained glass, or mosaic frescoes depicting revolutionary themes.

Finding food in Moscow is even more of a challenge. Scouting around the markets all we can find is caviar and vodka, while at grungy restaurants patrons line up for bowls of watery borscht (the food supply in Moscow has since improved, but good restaurants are the province of the privileged). We wind up eating at McDonald's where, at least, palatable food is served. Eventually we find out where the resident foreigners get their supplies – from a place called Irish House, a supermarket which deals only in US cash and has its own guards to keep an eye on the precious merchandise. We ransack the place for supplies for the long haul across Russia to Mongolia.

On the train platform Scott turns in to a condom vending machine: he dispenses condoms to those who've helped us out. Always handy to have a parting gift. Balloons for the children and, well, condoms for the adults. American-made condoms are superior quality; they don't break like the Russian ones, so they're sold at a premium.

We're off on the epic rail ride from Red Square to Tiananmen Square aboard the TransMongolian on Russian Train Number 2, the Rossiya. The first leg is a three-day journey to Irkutsk. Because it's actually cheaper to fly the route than take the train these days, you're in it for the thrill of overlanding. The 'Moscow Mafia' buys up large blocks of seats and sells them on the black market for this very popular trading (smuggling) run into China. So while the sleepers are worth maybe $3, they wind up costing us exponentially more than that.

From the window the main sight is a continuous blur of birch trees. Occasionally the train passes dreary logging towns – sawdust, junkyards, railyards, run-down wooden houses with corrugated roofs, the odd onion dome of a Russian Orthodox church. I'm reading a collection of Russian short stories I bought in Moscow for ten cents, a hardback English translation. The stark landscape perfectly matches the melancholy tone of stories about downtrodden serfs – classics by the likes of Dostoevsky, Turgenev and Pushkin. Life is still very tough in Russia. I cast my mind back to the family whose apartment we temporarily appropriated for our stay in Moscow, a university professor, Serge, and his journalist wife, Lena. His dream is to own a home computer; her dream is to travel to Paris; they figure it will take about five to ten years to realise those dreams. Serge is a blues fan;

the Russians didn't invent the blues, he told me, but they sure can identify with the lyrics.

Each car on a Russian train has several *provotniks*, usually women. *Provotniks* are supposed to provide linen, clean up, tell you when the train is arriving at a major station, and stoke the large *samovar* that provides hot water, but I suspect their real function is to maintain law and order among vodka-sodden passengers. Our *provotnik* has done over two hundred trips on this line, while her partner has clocked up fifty. He was an army officer who met her on this very train. A romance blossomed, they married, and he took to riding the rails with her.

Talking of romance, Scott is lovesick. All he can talk about is the woman he left behind in San Francisco. The TransMongolian ride covers three-quarters of Eurasia, so jokes abound about Scott holding his dick for three-quarters of the way across the Eurasian continent. Boredom at night is eased by the sport of train surfing: wait for the *provotnik* to take a nap, then open a door and climb onto the roof to take in the starry views.

Mafia types are getting bolder in Russia these days – or maybe more desperate – due to the collapse of the Soviet economy. When the train stops at one town, two thugs try to smash their way into the dining car to get alcohol. Apart from vodka and beer, the dining car only serves a mean-looking borscht, but you go to the dining car to chat with other passengers and stretch your limbs. Next door is a lazy concession to technology: half a car converted into a video salon, with awful films on show. The most exciting part of the day is when the train stops, giving you ten or fifteen minutes to rush around and buy whatever you can lay your hands on – hard-boiled eggs, wizened apples or piping hot potatoes – sold by motherly *babushkas* who operate out of large handbags.

★★★★★

We're making progress now, crawling across the map. We have even passed an obelisk that pretends to mark a dividing line between Europe and Asia. We have a frosty two-night stop in

Irkutsk: by day, we head off in a Lada taxi through snow flurries to visit Lake Baikal. By night it's a little warmer – in more senses than one – in an Irkutsk nightclub featuring near-naked go-go dancers.

At the station we are met by a woman who hands over the tickets for the fourth train of this rail odyssey, a local running to Ulan Bator. At the Mongolian border passengers get the smuggler's third degree from Russian military in greatcoats and fur hats. There's a definite change in the landscape, and we abruptly leave the Siberian forests behind. In Mongolia it's rolling hills and expanses of grassland dusted in snow, dotted with the herdsmen's circular felt tents and droves of goats and sheep.

'Pisspot!' snaps the guard. 'Pisspot pliz!'

The guard is intrigued by my passport, and I know why – it's the unicorn on the cover. This is a plum-coloured EEC passport bearing the United Kingdom's coat of arms, a lion and a unicorn upholding a crown with dual Latin mottoes. A Mongolian may never have seen a lion, but they grow up on horses; they ride before they walk.

*****

Ulan Bator, 6 a.m: Tumbling off the TransMongolian after the four-day ride from Moscow, things looked decidedly bleak. It was freezing cold, my head was reeling from too many rounds of vodka and, as far as the bleary eye could see, Soviet-style apartment blocks blotted the skyline of the capital. The four of us marched along the platform in silence, lugging our food and camping supplies. That morning, exotic-sounding Mongolia, which had lured us halfway round the world, didn't look exotic at all. It just looked terribly grey and dreary.

The first problem was where to stay. We asked a train conductor who'd just finished his shift. Solution: he took us back to his place where we occupied the carpeted living room for a couple of days. His family took care of us until we got our bearings and located a cheap hotel. The next pressing problem was visas: they were in danger of running out. They'd started running immediately in Budapest, and we'd spent about ten days getting to Ulan Bator, with stops in Moscow and Irkutsk. That meant we only had four days left.

One of the great sports of Mongolia is wrestling. We got a fine introduction to strangleholds at the visa office. The bullish man who dealt with foreigners was adamant that no extensions were permitted. Again I flourished our letter in Russian script and said we had a story to write and so much of Mongolia to see. Again he was adamant that there would be absolutely no extensions. Again I told him how big Mongolia was and how much time was needed to see it. And so it went, back and forth, this strenuous bout of visa-wrestling, for three hours, until suddenly he flipped: he abruptly picked up a pen, added a month to the visa in handwriting, and stamped it. Then he wanted to come on board as our guide for a trip to the north. Persistence pays.

We breathed a bit easier, and got around town to take in the sights, like the dinosaur museum, with its colossal rewired skeletons. Iconography of note: near the main hotel, a still-standing statue of Lenin. The one-tugrik note features the snow lion once found on old Tibetan money; the watermark on the tugrik is Genghis Khan. Scott left a few icons of his own – he put a *Free Tibet* sticker on the bumper of a Chinese consulate car.

Our self-appointed guide to the capital was Batman. It seems that every Mongolian male name has a 'Bat' or a 'Bold' in it, so 'Batmunh', or 'Batman', is just a bizarre coincidence. The first name is the most important in Mongolia, and Batman means 'Heavy Metal Hero' according to our new-found guide.

We met Batman on the street as we were trying to flag down a car near our hotel: there are very few taxis in the capital, so you just flag down any old vehicle and pay. Batman was short, with a crew cut and thick glasses, and a head full of English idioms that he was eager to practise in preparation for the time when he would make a pilgrimage to England to visit a British friend. Our part of the bargain was a free tour guide and translator.

Out with Russian, in with English. Learning English was all the rage in Ulan Bator, but few had mastered the basics. Batman

81

was at the advanced level, puzzled by idioms. We found out he had several love interests in the capital.

'I am playing the field!' he said proudly. 'I am, how to say? Sowing my wild oats!'

'Getting your rocks off.'

'Blowing your socks off.'

'Being a sexist pig.'

He had never heard so many wonderful idioms. He milked us for more. Like everyone else in Ulan Bator, he was desperate to change Mongolian tugriks for US dollars. One American dollar equals one big fistful of tugriks: the tugrik, like the rouble, had gone through the roof. Leading the way to economic disaster were two central bank governors who, in 1990 and 1991, gambled away the country's entire hard currency reserves – estimated at US$90 million – on international foreign exchange markets. They were thrown in jail, but rumour has it they soon had to be brought back to help sort out the country's tangled financial web as nobody else had the qualifications to do so.

'Frankly speaking, to tell you the truth, to be quite honest, to lay it on the line ...'

'Yes, man, cough it up!'

'Well, *to give you the real version*, the fact is that there are two hundred and fifty tugriks to the dollar,' Batman finally spat out, in his idiomatic mode. The year before, there were three tugriks to the dollar. Long queues for bread and milk, and a black market in fuel were tell-tale signs of a chaotic economy. Downtown, on shopfronts, linguistic chaos too: traditional Mongolian vertical characters are on their way in, while Cyrillic-scripted Mongolian is on its way out.

'The Russians are finished here,' said Batman. 'How do you say that with other expressions?'

'Gone ... Kaput ... History ... Toast ...'

'The Russians are *toast*? Toast!' said Batman. His face lit up – a new idiom – wonderful! 'It's toast! *The Russians are toast!*'

The Russians may be toast, but their 'legacy' lingers. Ulan Bator is an extremely ugly city of 500,000 – almost a quarter of Mongolia's population. In former times, the city was a sea of *gers* (the felt and lattice-wood tents used by Mongolian nomads). Now Russian-built apartment blocks dominate, towering over the odd Tibetan-style monastery, or the showy palace of a former khan. It's a curious blend of Russian, Chinese, Tibetan and Mongolian – with a touch of Disney. These influences can be seen in Mongolia's whimsical postage stamps: one features a Mongolian cosmonaut (sent into space with a Russian); another features Fred Flintstone riding a dinosaur past some *gers*; another depicts blissful Tara (goddess of compassion), and bodhisattvas of Tibetan origin.

But the real hero of Mongolia is Genghis (or Chinggis as he is known in Mongolia) Khan. Shopping for supplies at a shop that only accepted US dollars, I came across Chinggis Khan Vodka, 40 per cent proof, and labelled in English. Prominent on the label was Genghis' fat, bearded face, impishly smiling. All part of a determined effort to annihilate Mother Russia and revive the glorious days of Genghis way back in the thirteenth century. There was a four-hour Mongolian-made epic on the life of Genghis playing in cinemas in Ulan Bator.

★★★★★

Like Tibet, Mongolia severed links with the Chinese after the collapse of the Qing Dynasty in 1911. Formally declaring independence, Mongolia established a theocratic government under the leadership of the eighth Living Buddha, the Bogd Khan (Holy King). In a tussle between Chinese warlords, White Russians and Russian Bolsheviks, the Bolsheviks prevailed and, in 1924, Mongolia became the world's second Communist country, firmly under Soviet domination. When the Soviet Union disintegrated in 1989, Mongolia made a break for it, demanding independence. The last Russian troops left in 1992. The Tibetan experience under Chinese Communism is similar to that of Mongolia under the Soviets. There is no reason why Buddhism and Communism cannot coexist: both are rational, non-theistic (no belief in a superior god) and altruistic systems. The problem is Communist intolerance of Buddhism, not the reverse. In the

Stalinist era, the Russians tried to smash Tibetan Buddhism in Mongolia. Now, with independence, comes a revival.

A similar collapse of the Chinese Empire is the scenario that intrigues Tibetans the most. The Chinese authorities are upset with the Dalai Lama's visits to Mongolia, accusing him of stirring up anti-Chinese feeling. The Dalai Lama, in turn, points his finger at Inner Mongolia, a huge area that is now a province of China. In what seems to have been a deliberate policy, millions of Chinese were transferred into Inner Mongolia and today there is hardly any Mongolian presence left in the region.

On the map, Mongolia looks a fair distance from Tibet, but if you combine it with Inner Mongolia and take into account that Amdo used to encompass present-day Qinghai and Gansu, it is clearer that the Mongol Empire used to reach the edge of the Tibetan Empire. If the Himalayas formed Tibet's icy southern barrier, the opposite was true in the north, where relentless desert and grasslands are to be found.

In the thirteenth century, Tibet, like China, fell under Mongol domination, and the Mongols took a great interest in Tibetan Buddhism. Mongolia was, at the time, the sole superpower of Central Asia, with an empire that surpassed in size even that of the ancient Romans. In 1254, what is possibly the world's first inter-faith meeting took place at the Mongol court. Perhaps 'meeting' is not the right word: it was a showdown. Under the auspices of Mongke Khan, grandson of Genghis, a great debate was held between resident Christians, Nestorians, Muslims and Tibetan Buddhists. The Tibetans won the day, and Tibetan Buddhism was adopted as the faith of the khans.

In the fourteenth century, Tibet resumed its independent ways, but enjoyed a special patron-priest relationship with the Mongols over the next few centuries. Invited to educate the Mongols in spiritual matters, the Tibetans in turn accepted Mongolian guarantees to stave off would-be invaders. At Ulan Bator's Fine Arts Museum, the Mongol connection is vibrantly portrayed in *tankas*: *tankas* of Lhasa and the Potala, appliqué *tankas* of Tibetan deities. The museum offers a crash course in Mongol history, with lifelike portraits of the spiritual rulers, the Bogd Khans.

Masterful sculptures of Tara in bronze took my breath away. They were crafted by the revered seventeenth-century lama and ruler, Zanabazar.

Modern scholars come to Mongolia looking for precious *tankas* and texts that have disappeared without trace in Tibet itself, destroyed by the Chinese. Consider this find in the remote Russian province of Buryatia, populated by ethnic Mongolians: in 1985 a dusty box was opened in an Orthodox church. It was a complete set of the illustrated medical treatise known as the *Blue Beryl*, or *Tibetan Medical Atlas*. The 76 *tankas* which make up the treatise document the entire Tibetan medical system and were originally created to train medical practitioners. Somehow they made their way to Siberia, probably around 1900, were expropriated during Stalinist purges, and left forgotten in the church, lying there for over sixty years.

★★★★★

There's no nightlife to speak of in Ulan Bator, but sometimes you get lucky. The Mongolian Circus is the only place in the world where you'll see performing yaks. You have to take into account the fact that yaks are not very patient creatures, nor easily trained, so when you see a costumed performer walking a tightrope anchored at either end by the horns of live yaks, you can only be left enthralled. The concept of the circus is Russian in origin, but the repertoire of acts here is definitely Mongolian. An acrobatic team uses a springboard to somersault over a line of Bactrian camels in true Evel Knievel style. After each round of applause, another camel is added. This is followed by a brilliant display of trick horseriding.

Another night we gatecrash a musical soirée that is being staged for a visiting dignitary. This reveals unexpected gems: a haunting *khoomi* singer (performing throat singing, hitting high and low notes simultaneously), and an ensemble playing horse-head fiddles and other home-grown instruments. But the greatest surprise is a shamanic drumming dance, enacted by performers in reindeer skins. Up in the far north of Mongolia, the Tsatuun nomads depend on reindeer herds the way Tibetans depend on yaks; the Tsatuun even ride the reindeer like horses. The shamanic dance is obviously associated with inducing trances – it is visual voodoo, a window into arcane practices that have largely disappeared elsewhere. It is hauntingly primal and earthy, which is what shamanism is all about: a spiritual link to the environment, communing with the spirits of the forests, lakes and animals, being in tune with nature. These are ancient skills that sorely need to be revived in an era where the environment is everywhere under siege. Mongolia's great shamans were ridiculed as superstitious, and were systematically exterminated by the Russians.

★★★★★

It was our intention to get out of the capital at the first opportunity and travel the countryside at our own pace. This is where the true spirit of Mongolia lies. We struck a deal with a jeep driver called Ganbat. Our target was the far north-west, Lake Hovsgol. We would be riding in a Gaz, a sturdy Russian army jeep. 'Gaz' struck me as a kind of ironic brand name: it sounded short for 'gazelle', but it might equally have referred to 'gas guzzler', and to a chronic lack of petrol in Mongolia.

With the fuel crisis, we counted ourselves very lucky to have got a jeep at all. Cash US dollars helped along. Shaking off Russia had solved pride problems, but produced others: with Russia no longer supplying petrol, it seems logical for Mongolia to turn to China as a source of fuel, but Mongolia is suspicious – with good reason – of China's designs on the place.

Ganbat's entire family came out to wish us bon voyage. His girlfriend did more than that; she had decided to come along for the trip, complete with fashion outfits. A kind of last minute honeymoon decision, Ganbat explained (with four foreigners along – very romantic). Grandfather helped load up a dozen fuel jerrycans. Grandfather was an excellent mime: we didn't know it then, but the cans were all empty.

It quickly becomes apparent when you leave the capital that there are more animals than people in Mongolia – many more. On the grasslands you pass great herds of sheep, goats and horses. Here, in the wide open spaces, we sighted lots of birds too, pairs of hawks or demoiselle cranes. This is the Mongolia I wanted to see, the land of the nomads: the vast steppes, forests and deserts. In winter conditions are extremely harsh with ice, snow and bone-chilling winds. In the summer it actually gets hot.

This is something that puzzled me when I read books like Luigi Barzini's *From Peking to Paris* (written circa 1908): how, in the pre-road era, did primitive rally cars travel across Mongolia? The answer is grasslands. The cars could motor over the prairies. It wasn't entirely that simple; horses and camels had to haul the cars over some sections of the Gobi or when fording rivers, and camel caravans were used to lay down petrol depots. Mongolian horsemen entered the race, unofficially trying to outpace the cars. Another neat trick, further north at Lake Baikal, was driving along the tracks of the Trans-Siberian Railway, flying a red flag to stop approaching trains (which didn't always work).

In this great blank on the map – Mongolia is three times the size of France – there are few roads, but a jeep can go virtually anywhere on the flatlands in the summer. The problem is that there are no signposts, so which way do you go? Ganbat certainly didn't know; he kept getting lost, and had to ask local herdsmen for directions. He also obliquely asked us for directions, requesting a look at a large map that we had of the country.

As the Russian jeep bucked over the grasslands in the middle of nowhere, Ganbat announced that we were running out of fuel. And then a miraculous mirage appeared: on the horizon were two fuel tankers, which Ganbat flagged down. He paid for the fuel in cash, and we went running for our lives when the drivers lit up cigarettes during the refuelling operation.

The Chinggis Khan Vodka came in handy, we discovered, to seal deals and humour people along the route. It also had ceremonial uses: at strategic spots along the way were cairns of stones, called *oboos*, which Mongolians walk around three times and flick vodka at to ensure safe passage. And at each *oboo*, a few rounds of vodka went down the hatch for good measure too.

After a series of mishaps – jeep breakdowns, getting lost – we reached our target. Lake Hovsgol was frozen and starkly beautiful. We drove as far as the road went and camped at the edge of the lake. Nearby were a few *gers* with horse and yak herders. The herders were dressed in traditional garb – *del* and leather boots – the men sporting fedoras, the women dripping jewellery. The *del* is a long outer garment, held in place by a bright sash, and worn by both sexes with more intricate patterns for women. So they sit you down on a carpet in the *ger*, give you tea and yak milk: what do you talk about? Well, the most popular topics of conversation are animals, the weather and the family. Having exhausted the first two (*How are your yaks? Cold, isn't it?*), we proceeded to the third, which was more entertaining. The Mongolian words for the family had us in stitches. The word for mother is *ecchh*, father is *ow*, sister is *itch*, and brother is *ak*. We spent a pleasant afternoon sorting out the *itches*, *ows*, *aks* and *ecchhes* (I never did discover the word for mother-in-law).

Barbecues are a little different in Mongolia. They kill sheep with their bare hands. For spiritual reasons, they don't cut its throat; they just give it a heart attack instead by slitting a small hole in the stomach and reaching up to pinch a major artery.

We explored the Lake Hovsgol area on horseback – or at least tried to. A daytrip to the hills above the lake had me cursing my saddle, which was made of wood, topped with thin carpet. I kept wondering how Genghis Khan's hordes could've plundered Central Asia; if it was on saddles like this, they must've had rearends made of rubber.

★★★★★

Ten days later we were back in Ulan Bator, boarding a plane to fly south-west to the Gobi Desert. Or, should I say, trying to board a plane. We were late for check-in at Ulan Bator airport, and the surly clerk had resold our reserved seats. Great commotion ensued,

AT THE EDGE OF TIBET

with expletives hurled back and forth, and some frayed tempers. The next flight was four days away.

At this point the Mongolian pilot and crew strolled past. The pilot, readily identifiable by his sleek Ray-Bans, motioned for us to follow the crew. Straight into the cockpit of an Antonov-24, a 50-seat turboprop, with our luggage. The propellers whirled, the crew took their seats, the pilot indicated two flip-down seats for us – which still left me standing. An outstanding take-off, you might say. But you can't beat the price: the tickets cost us US$5 apiece, local price.

Our own crew was down to three – myself, Scott and Steve. Peter's time had run out – he had to get back to work in London – so he'd gone forward to Beijing and Hong Kong, and was thus missing out on this spellbinding flight.

Talk about dinosaurs: our plane was a vintage Russian model. There is only one thing scarier than a Russian plane: flying one with a Mongolian pilot, and being in the cockpit. Due to complete absence of computer controls, at the helm of this vintage Russian aircraft is a human decision-maker.

When the Soviet Union fell apart, so did Aeroflot. Once the world's largest fleet, the national airline splintered into hundreds of regional airlines, some little more than a single plane and pilot. This made matters worse for Russian aircraft, which already had a reputation for the world's worst safety records because of poor maintenance. Planes flown back to Russia for servicing might sit on the tarmac for up to a year, turning Russian airports into giant car parks.

As Eastern European countries shook off Soviet shackles, one of the first things they did was get rid of their ageing Russian aircraft and upgrade to American or French planes. They dumped their Russian museum pieces on impoverished Communist nations in the Far East, notably Mongolia, North Korea, Vietnam and Cambodia. The most common aircraft – Antonovs, Ilyushins, Tupolevs and Yakolevs – were mostly built in the 1960s and 1970s for military and cargo applications. The Tupolev-154 and Ilyushin-62 are notorious for engine failure, leading to several disastrous crashes in Russia and China. These older planes have little or no computer equipment; ours certainly didn't.

We broke every safety regulation in the book on the Gobi flight. The pilot clowned at the controls, the navigator passed around a bottle of vodka (the closest thing to in-flight service), we changed black market money, and then the co-pilot fell asleep – or appeared to have done so. Alarmed, I went to wake him up, only to find he was hunched over a handheld Russian arcade game, *Tetris*. At least he was honing his computer skills.

The landing at Dalanzadgad, in the Gobi Desert, was something else. As the Antonov wheels thumped up and down on the grass landing strip, luggage and contraband goods cascaded from overhead bins. On terra firma, men with horsecarts trotted across the field right up to the plane, looking for passengers with bulky luggage. We jumped out of the plane and started walking away from the chaos. Pretty soon we were running. Looking back, I spotted a man standing on top of the Antonov, positioning the hose from a large tanker for refuelling. He had a cigarette dangling from his lips.

In Dalanzadgad we hooked up with a driver, guide and jeep, all arranged from Ulan Bator. The driver picked up the local schoolmaster to provide translation, and off we drove into the Gobi, locked in a hockey dialogue (*LA Kings! Pittsburgh Penguins!*). Turns out Mongolia has its own ice hockey team, which plays in Ulan Bator. I asked them who their heroes were. Bruce Lee, said the driver. Jack London, said the translator – and Sir Walter Scott.

The Gobi surprised at every turn; it wasn't the lifeless environment I'd imagined, but rocky desert and grassland that supported abundant wildlife. There were valleys with deep green meadows and bubbling brooks; in the desert, wild flowers were in bloom. The Gobi functions as a vast wildlife sanctuary, like Tibet once was. Every day we sighted gazelles that clipped past the jeep at speeds of over forty miles an hour, or wild camels, or bands of argali sheep or ibex peering down from high rock ridges.

Our guides knew exactly where to find wildlife. They showed us magnificent sand-dunes; places where dinosaurs once roamed, where their bones have been discovered. Those may not be the only bones; our guides pointed out a site nearby where a huge monastery had been razed to the ground. In the Stalin era, seven hundred large and a thousand smaller monasteries were destroyed by the Russians, and thousands of monks were executed in an attempt to wipe out Tibetan Buddhism. A handful of the larger monasteries survived; out on the grasslands, *gers* are now converted for use as temples.

We stayed with families in *gers* on this trip, since our jeep crew had no camping equipment. When we asked about the availability of food, the driver abruptly changed direction, ploughed straight into a herd of goats, jumped out, grabbed one and negotiated a price with the herder.

We drove off to a nearby *ger*, where two women proceeded to make blood sausages from the goat right on the floor. This is meat-eating country: over the next few days we had goat dumplings, goat spare ribs, smoked goat and goat stew.

To cap the trip, a few days at a camel breeding station. It was run by Chjixian, a man in his forties with weathered features and an impish gleam in his eye. This was a two-*ger* family: the first belonged to him, his wife and the younger children; the second had been constructed for his grown son and family. The Bactrian camels at the station were surreal-looking – half bald, shedding great clumps of hair in readiness for the summer heat. In the afternoon, older camels returning to camp from a grazing sortie dolefully called out to their tethered offspring, separated for breaking in: the result was a cacophony of howls. By the end of the day I had a sore backside from camel-riding, I had camel hair all over my clothes, camel dung all over my shoes, and my eardrums were still ringing from howling camels.

There was no shortage of camel-related entertainment. The urchins of the family delighted in throwing camel ticks at us, which started off as a grand joke, but later necessitated serious self-examination before retiring (a tricky procedure as ticks like moist niches). Mum took us out to milk the camels, and later served up camel yogurt, which had a pleasant tangy taste, and some dried curd, which tasted horrible.

In the evening Chjixian proceeded to drink us under the table with fermented camel milk. He had a great sense of humour; he joked about our personal breeding power, or lack of it. He could breed, he claimed, *anything*; he was a strong man. He'd bred three hundred camels in the last twenty-five years, and reared dozens of horses, not to mention eight children. So what about us? How many children had we sired? How many camels had we propagated? How many horses had we broken in? How many *gers* did we own?

Chjixian crooked his forefinger and held it out like a limp penis to mock Scott's low breeding power – a weak man, completely lacking in prowess in bed. You boys are impotent! To turn the tables – element of surprise – Scott gave him a condom: here's how you stop breeding from happening.

We tried to explain what North American cities looked like, and how there were no goats or *gers* or camels, but the concept defeated him. Instead he settled for some family pictures, and was intrigued by a photo of a cousin with a Dobermann. On your next visit, he said, bring the dog along. It would have a fine time in Mongolia with so many new things to sniff at, and so many other animals to see. And so many wide open spaces to run around.

★★★★★

We make it back to Ulan Bator to board our last train for the crossing into China. Or, rather, we storm the train, forcing our way past the carriage guard, who has told us everything is sold out and he cannot honour our tickets. Once the train pulls out of the station, the same guard, when prodded, manages to find two free bunks. As the train rolls across grasslands and through the great Gobi Desert, smugglers work feverishly to stash their booty in the ceiling panels of the cars – cartons of cigarettes, deer antlers, even small live poodles.

Poodles, you ask? Well, yes, the poodles are destined to be illicit pets for rich Beijingers, who consider it chic to keep a show dog. The habit of keeping pets was outlawed during the Cultural Revolution, condemned as bourgeois behaviour. Now citizens can keep dogs, but only under a certain height at the shoulder, and it can only be walked at night after a certain hour. Basic freedoms that we take for granted in the West include the right to walk a dog of any height, at any time. Imagine this scenario: a Beijinger is out one night walking the dog when the Public Security Bureau swoops in, measures the dog at the shoulder and finds it exceeds the specified height. The PSB officer immediately stuffs the dog into a burlap bag and clubs it to death in front of the horrified owner. OK, that may be a bit exaggerated, but it's a scenario that's still plausible.

At the border there is a long stop while the bogies are changed – China has a wider gauge track – and while the Chinese on the train are subjected to various indignities like baggage checks and even random blood tests for AIDS.

The border change we're most interested in is the addition of a Chinese dining car. We stuff our faces on shrimp and vegetables, plates of stir-fried green peppers and mushrooms, items we haven't seen since Budapest. Unlike the bankrupt economies of Russia and Mongolia, China's economy is prosperous; the place is well stocked with goods and food. The section from Ulan Bator to Beijing takes more than a day: after the wild open spaces of Mongolia, there's a swift transition to densely populated areas. Villages flash by with throngs of bicyclists at the crossroads. We pass an ancient Chinese milestone, a section of the Great Wall, and finally the train pulls into Beijing Main Station.

At the other end of this trip – in Beijing – is Tiananmen Square, a vast desert of paving bounded by Mao Zedong's mausoleum, the entrance to the Forbidden City, and the Great Hall of the People. It is more than coincidence that the buildings and the square itself look Russian – they were built with Soviet know-how. Tiananmen Square was designed for mass rallies, but not for pro-democracy demonstrations. After the Tiananmen Massacre in 1989, a couple of big boards were put up detailing what Chinese people can or cannot do when visiting the Monument to the People's Heroes, a large obelisk that was the focus of the student demonstrations. Among the things you cannot do: no unlawful assembly, no spitting, no urination, even no joking.

We did one of the things you're not supposed to do. I guess we just got a bit too confident. The day before, I had been out at the Temple of Heaven, photographing Scott with his prayer flags – no problem. Scott is carrying a special set of prayer flags which he is intent on having photographed in different locations along the way in preparation for a national prayer flag day event in the United States, so he has been photographed in Red Square, in Ulan Bator's Sukhbaatar Square, and now the idea is to complete the set with Tiananmen Square. On 4 June, exactly three years since the massacre, we bicycled to the square. Scott started to pull the prayer flags out of his day pack. I started to bring the camera up to my eye. I say 'started' because neither action was completed. White gloves descended on my shoulder and on Scott's. The police were on us before we even took a picture.

Our first moments under arrest were pure Kafka: *This can't be happening to me. I'm not doing this. I can't be* ... disbelief, followed by denial, followed by shock. Everything seemed to be moving in slow motion. Now escorted by a phalanx of six policemen, we were marched off through the gates of the Forbidden City, passing under a giant picture of Mao, gazing sternly down.

'What's going on?' asked Scott, nervously. 'Where are we?'

'We're in deep shit,' I told him. I had thought of saying: *And we're going into much deeper shit*, but instead I blurted out that we were heading into the Forbidden City.

'You know, I've never been in the Forbidden City before,' said Scott.

'Hell of a way to get in,' I mumbled, quite perturbed now about my film and my camera. Curse this photography – it was a silly idea. Of course the police would all be out in force that day, looking for crazies, attention-getters and demonstrators.

Our escort frogmarched us past a bunch of foreigners, standing gape-mouthed. They were tourists: we were suddenly prisoners of some sort. Things looked quite different. Five minutes ago, I was happily riding a bicycle through Beijing traffic; now I'm under arrest and about to get a major grilling.

Arrest triggered shock, which now turned to apprehension, fear and helplessness – all at the same time. But mostly helplessness. We could disappear for a few months and nobody would be the wiser. All right, there was a third person, Steve, at the hotel, but they could take care of him too.

It's funny what goes through your head at times like this. I had sent out sixty rolls of film, mostly Mongolia pictures, by courier earlier that day, and I still had the receipt in my pocket. If they found the receipt, the police could seize the film on the grounds that it could be shots of similar prayer flags. I would never see the film again. My mind was racing, trying to resolve how to get rid of the receipt. Try and toss it down a toilet? Eat it?

We were ushered into a building, into a room full of chairs and large tables. Fortunately I wasn't asked to empty my pockets; however, I was asked to empty my day pack. As I did, a man followed my actions with a large video camera. These people didn't exactly bother to introduce themselves, so I'll call him Video-man. That morning I had photocopied my initial passport pages a dozen times as backups for visa applications. Video-man put all the copies in a long line, then taped the lot – incriminating evidence of some sort. Then he moved across towards Scott and taped the prayer flags, all laid out in a long line.

After Video-man came the Snapper. The interrogator reminded me of a snarly dog with loose jowls, ready to snap at you. Scott was separated across the other side of the room, delicately trying to explain how he came to be in possession of these prayer flags, which were by now Exhibit A. Nasty questions followed, designed to intimidate us. But I'd experienced this before: the important thing was to hold your ground.

A piece of paper was thrust in front of me. The Snapper motioned towards it.

'Sign it,' he said firmly, nudging me in the ribs.

'No way,' I shot back. 'It's in Chinese.'

'Sign it!' he barked, thumping his fist on the table.

I can't recall exactly what happened next. Rage creates memory gaps. Scott later assured me I went ballistic: I was apparently jumping up and down and yelling at him across the room not to sign anything, and yelling and swearing at the Snapper that I would not sign any piece of paper in Chinese and he'd better let me contact my embassy or I'd have his job on the line. Or something like that. This tantrum seems to have provoked some surprise among the Chinese interlocutors who were not used to such behaviour. We settled for a confession written by myself in English, in which I said I would never do such a thing again. I deliberately scrawled this in my worst handwriting. After a few hours they let us go, but confiscated the prayer flags.

★★★★★

'You were very lucky not to have been beaten up,' said the man at the US Embassy. One of the prayer flags bore the logo of Amnesty International, which – unbeknown to us – was a banned organisation in China. Scott was relieved that his pockets weren't searched; his money belt had Dalai Lama pictures and documents that were highly sensitive.

In case the authorities changed their minds and came looking for us again, we decided to leave the capital immediately to put some distance between us. We said goodbye to Steve and flew off to Lanzhou. From there we embarked on a haphazard overland route to Chengdu, skirting through the old Tibetan region of Amdo.

Amdo, north-east of Lhasa, was carved off by the Chinese into the provinces of Gansu and Qinghai, while the former Tibetan territory of Kham (east of Lhasa) was carved off into Sichuan and Yunnan provinces. There has been lots of Chinese infiltration since the 1950s, but on the plateau, Tibetan nomad culture survives. Few foreigners visit the Tibetan communities in these parts, but travel is easy enough as the Chinese government's stringent travel restrictions for Tibet do not apply here.

★★★★★

The fourteenth Dalai Lama of Tibet was born in a village near Xining in 1935, when the area was still in Amdo. Today, however, there are few Tibetans left in the village of his birth; it has been inundated by Chinese settlers, as has occupied Tibet. There is very much a frontier mentality among the Chinese settlers, this is their Wild West, complete with great windswept expanses of grassland and desert, gushing rivers, garrison-type towns, a strong Chinese army and police presence, and unruly minorities, like Goloks, who live on the grasslands in tents. Ethnically Tibetan, Goloks have never followed laws or politics from central Tibet, remaining aloof from the former Lhasa government. 'Golok' means 'those with their heads turned backwards', a tribute to the fierce independence of these people. To complete the Wild West picture, the high-cheeked Golok nomads herd what at first appears to be bison and turns out to be great hairy yaks.

The Goloks, cloaked in sheepskin jackets, unwashed, hair in wild disarray – the women with chunks of turquoise plaited in their hair – drift into town to buy supplies, or visit an important monastery. Taer Lamasery, fifteen miles south-west of Xining, is a sacred site for Tibetans. Inside a spectacular green-tiled building is a silver pagoda containing the earthly belongings of Tsongkhapa, founder of the Yellow Hat sect. Construction of the monastery began in the sixteenth century; it sprang up around a legendary pipal tree, said to have a Buddha-image on every leaf. The lamasery contains a wealth of Chinese and Tibetan styles of architecture, statuary and art, and is famed for its elaborate yak-butter sculptures, which can reach fifty feet in length.

In its heyday, the lamasery housed 3,000 monks, but under Chinese rule it is restricted to 400, so half the buildings now function as museum pieces. Numbers were further reduced through arrests in the late 1980s after demonstrations by the monks in support of those in Lhasa. In summer the place is full of Chinese tourists, many of whom demonstrate a profound lack of respect towards Tibetan culture, with photo opportunities at cardboard cutouts.

By contrast, another major Yellow Hat monastery, Labrang, is very active, with over a thousand monks in residence. Labrang Monastery is in the town of Xiahe, at the edge of the Aba Grasslands, a half-day bus ride from Xining to the south-east, crossing into Gansu Province. Founded in the eighteenth century, Labrang is as large as any temple complex in central Tibet, and bigger than anything in Lhasa. It is an entire monastic community

– a Buddhist university of sorts – with monks studying logic, medicine and astrology among other disciplines. The monastery was completely closed down from 1960 to 1980, but miraculously underwent a revival in the 1980s.

Just as fascinating as the monastery are the Tibetans who visit it, travelling great distances on pilgrimage. On reaching Labrang they walk a circuit of several miles around the monastery, stopping at various points to turn huge prayer wheels, or feed stray dogs that hang about for scraps. Other pilgrims fling themselves to the ground and prostrate themselves for the entire circuit. Inside the grounds, pilgrims visit sacred shrines or statues and leave coins, white scarves, or yak butter as offerings.

Xiahe has a beautiful location on a valley floor, surrounded by rolling hills. The town is part Chinese, part Hui Muslim, part Tibetan. The three sectors are distinct, but there is some curious commerce down the main street: Hui Muslims and the atheist Chinese are the ones selling Tibetan Buddhist artefacts and supplies to the Tibetan nomads. There is only one restaurant serving Tibetan food. I dined in a noodle house patronised by jolly old Chinese men – jolly because they spent all day smoking 'local tobacco' (marijuana) from long wooden pipes embossed with silver. After I'd eaten my fill of noodles, a beggar rushed in, grabbed my bowl and slurped down what was left.

Around the corner, another face of life in the Middle Kingdom: outside the Public Security Bureau pictures of criminal offenders were displayed, photographed shortly before they were executed. A bullet to the head is cheap enough, but the bill for the bullet is still sent to the family of the executed as further humiliation. The charge is usually ten yuan. A crimson tick is placed next to the criminal's mugshot to show that the execution has been carried out. This is a glimpse of the police state that instigated the Tiananmen Massacre.

*****

Rewind three years: my first visit to Xiahe. Flashing back to a scene that is stored in the darkest recesses of my mind. I am sitting in a noodle shop when a long line of children files past. Are they on their way to some kind of festival? I leave my half-eaten noodles at the table and follow them. Along the way I bump into Gerhardt, a German traveller. We follow the schoolchildren into an open-air arena, bounded by two- and three-storey buildings at the back of a small market. The arena is jam-packed with townspeople. The schoolchildren have been sent to witness the prelude to an execution.

Sitting on a balcony facing the crowd are Chinese judiciary officials in blue uniforms with red epaulettes. Below them are two trucks full of soldiers in green, machine guns at the ready, scanning the crowd. They are all wearing white face masks of the type usually worn if someone has a cold; here, the masks are worn so that the soldiers cannot be identified. In the truck on the left is a man with a shaven head, dressed in a shabby suit. He is firmly trussed up with rope, his hands bound behind his back. Around his neck hangs a sign in Chinese, and there's an army photographer snapping his picture. At ground level there are half a dozen other prisoners, surrounded by soldiers.

The judiciary officials deliver speeches. The man with the shaven head is Tibetan, about twenty years old, and he, along with his brothers, apparently carried out a revenge murder. They killed the man who had murdered their father. For this task, the brothers were groomed by their mother; the two brothers got long sentences. The speech-makers drone on. The prisoner remains mute, impassive, somehow detached from the proceedings. The schoolchildren shuffle their feet and look at him. The prisoner has perhaps an hour to live; the clock is ticking away. Public execution is a tactic known in Chinese as 'kill the rooster to frighten the monkeys'. Everybody gets the message: the schoolchildren, townspeople, would-be criminals.

No last-second reprieve. The last speech is made, and police motorcyclists with sirens lead a cavalcade of trucks out of the place. They roar off – sirens, clouds of dust, machine guns. Execution is swift. About five minutes after they leave the compound, the same army trucks return, minus the prisoner – or is he on the floor of a truck with a bullet in his neck?

★★★★★

On the home run: from Xiahe overland across the Aba Grasslands to Chengdu. We boarded a bus with a maniacal driver who careered around corners at suicidal speed and performed reckless overtaking manoeuvres. Our run-down bus was crammed with an ethnic assortment of passengers: Han Chinese with dowdy Mao suits, platform shoes and lurid longjohns visible under turned-up trousers; Hui Muslims with wispy beards and white skullcaps, accompanied by women in green headcowls; dignified Tibetan monks in maroon robes; and Tibetan herders sporting Stetsons and heavy sheepskin jackets trimmed with leopardskin.

For lunch – perfect timing – we stopped right in a village where a grasslands fair was in progress. These seasonal four-day fairs attract Tibetans who come to compete in horse racing and other events, to do some shopping, or indulge in matchmaking (which explains why the women are decked out in their finest). Our arrival in town coincided with the final of the men's basketball, which had a large crowd cheering the players on.

Moving on across the grasslands, the driver ran a gauntlet of mud and lost: the bus got hopelessly stuck in deep ruts. Some passengers assisted in trying to get the bus out; others fanned out across the countryside to perform ablutions or indulge in impromptu picnics. I made a beeline for the nearest yak-hair tent. These ingenious structures are a testament to the survival skills of the nomads, dependent on the yak for their livelihood. They use yak hair, hide, bone and innards to make household goods, and they eat yak milk, cheese, butter and meat. Here, in the treeless highlands, yak dung is the primary source of fuel for cooking and heating.

I was ushered into the tent, which had a cosy carpeted interior, somewhat smoky from the stove in the middle. I demonstrated the wonders of my Swiss Army knife to the assembled, and was rewarded with some awful butter tea, and dragged outside for a yak ride. The yak was at first cooperative, but quickly lost its temper, snorted, and threw me around; the nomad herders laughed themselves silly as they watched my rodeo antics.

Eventually our bus lumbered into Zoige, a town sited at 11,000 feet. Zoige looked like a set for a Luis Buñuel film, with animals wandering all over the place, yaks, cows, dusty horsemen coming down the main street with bags of produce and, in the middle of it all, Tibetan monks calmly playing billiards on open-air tables. The monks were from a monastery on the outskirts of town, which I spent an afternoon visiting; I lingered there, hypnotised by the deep chanting that boomed through the main prayer hall.

Back in town that night, we witnessed other strange rituals at the local hot spot, a disco. There were no couples on the floor – it was either women tangoing with women, or men arm-in-arm with men. And there was no alcohol, either; green tea was dispensed from large kettles to the needy. After the tangos and waltzes and green tea, a disco beat finally erupted, and the younger set rose to the occasion and boogied – not opposite a partner, but in a line, strutting their stuff in front of a mirror that ran the length of one wall.

The last major stop along this bus route is Songpan, an ancient garrison town with Chinese-style drum towers and walls, originally designed to keep bandits at bay. Songpan is a predominantly Hui Muslim town, but what catches the eye in the marketplace is the Tibetan women with elaborate headdresses of amber and coral, the likes of which are not seen in Lhasa nowadays. This peculiar jewellery style is a clue to another unusual facet of this area: the Tibetans here are Bon, members of the shamanist cult that predates Buddhism in Tibet. Outside Songpan is a Bon monastery, of a kind no longer found in central Tibet.

When Scott and I were returning to the hotel one afternoon, we ran into an agitated backpacker who warned us that the place was crawling with police. We went up to the rooftop section where we had a room, and witnessed a bizarre sight. An American was being held over the rooftop toilet vent by two police. Was this some kind of torture to exact a confession? No, it seems the confession had already been made. This was the re-enactment of a crime. The American in question, along with two companions, was working on behalf of a Christian mission group, distributing pamphlets printed in several languages to townspeople in the region. Spreading the faith – any kind of faith – is illegal in China. With the police hot on their trail, the trio of evangelists had thrown several bags of pamphlets down the toilet vent to avoid being caught red-handed. The police had traced passport registration records in hotels, leading them to this one. They quickly narrowed down the suspects, and they were now forcing the evangelists to re-enact their crime on video, prior to deporting them.

★★★★★

From Songpan, the road drops right off the Tibetan plateau through forested zones, following the banks of the fast-running Minjiang River. This is a rough road, prone to frequent landslides, a situation made worse by large-scale deforestation combined with torrential rains. This means a bone-jarring day and a half on the bus skirting past landslide debris along narrow cliffs until the crate finally rolls into Chengdu, the bustling capital of Sichuan Province. Chengdu's back alleys reek of deep-fried tofu, a pungent odour that indicates you are firmly back in the Middle Kingdom. When I turned on the TV in the hotel room, up popped Madonna, then Bruce Springsteen and U2, courtesy of a relay from Hong Kong, and I knew I'd reached the traveller's dreamland of clean sheets, hot showers and satellite TV.

★★★★★

Desert Mandala

The journey begins with maps. You pore over the maps, imagining what might be along the route. The finger traces the rugged terrain, feeling the numbness of icy slopes, feeling the harshness of desert wind. I felt like I'd travelled the edge of a vast mandala of sand – through India, Russia, Mongolia and China – arced around the periphery, skirted the great grasslands, caught up in a swirl of deserts and dust. Now it was time to head to the centre. To what the Tibetans know as Kangjen – the Land of Snows. To strike into Tibet.

PART TWO

HITTING THE ROOF

4

LHASA REDUX

Paranoia in the sacred city

One of the hazards of being a writer is that occasionally your mug pops up in the wrong place, like the front of a Lonely Planet guidebook, which mine did, in their China guide at the time. I could only hope nobody would put two and two together to blow my cover, because being a writer in Tibet could get you into deep water. Foreign journalists are virtually barred from visiting the region: the problem is that journalists tend to be sympathetic to the Tibetan cause of independence, and the rights to freedom of speech and the freedom to follow Tibetan Buddhist beliefs.

Merely being a writer by profession could get you unceremoniously dumped on the first plane out. I knew this happened. I'd met a Bangkok journalist and photographer team who had been on an innocuous assignment to follow the Mekong from source to sea. They got frustrated when official permission was slow in forthcoming, so they applied for regular tourist visas and flew into Chengdu, where they were detained, had their camera gear confiscated and their visas cancelled.

The Chinese could detain you and take away all your pens and paper, like they did to Chinese dissidents. Aside from executing more people every year than the rest of the world combined, China ranks very high up the international scale for having the most journalists in jail. All of which made me uneasy – actually, quite paranoid. I had gone through all written material in my pack, and pared down anything that linked me to writing. I had removed all research material, coded addresses into cryptic handwriting, gone to extraordinary lengths to divorce myself from writing.

Terry figured it out before the plane even took off, at the hotel in Chengdu. Yes, I was back in Chengdu four years later, ready to hit the roof. Terry, an engineer working in central China, had decided to take a break and show his teenage son James around. They were part of an impromptu group of ten that the Chengdu travel agent had assembled to purchase our plane tickets to Lhasa. Things were fine till Terry spotted my name on the list.

'I thought the name rang a bell,' he told me. 'You're a writer, aren't you?'

Shut the fuck up! I heard myself muttering under my breath. *Do you want the whole hotel to know?* 'Yes,' I said, then whispered, 'can you keep a secret?'

Writers, in their own way, are spies – always eavesdropping on other people's habits and conversations. Where else would they get their material from? But the Chinese have turned writers into full-blown spies. Writer equals journalist, journalist equals spy, ergo writer equals spy. Spy equals lengthy prison sentence. After being roundly criticised by the international community for sending people to prison on the charge of being 'counter-revolutionary', the Chinese settled on new terminology. They didn't want to call them 'dissidents' (which is what they are), so the next best thing they could think of was 'spy'. The Chinese have turned spying into an all-purpose reason for sending people to prison for lengthy periods. If a citizen of China merely passes along information to a foreign journalist, this act is viewed as leaking state secrets, which means that citizen can be convicted of spying.

Spying for whom? Well, this is never really clear, nor specified. But it could be for arch-enemy Taiwan, or more ludicrously, for the Tibetan government in exile – neither of which entities the Chinese authorities officially recognise. Or it could be spying for the Vatican. Before these options – long before them – it was spying for England or America. In the late 1940s, Hugh Richardson, a former British representative in Lhasa who came back to work for the Indian government, was accused of masterminding anti-Chinese activities. Lowell Thomas, an American journalist visiting in 1949, was accused of being an 'arch-spy' posing as a radio commentator. And in 1950, Robert Ford, a British radio operator working for the Tibetan government, was captured by invading Chinese forces at Chamdo and held on charges of spying. He spent the next five years in dark dungeons, dressed in rags, surviving on little more than boiled rice.

*****

For centuries, sealed in its mountain fastness, Tibet was only accessible to trading caravans of horse and yak, which had negotiated the high passes. Now things are different; you can fly straight over those passes, sharing a plane with Chinese military personnel, cutting an exhausting three-month overland expedition to a few hours in a reclining chair. To be more precise: the flight time is one hundred minutes. Heinrich Harrer, who managed to sneak back into Tibet in 1982 on a group tour, marvelled how he could fly right into Lhasa over such forbidding mountainous terrain. On his previous journey some forty years earlier, it had taken him almost two years to reach Lhasa on foot.

Flying into Tibet, I feel like an animated version of Tintin, the boy-journalist, landing in the middle of an intrigue. It's an unnerving experience. Our flight, a Boeing 757 from Chengdu, is chock-full of Chinese military personnel (checking in their weapons as they board?). The altitude on arrival – 11,800 feet – slugs you, and Chinese security and customs officials bamboozle you with weird questions (*Any books on Tibet? Dalai Lama pictures? Any biologicals?*). They're looking for subversive materials that are banned in Tibet. From Gonggar Airport it's a 50-minute ride to the capital, Lhasa, along the best road in Tibet, paved and four lanes wide.

First hurdle crossed. I have survived Chinese security checks in Chengdu and at Gonggar, so I can breathe more easily – or try to. I spend the first few days at Snowland Hotel, battling the altitude and waking up at night completely out of breath. And then I venture out, slowly, on brief forays.

It has been ten years since I set foot in Lhasa: I have a lot of trouble recognising the place. All the romance has gone out of it. What immediately strikes me is the Chinese-ness of the place. It feels like a theme park. The romantic view of Tibet is that of a vast region blanketed in snow, with lofty monasteries atop craggy peaks and hairy yaks roaming around – a land of monks and mystery. It can be all of this, what one Chinese promotional poster calls a 'fairyland'. Or is it 'the motherland'? What the glossy Chinese tourist brochures do not show you is a Lhasa overrun with soldiers, drab Chinese blockhouse apartments, girlie bars and glittering karaoke palaces.

This is the changing face of Lhasa: karaoke and concrete. In Lhasa they like concrete so much they've built a factory devoted to it, right near Lhasa Beer Brewery. Chinese contributions to Tibetan culture: karaoke bars, concrete, blue-tinted glass and the mini-brothel. A taxi driver tells me in broken English supplemented by crude hand gestures that whores are definitely an incentive for workers like himself. The salary for Chinese working in Lhasa is three to five times higher than in mainland China, with preferential tax and loan policies. And there are cheap whores into the bargain.

From the top of the Potala, my suspicions are confirmed: there's a sea of Chinese concrete buildings all the way to Sera Monastery; there are high-rise buildings with bathroom-tiling exteriors and blue-tinted glass; there are Chinese flags and little Chinese lions all over the place; there are heroic Soviet-style statues in the middle of roundabouts, one showing victorious Chinese mountaineers atop Everest, which they conquered from the north face.

Lhasa used to be the home of a privileged elite – those in the service of the Dalai Lama – and Tibet was the seat of the most unusual form of government the world has seen, a Buddhocracy ruled by reincarnate lamas. Before 1950 Tibet was never colonised or modernised, so it took a completely different route to other countries in Asia. Lhasa's design was based not so much on practical aspects as sacred considerations. The seat of government was the Potala, and across town, separated by meadows, was the Jokhang Temple, with a market and artisan section. Lhasa was never a big city: prior to 1949, the population was estimated at only 30,000, with an additional 16,000 monks at the great monasteries of Sera and Drepung on the outskirts. Today, with a population of around 250,000, Lhasa remains the biggest 'city' in the entire Tibetan realm if you discount the Mongolian capital of Ulan Bator.

Old Lhasa was romanticised by early Western explorers. Though it was the dream destination of both Tibetan pilgrims and explorers, it was not exactly paradise. In 1904 the invading English under Francis Younghusband found their triumphal march into Lhasa impeded by piles of refuse, stagnant pools of water, open sewers, and various rabid animals and mangy dogs foraging for putrid scraps of food – not to mention beggars. The present Dalai Lama recalls the Potala being cold, gloomy and full of rats. He much preferred to spend time in the gardens of Norbulingka, the smaller-scale summer palace.

If he were to visit today the Dalai Lama would have trouble getting his bearings. The new navigation landmarks are all Chinese. The transformation of Lhasa began in earnest in the early 1960s, but really it is from the early 1990s that Chinese building gathered momentum with the construction of downtown offices and karaoke bars, whole suburbs of concrete apartment buildings, an outer industrial fringe and a final ring of army bases.

It seems absurd to put it this way, but you really have to visit the 'Tibetan Quarter' of Lhasa, around the Jokhang Temple and the Barkor, to catch any Tibetans in action. Think of Lhasa as one large Chinatown, with the Tibetans reduced to a minority in their own capital. Their last bastion around the Jokhang comprises less than a quarter of urban Lhasa. Of the estimated 250,000 residents of Lhasa, two-thirds are reckoned to be Chinese.

To assist the paranoid Chinese authorities in their endeavours to snoop on the Tibetans, there is a nefarious network of informants – human listening posts – and video surveillance cameras. The video cameras are mounted around the Barkor area, within the Potala and at major intersections of the city. The cameras were initially sold by Western countries to monitor traffic flow, but since Lhasa doesn't have a significant traffic flow problem, they are obviously put to other uses here.

The murder of Lhasa. I've been trying to put words to what has happened here. The city has been murdered. In fifty short years the authorities have attempted to dismantle the thousand-year-old Tibetan culture. Ancient Lhasa is now buried under a Chinese layer.

You can see this layering at work at the Potala Palace, still the dominant architectural presence in Lhasa. It is a 13-storey castle, built of rammed earth, wood and stone, thought to contain upwards of a thousand rooms. When it was completed in 1694, this Tibetan 'skyscraper' was grander than anything in Europe. Quite an achievement when you think that the Tibetans used no steel frame, no nails in the woodwork and no wheeled devices to lug stones. Deep in the bowels of the Potala is the oldest chamber, the Chapel of the Dharma Kings, with niches filled with statuary of past kings. The statue most highly revered by pilgrims is that of Songtsen Gampo, the seventh-century king who moved his capital from the Yarlung Valley to the site of Lhasa.

The word Lhasa is thought to derive from the Tibetan words *lha* (the gods) and *sa* (earth), meaning ground of the gods, sacred earth, sacred turf: the Holy City, abode of the Dalai Lamas. Under successive Dalai Lamas the Potala Palace grew larger and larger. The tombs of the Dalai Lamas, from the fifth to the thirteenth, all lie within the Potala (with the exception of the sixth, who disappeared). These elaborate tombs, made partially of gold or silver, are encrusted with precious jewels. The Potala's maze of rooms is thought to house some 10,000 shrines and 200 statues.

And now we come to the layering: on the inside, fire extinguishers and electrical wiring have been installed, and video surveillance cameras all over the place check on the monk-caretakers. Monks are no longer allowed to wear robes in the Potala and the Dalai Lama's personal monastery within the walls has long been disbanded. On the outside, the walls have been strengthened and Chinese banners hung from them to welcome visiting dignitaries, because the Potala is now no more than a haunted castle – a tourist photo stop. Then, to make it easier to photograph, the area facing the Potala was levelled to create Potala Square.

Within the front walled section of the palace are scattered buildings that now function as Chinese-run souvenir shops and art galleries, and a small hotel. The buildings were once part of Shol, which housed one of Tibet's greatest woodblock printing presses. The entire Tibetan administration was quartered in Shol, along with Tibetan Army officials, guard offices and a prison (most of Shol has been demolished).

But the most obvious Chinese handiwork is Potala Square, a wasteland of paving facing the Potala. It was completed in 1995 to commemorate the thirtieth anniversary of the founding of the Chinese-designated Tibet Autonomous Region. A large area of ramshackle Tibetan housing was razed to create this square. But the concept of a large square is alien to Tibetan town planning: this is a purely Chinese idea. Potala Square has a lot in common with Beijing's Tiananmen Square, including the same chandelier-lamp fixtures with propaganda speakers attached. Tiananmen Square was designed for military and mass solidarity parades, and meanwhile used for weekend amusements like photo taking or kite flying.

This is what Potala Square is used for: the military use it as a big car park; concerts for the military have been staged here; shows of force by the PLA have taken place here. It is the number one Chinese photo opportunity site. There is a slew of photographic shops just to the west of the square, catering to tourists. A flagpole at the front of the square is a favourite place for Chinese soldiers and tourists to have their photos taken. Motorcades of arriving Chinese dignitaries make this their first stop when they come from the airport. Escorted by the dreaded PAP (People's Armed Police) dressed in white uniforms and on motorcycles, the dignitaries alight for photo sessions in front of the Potala, whose outer walls are inevitably draped with long red banners with Chinese characters welcoming them.

At the back of the square are amusement rides for children and a fountain with a Chinese dragon sculpture. There's an old Soviet aircraft which is used as a photo prop: for a small fee, tourists can mount the aircraft, stand up like invading conquerors in the cockpit and wave, with the Potala in the background. This is reputed to be the first Chinese airforce plane to have landed in Tibet.

The more you look at it, the more of a puzzle Lhasa becomes. There is no Tibetan building going on; in fact, the bevelled two-storey dwellings around the Jokhang are being knocked down and replaced with newer structures. However, at the west side of the Potala, miraculously, the West Gate has popped up. The shrine-like gate was the coveted entryway that explorers in earlier times dreamed of passing through. It was levelled during the Cultural Revolution. Now you see it, now you don't; I later discover that it has been resurrected as part of a multi-million dollar restoration of the Potala, completed in 1995. But why spend millions on restoring the palace of Public Enemy Number One? Partly because the Potala has been declared a UNESCO World Heritage Site, but ultimately it all comes down to tourism.

According to the Tibet Tourism Bureau, arrivals in Tibet in the mid-1990s averaged 30,000 foreign visitors a year, probably supplemented by an equal number of domestic Chinese visitors. The bureau hoped to double or triple that number, generating at least US$30 million in foreign exchange.

Tourists love monks. One of the great anomalies of tourism in Tibet is that the monasteries are kept open and operating only because of tourist demand to see them. Tourism in Tibet, however, puts the Chinese authorities in an awkward position. When individual tourists were allowed in for the first time in 1984, and the Tibet-Nepal border was opened, the Chinese believed that the large number of Westerners would engulf the battered Tibetan culture. But the opposite has proved true: visitors bolster pride in things Tibetan; they come to see Tibet, not China. They come to see the great monasteries, the Tibetan way of life – the very things that the authorities want to eradicate. Individual tourists are more likely to have links with Tibetan refugees in India, and are able to interact with the locals in Lhasa more than sequestered group tour parties.

Hinting at perhaps too much interaction are signs posted on the walls of budget hotels around Lhasa, like the Yak Hotel, the Kirey or Snowland. These start off with *Welcome to Lhasa* and go on to warn Aliens (foreigners are always referred to as 'Aliens') *Attention Aliens! Whatever planet you are from, pay attention!* There are warnings not to join in or photograph any demonstrations, or distribute pro-independence literature.

If tourists indulge in any of these pursuits Chinese retribution is swift: the darker side of life in Tibet surfaces. When a foreign student videotaped demonstrators protesting price increases in Lhasa, she was hurled into a police wagon head first, causing injury. She was later strip-searched, her video equipment confiscated, her hotel room ripped apart and she was taken in tears to the airport and put on a plane to Kathmandu. A group tour leader experienced some tense moments outside the Jokhang Temple in Lhasa when a handgun was pressed against his head. Some monks had started parading the outlawed Tibetan flag nearby, and members of his group, thinking this was a Tibetan ceremony, started to take pictures. A Chinese army officer held a gun to the leader's head and told him to collect the film that had been taken. In another incident, horrified group tour members stumbled across a public execution in Lhasa.

★★★★★

Distributing 'propaganda' is a serious matter, particularly handing out tapes with the Dalai Lama's voice or printed matter bearing his signature or picture. An American I met in Lhasa was given his marching orders because he had scribbled some pro-independence suggestions in a comment book at a local bank. He was on a plane out of the city three days later.

But that doesn't mean you have to remain totally silent. In a restaurant, I got into a conversation with a woman who worked at the nearby Xizang Television studios. She started asking me the usual boring questions: *Do you have a car? How much money do you make?* Things like that. And then, by way of talking about the Potala, I manoeuvred into this question: 'What do you think of the Dalai Lama?' She looked stunned for a few seconds, and then came back with this curious response: 'Only educated people speak about this topic.'

'But you are educated, aren't you?'

Seeing no way out of this, she got up and left the restaurant in a huff.

I tried that question on several Chinese living in Lhasa after that. The response was invariably to try to dismiss the subject, so I grew bolder. Sitting out the rain in a shelter at Drepung Monastery with a young couple from Guangzhou, I ventured this: 'Why is it that a billion Chinese are afraid of one man?' This got their blood going – they adamantly insisted it wasn't true. 'Then why won't you talk about it?' I asked. Testing the waters, the man asked me what I thought of the Dalai Lama. I told him the Dalai Lama was a Nobel Peace Prize laureate who worked hard for the cause of world peace, and I admired that.

Turning this over carefully, the man came back with another question.

'How would you feel if part of your country wanted to break away, splitting up the nation?'

'Normal,' I answered. He had chosen the wrong country. I live in Canada: Quebec has been trying to break away for ages. 'At least we let them conduct a referendum,' I told him. I was going to add: *and we don't shoot them*, but I thought that might be pushing my luck.

So thoroughly is the Chinese position drummed into the minds of its citizens that you would be very hard-put to find anybody even remotely sympathetic to the Tibetan position, or well informed enough to be able to present any kind of coherent opinion. Most are terrified of expressing any opinion that deviates from the norm. The rare voices raised on the contentious issue of Tibet belong to a handful of Chinese dissidents living in exile in the West. Says New York-based dissident writer Cao Chang-ching (quoted in the *Tibetan Bulletin*): 'Unless Tibet regains its independence and becomes a member of the United Nations, its position will never be safe. How can a mosquito trust an elephant?'

Tibet is a colony, and the Chinese living there have a colonial mentality: soldiers, hard-nosed administrators or wheeler-dealer settlers out to make a fast buck. So the closest you come to getting the perspective of the 'ordinary' Chinese is … from Chinese tourists. Whenever I asked tourists about what brought them to

Tibet, nine times out of ten they would completely shut down. Out at Sera Monastery, I joined a man from Shanghai at a tea stall and broached the subject of his visit: 'Oh, yes, very interested in Buddhism, all the temples, the ceremonies,' he told me.

'But isn't China officially atheist?' I asked him. 'How does that work?' He gave me a strange look and said he couldn't speak about such things. This topic was now closed. He looked furtively around, slurped down his tea and did a fast exit stage-left.

Most Chinese see the Western preoccupation with Tibet as part of a massive conspiracy to demoralise the People's Republic and weaken the nation. Or so I learned later from a businessman who spewed forth about it, if only because he was drunk. He wanted to practise his English, so bored with his humdrum dialogue, I fired some radical questions at him to see what he would do. And to my great surprise, he answered them very frankly. He started talking about everything that was taboo: about Taiwan and Tibet. He told me that Tibet had been part of China since the thirteenth century. I told him that this was not possible, because in the thirteenth century, China was not run by Chinese but by Mongols. If China was itself occupied by a foreign power, how could it possibly have claimed sovereignty over Tibet?

He paused to dwell on that for a minute, and then proceeded to lecture me about the happy Chinese family of minorities and how the Tibetans should be grateful for all the advances made in Tibet through the goodwill of China. Anyhow, he insisted, talking of happy families, back in the seventh century, the Tibetan king married Chinese Queen Wencheng. She 'enlightened' the Tibetans: didn't that show that Tibet was indeed part of China? Not at all, I told him. Wencheng was a gift – of sorts – donated by the Tang royal family to placate the marauding Tibetan warriors on their doorstep. And she was only one of five brides of the Tibetan king: there was a Nepalese queen and three Tibetan queens as well. The man was stunned to learn this version of history.

When I brought up the topic of the Dalai Lama, my companion turned and raised his voice: *Bad man! Very bad man!*

'But why?' I asked. He scratched his head. It turned out he knew nothing about the Dalai Lama beyond the standard propaganda spiel about the worst traitor in the world. I guess you could blame this ignorance on lack of access to any kind of independent media. Probably you couldn't blame the Chinese for thinking the way they did; instead, you could congratulate those in charge of education curriculums and those controlling the reins of the media for doing such a terrific job of warping everything.

★★★★★

There is one guesthouse that has me foxed, because it is run by foreigners. The Pentoc Guesthouse has its own fax machine. Not only that, they appear to have e-mail access. Foreigners with fax machines and e-mail access in Lhasa are an incredible bending of the regulations; they must have extra-special connections with the authorities. To have a fax is a privilege that requires a restricted licence, and you can be sure the owner of that machine is carefully screened. There are no foreign news representatives in Lhasa: no CNN, no BBC, no Reuters. There are hardly any NGOs; those that exist (mostly medical health groups) are closely monitored and their members are swiftly kicked out if they dare to step over the line of political activism.

But the Pentoc is not NGO-related. I discover it is linked with an evangelical group from northern Europe, so while I have seen foreign evangelists arrested in Sichuan for spreading the gospel – and promptly booted out – it's quite a different story in Tibet. Here they are welcomed with open arms in a complete about-face. All part of the destruction of Tibetan cultural identity, this time an attack on Tibetan Buddhist religious values. The authorities don't care if these evangelists convert Tibetans as long as they don't try the same thing with ethnic Chinese.

Reassuring foreign guests that all is fine in Tibet are slick brochures about human rights prominently displayed in the lobbies of higher-end hotels. Human rights problems? What problems? The Tibetans enjoy many more human rights now than they used to in pre-1950 Tibet, claim the brochures: in that era, ordinary Tibetans were serfs, locked into exploitation by Tibetan nobility and monastic overseers. The Chinese broke down this class system. But how? By replacing Tibetan masters with harsher Chinese ones? The pamphlets seem to equate human rights with food, shelter and the availability of material goods. But as the French explorer Michel Peissel puts it, 'the Tibetans still preferred independence to electricity, and freedom to sewers'.

The glossy brochures brazenly quote sections of the Universal Declaration of Human Rights, claiming that these rights were violated in pre-1950 Tibet, with its medieval punishments, serf labour, and lack of healthcare and other social services. Black and white pictures from the time show starving beggars in rags, while modern colour pictures show laughing well-dressed Tibetans enjoying life under the Chinese. But the brochures don't explain why Tibetans have been given lengthy prison sentences for translating the Universal Declaration of Human Rights into Tibetan; or why they are no longer accorded the right to choose their own incarnate lineages; or why the computers in Lhasa rarely employ Tibetan script – everything is conducted in Chinese characters. Tibetan rights activists complain that China has a policy of trying to eradicate Tibetan script, which derives from Sanskrit. In order to get a decent job or pursue further studies, candidates have to speak Chinese. Any official paperwork and red tape – contracts, licences and so on – are exclusively in Chinese.

In the bookshops, Tibetan-language books are mostly ancient religious texts, the equivalent of cosmetic wallpaper. Hardly any modern textbooks are written in Tibetan, and there are no Tibetan-language maps. Bookshops do, however, carry some maps and magazines in English. A corker is the monthly Beijing-produced magazine *China's Tibet*, which specialises in the kind of rhetoric I call 'Chinaspeak'. It tells you how wonderful life has been in Tibet since its 'peaceful liberation' by the PLA in 1950, and how much the Tibetans love the regime (some Chinese sources admit that the invasion was in fact not entirely peaceful, and that the PLA was reluctantly forced to machine gun the hapless Tibetans to clear them out of the way). The magazine blithely tells you how 'the Dalai clique' tried to interfere in the selection of the

'Soul Boy' (the eleventh Panchen Lama) in 1995. The short form 'Dalai' is considered insulting by Tibetans, and they find the term 'Soul Boy' annoying and misleading (the term is applied by the Chinese to reincarnates, and comes from *lingtong*: *ling* being soul, *tong* being boy or child). The 'Dalai' is described as a 'fox in monk's robes' and a 'splittist', shorthand for an advocate of Tibetan independence. The idea here is that the 'motherland' must stay whole; anybody that splits off a piece will ruin the symmetry. With a unique brand of twisted logic, the Chinese propagandists make a strong case for 'ethnic unity', when in fact 'ethnic cleansing' would be closer to the truth.

Assisting the 'splittists' are 'foreign imperialists'. It is never specified which country these all-purpose scapegoats are from, but popular candidates are 'bad elements' from Taiwan, the United States, the United Kingdom and Germany. After the Dalai Lama received the Nobel Peace Prize, Norway was added to the blacklist.

Chinese sources occasionally admit it's not always peaceful in Tibet. Here's how one magazine, the *Beijing Review*, in 1983 summed up the March 1959 Lhasa rebellion:

> The imperialists and a small number of reactionary elements in Tibet's upper ruling clique could not reconcile themselves to the peaceful liberation of Tibet and its return to the embrace of the Motherland. The reactionary elements were intent upon launching an armed rebellion, negating the agreement and detaching Tibet from China ... They finally launched an armed rebellion on March 10 1959. But, contrary to their desires, this rebellion accelerated the destruction of Tibet's reactionary forces and brought Tibet onto the bright, democratic, socialist road sooner than expected.

The rhetoric remains little changed in the following piece, written for *Beijing Review Press*, except that the main 'troublemakers' are Tibetans from abroad – agents of the Dalai Lama – who reside in foreign countries:

The demonstrations which occurred in Lhasa in September and October 1987 and March 1988 were by no means peaceful. These riots were deliberately instigated by a handful of separatists, who waved flags of 'independence' and shouted slogans clearly aimed at separating Tibet from China and threatening national unity and stability. The rioters also committed a series of criminal activities … A host of facts have revealed that the Lhasa riots were caused by a handful of separatists at the instigation of the Dalai clique.

★★★★★

A significant percentage of the Chinese population consists of soldiers and security forces; Lhasa is ringed by huge military compounds. The military presence is everywhere: you see men in green jogging down the streets in tight formation in the early morning, soldiers in camouflage fatigues on mountain bikes, officers snapping souvenir pictures at the Potala Palace. There are so many men in green that you have trouble taking a photo without one or two – or even a truckload – popping up in the viewfinder. Photography of military activity in Tibet is forbidden, of course, and it can lead to the confiscation of your film, or even your camera.

A lot of the military activity is removed from prying tourist eyes anyway, hidden behind the high walls of compounds dotted around Lhasa. Two hundred years ago, not even the exact location or elevation of Lhasa was known. Lhasa's mysteries today are quite different: sentries with Kalashnikovs or handguns guarding military compounds. I cannot reveal how, but I managed to enter a military compound out near Drepung. It was like a self-contained citadel, and large numbers of trucks and jeeps were parked in an inner courtyard. The compound had its own shops and cinemas. Satellite dishes sprouted from the rooftops.

Giving the military some cause to be paranoid are the mystery bombers of Lhasa. There have been sporadic reports of bomb blasts around Lhasa since the mid-1990s. The authorities have largely remained silent on the subject, but in May 1996, they admitted to three bomb blasts in Lhasa, blaming them on separatists. The blasts appear to have been small, set off in protest rather than to cause injury or loss of life. The Chinese described subsequent blasts as 'an appalling act of terrorism'.

*****

Barkor Bazaar, Lhasa's lively ancient open-air market and inner pilgrim circuit, is a barometer of what's in – and what's out. That applies in spiritual terms too. Apart from a trade in *khatas* (sold, curiously, by Chinese entrepreneurs), prayer wheels and other pilgrim gear, there are vendors of iconography. At a table of framed photos and posters, I pause to check 'the news'. Ugyen Trinley Dorje, the seventeenth Karmapa – a boy approved of by both the Chinese and the Dalai Lama – is prominent: several pictures show his 1992 enthronement at Tsurphu Monastery outside Lhasa. The chubby-faced tenth Panchen Lama, who died in Shigatse in 1989, is prominently shown too. But nowhere to be seen is an image of the Dalai Lama, which would have been all over this table several years ago. Instead there are numerous images of Gyaltsen Norbu, the young boy chosen by the Chinese to be the eleventh Panchen Lama.

All this imagery – or absence of it – is connected. The Dalai Lama's image has been banned, along with pictures of his choice for the eleventh Panchen Lama. The same purge of Dalai Lama pictures is taking place on a much larger scale at monasteries throughout Tibet. This campaign has been simmering for the last forty-five years, and reached boiling point in early 1996 on the heels of the bizarre 'battle of the incarnates'.

After the Dalai Lama, the second highest religious authority in Tibet is the Panchen Lama, with a seat at Tashilhunpo Monastery in Shigatse, central Tibet. When the tenth Panchen Lama died in 1989, the exiled Dalai Lama asked for cooperation from the Chinese to find the reincarnation of the lama. His request was rejected, and instead, the Chinese embarked on their own hunt. In May 1995 the Dalai Lama announced that six-year-old Gedhun Choekyi Nyima from northern Tibet was the next Panchen Lama. The Chinese were infuriated. The young lama disappeared, along with his immediate family, becoming the world's youngest political prisoner.

In December 1995 the Chinese installed their own choice, six-year-old Gyaltsen Norbu. Thousands of posters of the Chinese-appointed lama were distributed, replacing images of the Dalai Lama in temples: a new campaign was unleashed by Beijing to discredit the 'Dalai clique'. The magazine *China's Tibet* even went as far as asserting that because of the Panchen Lama incident, the Dalai Lama was 'the main hindrance to normal order in Tibetan Buddhism'. This is odd coming from atheistic Chinese, who for a long time dismissed reincarnates as 'feudal superstition'. They only became really interested in the incarnates in the 1990s, when they seemed to embark on a strategy of controlling the figureheads. But the Panchen Lama debacle may be a dress rehearsal for what the Chinese authorities really have up their sleeve: the choice of the next Dalai Lama. Traditionally, the Panchen Lama has influenced the choice of the Dalai Lama and vice versa. The Dalai Lama has said that since he has spent so long in exile, logically his reincarnate would be born outside Tibet, but the authorities have challenged this, insisting that a real Dalai Lama would only be born in Tibet.

Near the front entrance to the Potala, Chinese vendors sell books on Tibetan culture, written and printed in Beijing. I was curious to see how the editing went when it came to the Dalai Lama's image. Would older glossy books have certain pages missing or have his picture cut out? I pick up a glossy hardback book on the Potala, obviously an expensive production. In the entire book there's only one image of the Dalai Lama, a small black and white picture that shows him when he was much younger, talking with Mao Zedong in Beijing. A politically correct image.

In the Potala Palace itself, all Dalai Lama images have been removed from the walls and shrines. The whole trade has gone underground with vendors and buyers risking prison if found in possession of a picture. But Tibetans are willing to take risks. In a temple, a monk takes me aside to view a *tanka* in a dark corner. He lifts up the silky covering for the artwork and there, under the exterior image, is a big portrait of the Dalai Lama. A beatific smile creases the monk's face.

★★★★★

Two months before I came to Tibet I was heading up to my hotel room in Bangkok when the lift got stuck somewhere between the fourth and fifth floors. At first I thought that I could get the old contraption moving by fiddling with a few buttons. Then I started pounding on the walls and the doors, but no one heard. I passed the next four hours tearing my hair out, wondering if I would ever get out of this metal box and how long I could last without food or water. I wondered if I would be found; how much time I would waste; what would happen if I needed a piss. It is highly traumatic to be trapped. Those hours seemed like an eternity. Eventually, one of the hotel staff realised my predicament and prised open the door just wide enough for me to get out.

The reason I flash back to this is that in Tibet, prisoners can be boxed in like this for ten or twenty years, not just a few hours. And nobody hears their cries. Tibetans who have taken part in pro-independence demonstrations in Lhasa languish for years in prison, often subjected to brutal physical and mental torture. Or they just die in this hell.

In the past, monks and nuns have spearheaded demonstrations in Lhasa, perhaps because their faith is under attack; perhaps because they are not afraid of dying; perhaps because they have no immediate family to support. Invited back to a monk's room in Lhasa, I am alarmed to see slogans on the walls – written in English – about a free Tibet. Any of these signs would be enough to put him behind bars for ten years, but he doesn't seem concerned. He pours me some butter tea and casually enquires about news from the West. I am afraid for him; afraid because of his lack of fear. I am afraid to be associated with him; afraid that he might be investigated for having contact with a foreigner and that the trail will lead back here.

★★★★★

Traditionally, pilgrims arriving in the holy city of Lhasa would perform three clockwise walks: the inner circuit of the Jokhang Temple; the twenty-minute outer circuit of the same temple (Barkor Bazaar); and the ninety-minute circuit around Lhasa itself, known as the *Lingkor*. Within several days of reaching Lhasa, I set off on this longer route with Terry.

We follow a group of pilgrims, spinning prayer wheels and murmuring the sacred mantra *Om Mani Padme Hum*. Nobody is quite sure what the mantra means: some say it has sexual connotations concerning the jewel in the lotus; others say it is supposed to open heaven and close hell. If this is the case, on the *Lingkor* the chant should be used as an incantation against prostitutes because they now occupy parts of the route. Little of the original *Lingkor* retains its religious significance; today, much of the route passes Chinese shopfronts and government offices. Chinese small businesses have mushroomed in Lhasa in the wake of 1992's economic reform policy, which encouraged large numbers of Chinese settlers to move to Tibet.

Despite the changes, Tibetan pilgrims still make the rounds – old women spinning prayer wheels and mumbling mantras, and the occasional prone prostrator inchworming his way around the route, wearing a rubber apron to prevent his clothing being ripped to shreds. Keeping these pilgrims in view, we work our way east to the Telegraph Office. South of this the way is lined with girlie bars and hair salons. It is a shock to see pilgrims filing past Chinese prostitutes sunning themselves outside bars, or knitting, or getting their hair permed to while away the daylight hours. One bar with a smoked blue-glass veneer features a marble Venus de Milo in the lobby to set the mood. Nudes or noodles? A bit of both, I imagine, served up in private booths at night, along with copious quantities of beer.

These tiny bars, stocked with women in black lace and hotpants from Sichuan, have proliferated around Lhasa since 1992, turning the holy city into a whorehouse. Some Tibetan women are also involved in the trade, which caters to Chinese government officials, army officers and businessmen. Hairdressing salons – sometimes fifteen in a row – often act as fronts for prostitution, with private booths in the back. And certain Chinese restaurants provide female company as part of their service. Lhasa has morphed into a cityscape of parlours: videogame parlours, massage parlours, hairdressing parlours, late-night drinking parlours.

Onward along the *Lingkor*, pilgrims pause to burn juniper at clay urns and gaze in wonder at the new mock-Tibetan Tibet Royal Hotel. This has a Tibetan exterior decor, but the heart is Chinese – a rabbit warren of karaoke salons, and the most-frequented Chinese disco in Lhasa, called the Top View.

Down the road, we pass Jarmalinka Island. Once untouched, this island in the Kyi Chu River was a popular picnic spot for Tibetans, connected by a rickety wooden footbridge festooned with prayer flags. The footbridge is gone, replaced by a double-lane cement bridge decorated with Chinese lions. A sentry box prevents Tibetans from visiting – Jarmalinka is being 'developed' by the Chinese as some kind of resort, with trucks rumbling across the bridge and ominous concrete buildings sprouting up. The structure is rumoured to be a casino, a joint venture with a company from Macao.

On the walkways to the west side of the *Lingkor*, the Tibetan pulse finally picks up: rocks engraved with images of Tibetan deities, garlands of prayer flags, piles of mani stones engraved with hallowed mantras, and a huge blue-faced Buddha gazing down from a rock wall. A blue Buddha, I reflected, could not be more appropriate – what I've seen on the *Lingkor* is enough to give any Buddha the blues.

Seeking solace, I escape to the inner sanctum of the Jokhang Temple, where the Tibetan pulse is still strong. It is dark and smoky inside. Dim light is provided by a galaxy of butter lamps; the air is thick with the odour of yak butter and incense. The deep, hypnotic chanting of monks at prayer reverberates through the inner sanctum. Echoing through the halls is the sound of murmuring from throngs of Tibetan pilgrims as they pay homage to the myriad icons found here.

I make my way up to the flat rooftop to take in the fine views over Lhasa and the Potala in the distance. Strange things are afoot on the rooftop. Even here, at the sacred heart of Lhasa, the banality of Chinese occupation creeps in. In a tented enclosure is a teahouse, serving drinks to Chinese army officers, and Chinese and Western tour groups. No pilgrims are visible; access to the rooftop seems to be a privilege reserved for tourists. Tourists get tired, and this is a good spot to take pictures and take a break, it appears.

Even stranger, I find a monk sitting here with a can of Coke, engrossed in a laptop computer. I peek over his shoulder: he is typing away in Tibetan script. This is the first time in Lhasa I have seen a computer being used for this purpose. What kind of phantom is this?

'I am from the States,' he says with a broad grin, startling me with his excellent English, 'but originally from Amdo.'

He somehow obtained permission to visit his home town, and then just extended his stay and wangled his way through to Lhasa. I spend a long time chatting to him and sipping tea; he's a goldmine of information. He tells me the tale of Monlam Chenmo.

Monlam Chenmo, the Grand Tibetan Prayer Festival, coincides with Lunar New Year celebrations, and takes place around February or March. Or used to. There have been no full Monlam celebrations since 1988, after a series of explosive events.

In 1986, for the first time in over twenty years, Monlam was revived at the request of the Chinese. Whether this was as a spectacle for tourists, or to show the world that religious freedoms were being resumed, is not clear. But Monlam was potentially a troublesome period: the 1959 Lhasa Uprising took place on 10 March, at the tail-end of Monlam when the city's population swelled for festivities.

In 1986 over a thousand monks from the different monasteries around Lhasa got together for rites. Huge butter sculptures were displayed outside the Jokhang Temple at the heart of Lhasa, attracting crowds of up to 10,000 people from Lhasa and the valleys beyond.

Versions vary as to exactly what happened at the third Monlam to be staged. The last day of Monlam, 5 March 1988, turned into a riot, close on the heels of the pro-independence riots of 1987. Apparently, when a procession was in progress around Barkor Bazaar, some monks chanted independence slogans. Stones were thrown at them and they were warned to keep quiet. When they repeated the slogans, a Chinese policeman advanced, drawing his pistol. A Khampa tribesman from eastern Tibet stepped in to defend them, and was shot in the head at point-blank range. Infuriated, the monks paraded the dead man's body around the Barkor. At first the Chinese did not interfere, but by the third circuit of the Barkor, they were using batons and tear gas – then guns. Eighteen Tibetans died that day: Chinese troops stormed the Jokhang Temple and beat a number of monks to death with iron bars; other monks were thrown off the rooftop. Some eight hundred Tibetans were arrested.

The following year Monlam was boycotted by the monks. On 5 March 1989 the most severe rioting erupted. As many as a hundred Tibetans were killed, Chinese shops were burned, a state of martial law was declared and all foreigners were ordered out of Lhasa. No more grand Monlams have been staged since, although Chinese-produced brochures show the ceremony in progress to bolster the Chinese claim that there is complete religious freedom in Tibet.

Martial law was not lifted in Lhasa for thirteen months. By late 1991 the situation was back to normal, according to the Chinese. The place was open to tourism: business as usual, albeit with lots of permits, restrictions, checkpoints, and frequent chopping and changing of regulations. China favours group tours – members are easily controlled, stay a short time, shell out big bucks and have little contact with the locals.

Despite restrictions, individual travellers still manage to get into Tibet and run around, exploring loopholes – riding local buses, sneaking around by bicycle, trekking and camping with nomads. The most common method of travel for individuals is to band together in Lhasa and rent a Landcruiser. Which is what four of us did to sneak out to Ganden Monastery, twenty-five miles east of Lhasa.

Ganden was off-limits to tourists because rioting had taken place there a few months before. No monks would talk about what happened (probably from fear of 'undercover monks') but the presence of twenty soldiers armed with Kalashnikovs at the monastery gates was eloquent enough. Surveying this area from a ridge above the monastery with binoculars, I was startled to find a PSB officer staring back at me – through binoculars. Ganden is a mix of ruin and renovation; the entire place was dynamited to rubble during the Cultural Revolution and then, in the interests of tourism, sections were rebuilt.

The May 1996 riot at Ganden apparently broke out over the brusque removal of Dalai Lama pictures by Chinese officials. Two monks were killed, another seriously injured, a further ninety monks were reported arrested, and several hundred others fled into the surrounding hills.

In mid-1996 large contingents of PSB officers moved into the grounds of Sera and Drepung monasteries on the outskirts of Lhasa to 're-educate' the monks. 'The Chinese say there is religious freedom,' a monk confided to me, 'but there is none.' Foreign visitors to Drepung were treated to the spectacle of PSB squads telling monks what to believe, then shooing away tourists if they tried to take pictures. The Chinese adopted a new tactic: forcing monks to sign documents to denounce the Dalai Lama, confirm that the Chinese-backed Panchen Lama is the only one, and deny that Tibet was or should be independent. They also pledge not to listen to any Tibetan-language broadcasts from abroad. At Sera Monastery, when they refused to sign oaths, seven monks were arrested for 'leading a rebellion'. All this is a flagrant violation of the right to religious belief – but then, China has violated just about every single article of the Universal Declaration of Human Rights in Tibet.

5

MOTORING OVER THE HIMMIES

Where the yaks and the snow lions roam

The history of wheels in Tibet is a very short one. Hardly any. Not until the Chinese invaded, anyway. The monks had a virtual patent on the wheel: the eight-spoked wheel of the dharma is a revered symbol, seen atop all Tibetan monasteries nestled on a lotus base and flanked by two deer. The wheel is an ancient Indian symbol of the sun, of creation. In Tibet it is symbolic of the first turning of the wheel of dharma, the first teachings by Sakyamuni Buddha at Deer Park in Sarnath, setting everything in motion. The eight spokes signify the Noble Eightfold Path. This is the wheel of the law, the wheel of rapid spiritual transformation due to Buddha's teachings; the wheel of overcoming obstacles. A thousand-spoked wheel made of gold is said to have been presented to the Buddha after enlightenment, and is also the emblem of Tibet's religious kings.

The only wheel in constant use in old Tibet was the prayer wheel: either the huge fixed prayer wheels, embossed with sacred mantras that were spun by pilgrims at monasteries, or the miniature handheld prayer wheels. The monks were none too keen on seeing the wheel, or close replicas of it, used elsewhere, such as barrelling along a road. An ancient prophecy held that the use of the wheel would scar the surface of the earth, releasing evil spirits and destroying the social fabric of Tibet (and that may yet prove correct).

So here's a culture that knew about the wheel, and knew what it could do, but chose to ignore this technological advance because the wheel happened to be a sacred symbol. In the 1930s the British started running mail vans along part of the route to Gyantse, but reaction from the monks was so strong they had to revert to horse relays again. A few Nepalese merchants used bicycles in Lhasa, brought in from India, but bicycles too were rare in pre-1950 Lhasa.

The main mode of travel in Tibet back then was by horseback or on foot. Caravan routes snaked south from Tibet into Ladakh, Mustang, Sikkim and Bhutan, and north into China and Mongolia. Trade with Bhutan relied on barter: wool, salt and yak tails would make their way to the Bhutanese border, and were traded for hand-woven silk fabric, bamboo baskets and red chillies. During the Second World War, when the Japanese cut off supply routes to China through Burma, the Americans secretly arranged to fly over Tibet, ferrying supplies from India to south-west China. The Tibetans stipulated that supplies were restricted to the non-military variety. In the early 1940s, Chinese-initiated supply caravans also proceeded overland from India to Yunnan Province. These consisted of large numbers of Bactrian camels from Sining (Turkestan), with additional Tibetan mules. When the Chinese invaded Tibet, reaching Lhasa in 1951, they still relied on pack animals: soldiers mostly arrived by horse or camel.

Out at the Norbulingka, the Dalai Lama's former summer palace, I went looking for the cars that were once garaged there. After asking around, a Tibetan who lived in one of the buildings pointed at a woodpile. No, no, I said, not wood – I want to see a car, and again pointed at a picture I had of one of the cars. Again he pointed at the woodpile, and then I noticed a trace of orange. It was the body of the old yellow and orange American Dodge, buried under the woodpile. Nearby, in overgrown grass, lay the rusted remains of a baby-blue Austin. My mind flashed back to my interview with the Dalai Lama in McLeod Ganj, and I could hear his booming laugh as he told me of his teenage pranks in the 1940s, including crashing the Austin into a tree.

The cars were gifts from British political officers, carried in pieces by yaks and mules over the Himalayas from India and reassembled by an Indian chauffeur and mechanic. The thirteenth Dalai Lama was given three cars: a 1931 yellow and orange Dodge, and two 1920s Austin A-7s, one yellow, the other blue. All three were parked at the Norbulingka. The yellow Austin was used by the thirteenth Dalai Lama within the palace grounds. The blue Austin, which simply bore the number plate *Tibet No.2*, was used by officials at the Norbulingka.

The cars were mostly used for ceremonial occasions, and apart from an American jeep, these were the only cars in Lhasa at the time. Their range was limited by lack of roads, and, more to the point, lack of fuel, which had to be carried in from India. By the 1940s they had fallen into disrepair, but the young fourteenth Dalai Lama managed to get them running again. One of the cars was later adapted to power a generator for the fourteenth Dalai Lama's private cinema, hooked up by Heinrich Harrer.

Unlike the Tibetans, the Chinese are very highway-oriented. An invading force needs good roads to maintain its presence. Within a few short years of entering Tibet, the Chinese had engineered two major highways linking China to Tibet. And like Imperial Rome, the Chinese painstakingly maintain these links: there are road stations at ten-kilometre intervals all the way along major routes, as well as kilometre marker stones.

Lhasa is not Tibet – it is too heavily Chinese-influenced for that. So I was keen to get out into the countryside. The only sanctioned way to do this is to go by Landcruiser with a small group, driver and guide. Japanese-built vehicles rule the road in Tibet, the Toyota Landcruiser and the Mitsubishi Pajero. The vehicles take terrific punishment and are thus in various states of falling apart. You have to size up a rented vehicle carefully before embarking on a week's foray. How bald are the tyres? Does it have any suspension? What about the driver – how bald is the driver? Does he have any kidneys left? How many dials on the dashboard are still functioning?

I insisted that any group I joined had to have a Tibetan driver and guide, for the simple reason that the group could interact better with Tibetans in the countryside. And hopefully the money would go into Tibetan pockets. Another significant difference: the Tibetan guides and drivers know how to laugh. Their sense of humour and their wide smiles speak volumes about the amazing resilience of the Tibetan people in the face of extreme adversity.

★★★★★

Our driver on the first foray out of Lhasa looked exactly like Yoda in *Star Wars*, short and stocky with big pointy ears that jutted out, a high raspy voice and a certain wisdom engraved on his face. His real name was Rinzin, but Yoda became his nickname. He was steady on the wheel, and made all the right decisions about where to stop, where to eat and where to stay the night. Yoda was simply superb at what he did. Nima, the guide, on the other hand, was absolutely useless. If you asked this punkish youth to identify a particular statue, his eyes would glaze over and he would laconically say *Metal Buddha*. And this one? *Wooden Buddha*. And that one? *Painted Buddha*. Nima's main preoccupation was visiting bars or discos and chasing women. If there were no discos or bars in town (which was frequently the case), he lost interest and grew morose. All he wanted to do was get back to Lhasa, where there were lots of bars and discos, and shops with designer-label clothing for sale.

Aboard for this trip: Terry, his son James, myself, and Peter and Sophie, a young couple teaching at an institute in China. Peter was Australian, Sophie was French, and Tibet was clearly part of a romantic fling. You would need a crowbar to separate the two: they cuddled in the car, they cuddled in monasteries, they cuddled in restaurants, they giggled in hotel rooms (where super cuddling took place, we assumed). High altitude, however, is not conducive to romantic endeavours – too much stress on the lungs and heart rate – and Tibet offers little in the way of privacy.

Terry was an old road warrior. He travelled with a canvas-and-wood rucksack – and a ribald sense of humour. We kicked off the trip with a glorious diversion. Along the road, Terry spotted a Tibetan rider in full festival regalia (tasselled red hat and yellow jacket) so we asked Yoda to follow him. Yoda grinned, geared down, and left the highway. Down a winding track we came upon a horse racing festival, and were liberally plied with picnic food and *chang*. Warm-up event: riders with jingling bells launched their mounts along a track and performed acrobatics, letting go of the reins, leaning over to touch the ground, leaning right back in the saddle. The main event featured costumed riders who thundered along the same track and each fired two arrows sideways at a target. One arrow was primed in the bow; the second was held in the teeth. All the spectators were arrayed along the target side, but we stayed well clear of the landing zone. The costumed riders, we noticed, were liberally plied with *chang*, and an arrow to the forehead on day one of the Landcruiser trip would not have been auspicious.

★★★★★

If you want to get to the heart of a culture, delve into its mythological database. In Tibet's case, Samye would make a fine starting-point. We leave Yoda to guard the Landcruiser on the north banks of the Yarlung Tsangpo, and proceed by barge to Samye for an overnight stay.

Samye is thought to be Tibet's first monastery, and its first university. There are about a hundred monks in residence within a walled monastic compound, and several hundred villagers resident outside the walls. The entire monastic complex of Samye has been constructed according to the principles of geomancy, a concept borrowed from India. Samye is a piece of cosmic architecture. Seen from an aerial perspective (which is quite possible from nearby peaks), it is a mandalic 3-D replica of the Tibetan Buddhist universe – the architecture of enlightenment. The monastery is believed to have been founded in the eighth century, and has been demolished and reconstructed a number of times due to civil war, fire, earthquake and, more recently, Mao Zedong's fanatical hordes.

At the centre of the Tibetan Buddhist universe, on top of sacred Mount Meru, lies a mythical palace, which at Samye is symbolised by the three-storey main temple, Samye Utse. Outlying chapels in the cardinal directions symbolise four great island-continents, and eight subcontinents (curiously, the main cardinal direction for alignment in old Tibet was west, not north). The complex is bounded by an oval wall, pierced by four gates and topped by 1,008 small *chortens* (bell-shaped shrines) representing Chakravala, a ring of mountains surrounding the universe.

The ground between the main temple and the satellite

continents is meant to represent a 'great ocean', which may once have been hallowed ground, but is now a muddy wasteland. Following the Chinese occupation, villagers (who live outside the walls) were encouraged to treat the walled sanctuary of Samye as just another part of the village, so pigs, cows, chickens, braying donkeys and sheep are herded through. This gives Samye a somewhat earthy and surreal air; you round a corner looking for a sacred temple, and instead stray across a pig wallowing in the mud. And there are, I swear, more dogs at Samye than people; a roving band of dogs lays claim to the territory of the flagstones outside Samye Utse.

There is nothing cosmic about the guesthouse except, perhaps, the canopy of stars visible from the rooftop open-air squat toilet. It is a former monastery building with lots of character, but the dorm we're assigned to is spartan and chilly, with musty quilts as bedding. Luckily, we've all brought sleeping bags along.

★★★★★

Within the 'cosmic city' of Samye, there are frescoes of other legendary realms, such as the kingdom of Shambhala, shown in a mural in the main monastery. The inspiration for Shangri-La, the Tibetan legend of Shambhala can be traced to the eleventh century. The first Western reference to Shambhala was in a letter by Portuguese Jesuits in the early seventeenth century; they referred to 'Xembala'. In 1819 Hungarian scholar Alexander Csoma de Koros set off with a backpack to search for the ancestral homeland of his people, reputed to be in Central Asia. He never found it, but he did reach Tibet and became the foremost Tibetan language expert of his time. He wrote on the origin of the esoteric Kalachakra teaching, saying it derived from Shambhala.

Shades of Shangri-La: Shambhala is believed to lie somewhere to the north or north-west of Tibet, hidden behind high mountain ranges and glaciers. The kingdom is shaped like a huge lotus and filled with lotus lakes and sandalwood forests, all encircled by great snowy peaks. The people of Shambhala live free of disease and poverty, are wealthy and beautiful, and follow the practices of tantric Buddhism. Palaces made of gold and silver, studded with precious jewels, outshine the moon.

At some point in the future, barbarians (unspecified which ones) will set out to destroy Shambhala and its faith. King Rudracakrin, twenty-fifth in the lineage, will ride out of the gates of Shambhala with his armies and engage the forces of evil in apocalyptic battle, and Buddhism will reign victorious. This will usher in a golden age where people will live longer and crops will grow abundantly.

★★★★★

Mythological database entry: *snow lions*. Also depicted in frescoes at Samye Utse. Found only in Tibet. When the lion made the leap over the Himalayas from India, it became the residing deity of Tibet's snowy ranges, able to bound from snowpeak to snowpeak. Shown in frescoes with a white body and turquoise mane, or a blue body with vermilion mane and green eyes. Symbol of fearless joy – a mind free of doubt, clear and precise. The snow lion dance is performed at special events by performers in snow lion costumes. Snow lions are shown upholding the three precious jewels of Buddhism on the forbidden Tibetan flag. The snow lion is one of the clawed supernatural animals of the four directions appearing on prayer flags. If shown in pairs, the one on the left is male, the one on the right, female. Snow lion statues, depicted with cubs, stand guard at the gates of Norbulingka. Snow lions appear on the crest and seal of the Dalai Lama; they appear on Tibetan government seals of office, on old bank notes and stamps.

There's a curious ideological battle involving snow lions, possibly because of their close association with Tibetan nationalism. Outside the front gates of the Potala stand statues of Chinese imperial lions, the same symbols of Chinese emperors found at the Forbidden City in Beijing. Chinese officials have objected to a logo at a conference in Europe; the image in question was not the Tibetan flag, nor an image of the Dalai Lama, but simply a pair of snow lions.

*****

Tibetan cosmic architecture stands in jarring contrast to the Chinese bathroom school of design. In the town of Tsedang buildings with white-tiled exteriors and blue-tinted glass line the boulevards. Unlike Tibetan buildings, which blend in with the environment and are made of natural materials like stone and wood, the Chinese structures are the same as the ones all over China, and make no attempt to blend in. The blueprint for large towns is not Tibetan: it is a Chinese import. And Tsedang is a prototype for what may come to pass in the rest of Tibet: concrete blockhouses, brothels, karaoke bars, army barracks, crowds, trucks and traffic.

If you're a plumber, don't take a holiday in Tibet. Terry, who usually brings along a set of plumbing and electrical tools when travelling in China, takes one look at the bathroom in the Friendship Hotel in Tsedang and gives up. Our jerry-built hotel is full of fancy gadgets that don't work. The toilet, which looks modern, has a plastic bucket next to it. The idea is to fill up the bucket from the shower and use that to flush, because the flusher doesn't work. The more non-functioning gadgets you have in the room, the more you pay. This one has a TV set, but that doesn't work either, showing a screenful of static when you turn it on.

Entering a Tibetan restaurant in Tsedang, we are refused service. The owner says it is because he is afraid of the PSB, who have a deal with certain Chinese-run restaurants in town. Incensed, we wander off to a Tibetan teahouse to cool our heels. Within ten minutes two PSB officers in sunglasses materialise. We make life difficult for them by pretending not to understand any Chinese. One officer produces a booklet designed for situations just like this. It is titled, *Conversations for Aliens and Public Security*. Intrigued, I wait till his attention is diverted, and pick it up. I flip to a page stocked with phrases like *Aliens must comply with local regulations*, and *Please sign your interrogation here.* The PSB man turns around and snaps it out of my hands. A terse conversation follows, something along these lines:

'Where is your permit?' he barks.

'The guide's got it.'

'Where is your guide?' he barks again.

'No idea,' I venture.

'Probably down at the local disco,' chips in Terry.

'What is there to see in Tsedang?' I ask. 'I mean, why do we need a permit?'

I already know the answer to that question, but I ask it to rile them anyway. There is nothing to see in Tsedang. The permit is for sites further south, which have no hotels. Tsedang is a stepping stone to our real destination, the ancient fortress of Yambulagang, which is actually not that ancient any more. In fact it's a pretty good 1982 copy of a fortress built by the kings of the Yarlung Valley back around the seventh or eighth century. Now you see it, now you don't: Yambulagang Fortress was completely destroyed during the Cultural Revolution, and then, realising this was a rare architectural style and thus a major tourist draw, the Chinese ordered a complete reconstruction job. If you want to be king of the castle, you clamber up stairways through several storeys to the very top of the fortress tower, where observation windows give fine views of the patchwork of fields in the village below.

Three village children act as our guides. For some reason they do not demand pens or bon-bons. In the places along the way where we have stopped, children usually crowd around the Landcruiser clamouring for these items, an unfortunate pattern fostered by group tourists who readily dispense such goods. The Chinese think of foreigners as cash dispensing machines, while Tibetan children think of them as ballpoint pen dispensers. Our little guides, however, are very good company – they are pleased by the simplest of things. They are ecstatic to gaze at the valley through my binoculars; they are fascinated listening to tapes on James's Walkman. And they teach us Tibetan songs.

★★★★★

From Khamba La Pass there are aerial-type vistas over the turquoise waters of Lake Yamdrok Tso, and beyond to the snowcapped peak of Kula Kangri on the Bhutanese border. One day, I know, I will get to the other side of that view. Prayer flags flap from stone cairns at the wind-buffeted pass, some with colours faded by the sun, others in vibrant blues, reds, yellows or greens, newly placed by Tibetans to give thanks for safe passage.

On the other side of the pass there's something very disturbing on the horizon. It's a hydro-electric power plant on the shores of the lake. Through binoculars I can make out the turbines. I've read about this: the plant is part of a hare-brained Chinese scheme that drains the lake water to produce electricity for Lhasa during peak demand. The scheme has been a total disaster. There are concerns that the water level at Yamdrok Tso will drop significantly, or possibly even completely drain away. Authorities in Lhasa insist this is not the case: they say they will pump water back from the Yarlung Tsangpo River to replenish the lake water. But even if this were true, it means snow-fed lake water would be replaced with muddy river flow, with uncertain ecological results.

Solve one problem, create a bigger one: the scheme will increase Lhasa's electricity supply, but it will jeopardise the water supply in Yamdrok Tso, Tibet's largest freshwater lake. The fate of the lake is in the hands of bunglers who have one of the world's worst environmental records. China's rivers are in dire straits: some 80 per cent are so degraded they no longer support fish. China's forest cover has largely disappeared, and as loggers clear the forested slopes of the Tibetan plateau, more flooding and degradation of the rivers will occur. It is estimated that over 50 per cent of Tibet's forests have been cut down since 1959, mostly in eastern, north-eastern and south-eastern Tibet. If deforestation continues at such a pace, there will be nothing to stop landslides and mudslides cascading down during monsoon season not only into China, but into neighbouring nations like Burma and India.

In the village of Nagartse we make a pit stop at a tent teahouse. A crowd of Tibetans gathers as Yoda wheels and deals, buying wild mushrooms and strings of hardened yak cheese from the locals. The cheese is inedible, but the mushrooms are promptly added to soup; they taste delicious. Yoda is fast becoming our real guide. Nima merely acts as a medium to communicate with Yoda the All-Knowing. Yoda seems to know everybody along the way. And he knows every single rut on the road. When I inquire about visiting the monastery of Samding, for which we have no permit and which is technically off-limits, he simply nods and points to a distant ridge. Then he drives from Nagartse right up to the front gates of Samding, something that I did not know was possible. I was expecting a hike of a few miles.

Samding has a very odd background. It was run by an abbess, one of the few female incarnations in Tibet. The lineage goes back to the eighteenth century when, according to legend, she and her cohorts transformed themselves into pigs to save themselves from a Dzungar Mongol attack. Thus she earned the name Dorje Phagmo (Thunderbolt Sow). The lineage fell into dispute in the late 1930s; later, the sixth Dorje Phagmo sided with the Chinese and left the monastery. Out here in the middle of nowhere, parked improbably on a mountain top with expansive views, the rebuilt monastery imbues an air of mystery.

More mysteries: further down the line, a mystery town pops up. About twenty miles from Gyantse, we motor through a town that does not appear on any map. Not yet, anyway. It is a sea of corrugated tin roofs. We pass a huge hole being bored into a mountain side by Chinese workers – it looks like a railway tunnel. But there is no railway anywhere in Tibet. Inquiries to Nima yield a blank. Terry's engineering instincts tell him the construction is part of a dam connected with the electricity-generating scheme at Lake Yamdrok Tso. Yoda grimaces, making gestures that indicate craziness.

★★★★★

In Gyantse you can still get a feel for what old Tibet was like. The Tibetan quarter of town is fairly well preserved: a monastery complex up one end, a colossal fort up the other, and a dusty market and residential area of flat-roofed housing between the two. On the fringes of town are brilliant yellow mustard fields; ox carts and horse carts jingle by. The Landcruiser ploughs past herds of sheep and goats, and donkeys loaded with pots. There's no plumbing in the old quarter – water comes from street taps. However, solar cookers have been introduced by the Chinese: along with mounds of yak dung, these concave-shaped reflectors are found on numerous rooftops, and can bring a kettle of water to the boil in a few minutes.

Gyantse's monastic complex suffered great damage during the Cultural Revolution, and the fort was bombarded by the invading British in 1904. Dedicated to the latter topic is a two-room display inside the fort with a sign, 'Memorial Hall of the Anti-British'. A Chinese guide who was shepherding some group tourists seemed to think that the Tibetans won the battle of the fort in 1904 with Chinese assistance. Terry, born and bred in England, puffed up and loudly called this interpretation into question, stopping the guide in his tracks.

As Terry raised his camera to his eye, a museum attendant made a grab for it. Terry bristled fiercely and told him to back off. I jumped in between them, assuring the attendant there was no problem, when in fact a major dust-up was brewing. Within twenty minutes, as we were sauntering down to the entrance gate, a Chinese official materialised to question Terry, who feigned ignorance, but nevertheless remained aloof and unrepentant about his visit to the memorial hall. History, it seems, undergoes constant revision in the People's Republic of China. Sensing big trouble, I picked up my pace and left Terry behind with the official, still arguing. This was cowardly of me, and Terry ribbed me for it later, but I couldn't afford to get kicked out of Tibet just yet.

Gyantse's street markets are quiet and there is little evidence of the bustle of the past. Gyantse once flourished as a funnel for the export of sheep wool due to its location – wool was brought here from outlying areas in Tibet. By the 1930s, a great deal of Tibet's sheep wool production was slated for export to British India. There was little interest in yak wool, which was too harsh in quality, although in the pre-synthetic era, the beards worn by Santa Clauses in US department stores were made from yak tail hair.

Wandering the back alleys of Gyantse's old quarter, I chance across a carpet factory. The small operation is a shadow of what Gyantse once was, but stepping into this space is an extraordinary feeling, as if the hands of time have been turned back. As in the old days, work is done by hand, by women carding the wool, spinning, dyeing, weaving on hand looms and trimming the final product with shears. There's one dimension to traditional weaving that I had not envisioned: sound. The women sing raucous ballads as they work, keeping up a steady rhythm while they weave. There's a clacking of wooden loom parts, and while all this is going on, they take the opportunity to joke and flirt outrageously with me, demand that I send photos, try to barter for my day pack. I am trying to work out how they can weave from memory, quite a feat considering the complex designs. Even the smallest pieces – the horse carpets, used as a saddle base – are quite intricate.

In the early 1930s, riding on one of these carpeted saddles came British journalist Robert Byron. By promising to write pieces for the *Evening Standard*, the *Daily Express* and other journals, Byron – starting in London – smooth talked his way onto a series of planes that took him to India. That alone was a huge adventure: Byron had never flown before and now found himself up in the air on a variety of craft ranging from a 'flying boat' (seaplane) to an Italian monoplane. Enduring the constant roar of propellers, he spent a week hopping from aerodrome to aerodrome. From Kalimpong, Byron and two companions skirted official obstacles, forged across the Tibetan border, and rode ponies along the trade corridor permitted to the British as far as Gyantse, where there was a British Trade Agency.

'The supreme moments of travel are born of beauty and strangeness in equal parts' Byron once wrote. In Gyantse he found both beauty and strangeness – and pleasure. 'Looking back on Gyantse now,' Byron wrote as he wistfully turned back to Sikkim on his pony, 'I realise what a precious glimpse that week gave us of a way of life which the world has nowhere else preserved. In European parlance it is a medieval way of life, a stage through which we ourselves passed long ago, but from which, nevertheless, the roots of our tradition still draw much of their strength.'

Byron wondered how long it would take Western materialism to penetrate the isolation of Tibet, and how long Tibet could remain free from the military menace of China and Nepal without raising a properly trained army (the formation of which the Tibetan clergy opposed). In a nation where 'justice is cruel and secret, disease rife, and independent thought impossible, Western ideas might bring some benefits'. However, he hoped that the life he saw in Gyantse would endure, because Western civilisation suffered from a quite different malaise – spiritual emptiness – which Gyantse did not.

★★★★★

A gilded jewel-encrusted *stupa* encloses the embalmed body of the tenth Panchen Lama, who died in 1989. The body was embalmed according to traditional Buddhist rites. The internal organs were removed, and moisture was taken out of the body; it was then rubbed with saffron, spices and salt, and wrapped tightly in silk. After five months the dried shrunken body was repeatedly coated in gold, ready for entombment. The tomb of the tenth, completed in 1993, is the newest building at Shigatse's sprawling Tashilhunpo Monastery. No expense spared here: brochures boast of the half a ton of Chinese gold used in its construction, which may explain the Chinese-style roof. A life-sized statue of the Panchen Lama is shown at the front of the tomb.

It is supremely ironic that a man vilified by the Chinese while he was alive should be deified as a saint at Tashilhunpo. Chokyi Gyeltsen, the tenth Panchen Lama, was born in 1938 in the Kokonor region of Amdo. Actually, he was born several months before the ninth Panchen Lama died. This anomaly is explained by a secondary type of reincarnation whereby the ultimate source of the reincarnate can multiply simultaneously, and not necessarily after death. The tenth Panchen Lama was the third choice for the role and was enthroned in 1952 after two other boys died. He was brought to Shigatse by the PLA as the Chinese were determined to belittle the Dalai Lama's authority. After the

Dalai Lama fled Tibet in 1959, the tenth Panchen Lama by early accounts became a mouthpiece for the Chinese. However, after the PLA raided Tashilhunpo Monastery in 1960 and disbanded the monks, the Panchen Lama changed tack. In 1961, when asked to move to the Potala to replace the Dalai Lama, he flatly refused to do so.

In 1964 the Panchen Lama was asked to denounce the Dalai Lama at the height of the Monlam Festival in Lhasa. A crowd of 40,000 gathered outside the Jokhang; he delivered a stunning speech of solidarity with the Dalai Lama, in favour of Tibetan independence. He was promptly placed under house arrest, denounced as a reactionary, and brought to trial. After being beaten to induce a confession, he disappeared, along with his parents and entourage. He was taken to Beijing and sentenced to ten years in prison in 1967, most of it spent in solitary confinement.

By 1978 it was thought that he had died in prison, but that year he miraculously surfaced again – supposedly free and fully reformed. He was refused permission to travel to Tibet and continued to live in Beijing, where he held a government post. Then he did the unthinkable: he married a Chinese woman, Li Jie, with whom he had a daughter. Since none of the Panchen Lama lineage holders had married, and to preserve his spiritual standing among the Tibetans, his wife pretended to be his personal secretary. He had not only abandoned his vows of celibacy, he had compounded the deed, in the eyes of the Tibetans, by marrying a Chinese woman. The only way the Tibetans could explain this aberration was that the Chinese had forced the marriage on him.

Eventually, he managed to return to Lhasa and Shigatse for extended visits, during which he again became increasingly critical of Chinese policy in Tibet. In 1989 he was found dead of a heart attack in Shigatse, at age fifty. Although seriously overweight and a prime candidate for a heart attack, many Tibetans believe he was poisoned.

The Chinese have not exactly laid the matter to rest. In 1995 the choice of two Panchen Lama successors triggered a fierce battle of wills between the Chinese and Tibetans. The Dalai Lama's boy-candidate, Gedhun Choekyi Nyima, disappeared in Chinese hands. The Chinese-chosen candidate, Gyaltsen Norbu, was in Beijing, supposedly furthering his education, but most likely because his safety could not be guaranteed at Tashilhunpo. In the events leading up to Gyaltsen Norbu's enthronement at Tashilhunpo in November 1995, the leading lamas at the monastery were sacked, the head abbot was thrown in jail, and scores of monks arrested. Security for the enthronement ceremony was tight, with hundreds of PLA troops deployed. In the aftermath, Chinese work teams moved into the monastery to force monks to pledge their loyalty to the new Panchen Lama; those refusing to do so were expelled or imprisoned. Under these circumstances, you wonder if there is anything normal going on at the monastery, with monk-spies out in force. And you wonder exactly what the monks are debating about in their ritual afternoon sessions.

I can get nothing from the monks about the choice of Panchen Lama. But in a local photo shop, the Tibetans are more direct. There's a large poster of the Chinese-chosen Panchen Lama on the wall, and when I point to it, one Tibetan throws up his hands in despair and shouts *No! No! No!* A woman lifts her crooked little finger to her eye giving the evil-eye gesture; the little-finger-up means 'bad' in Tibet. And a third customer points to his mouth and then puts his wrists together; he is telling me that if he talked about it, he would be in handcuffs.

In Shigatse we stay at Tenzin Guesthouse, run by a Tibetan family. The place is multilevelled: a courtyard in the centre, galleries arrayed around it, and rooms further back. On the entrance floor, cows and goats are quartered, and sometimes you have to squeeze past some large animal to gain the upper levels. The extended family occupies the next floor up: the gallery here is busy with activities like carding and spinning wool, washing, or churning tea. On the top deck, there's accommodation in dorms for foreigners. At sunset we hang out at the rooftop gallery, drinking beer. Kat, a French woman researching Tibetan artwork for her thesis, has been in Shigatse for several weeks. She knows the best places to eat so we all follow her down the street to dine at Greasy Joe's Café. The menu is simple: you select the vegetables, and Greasy Joe runs back to the kitchen and stir-fries them in the wok, along with tofu, meat, or whatever else you care to add.

Stir-fries. Terry launches into a story about the ultimate stir-fry experience. Picture this: he's guest of honour at a banquet in Zhengzhou, where he's working. It's an elaborate affair, starting out with seahorse soup – Chinese medicinal fare – washed down with that virile delicacy, five-penis wine. And then, a hush descends as a large dish is brought out: stir-fried scorpions. All eyes turn to Terry: will he be intimidated? They have obviously underestimated him. He takes one look at the scorpions and booms, 'You bunch of sissies – you eat them dead? I thought you ate them live!' He is obviously under the weather from the drink, but it's too late, the host must not lose face. Losing face is very bad at a banquet. The challenge has been thrown out, and the banquet maestro orders a round of live scorpions.

'The trick to eating a live scorpion,' says Terry nonchalantly, 'is to bite its head off before it sends its tail-stinger into your lips.' When you pick up the scorpion with your chopsticks, it starts snapping its tail. To get around this, to slow the speed of its reflexes, you immerse the scorpion in rice wine, which sends it into a temporary coma. Then you have to move quickly, biting off its head before it comes around. Hopefully the chef has removed some poison, but according to Terry, judging from the ashen faces around his table, perhaps not. Terry survived the banquet, but one of the diners had to be rushed to hospital after getting a stinger to the lip.

Traveller's Digest: the name of a specialist magazine that should be launched, catering to the subject of the intestines and the effect of foreign food on them. The magazine would feature eloquent essays on Giardia (which is a spectacularly unpleasant digestive upset), flamboyant tracts on better digestion, ominous warnings about dire rear. It's truly astounding how much travel talk revolves around food and drink – and the stomach, the intestines, bugs in the intestines, explosive guts. You abandon your humdrum home environment and end up becoming preoccupied with your own stomach. Here at Greasy Joe's, the topic turns to mystery meat.

We are trying to identify the meat in the soup – yak, sheep or goat?

If the Chinese are not fastidious eaters, the Tibetans are when it comes to taking the life of any sentient being. In an ideal world, Tibetans would be vegetarian, completely avoiding the taking of animal lives. But the reality is that meat is an essential part of their diet on the plateau. Buddhist teaching does not prohibit eating meat, but Tibetans will make varying degrees of effort to minimise the karmic damage involved in slaughtering animals. There's a kind of sliding scale: larger animals are preferred for slaughter, because they will feed many more people than a small animal. Thus Tibetans would rather take one big life (a yak) than lots of smaller lives (fish). Prayers will be said in compassion for the departed yak; Tibetans wish it a better rebirth before dining on the meat.

It was curious, therefore, to see a sign in Shigatse advertising fish from the Yarlung Tsangpo River on the menu. The restaurant had to be for Chinese patrons. As vultures consume the deceased on land (sky burial), fish are relied upon to consume the deceased in the water, a process known as 'water burial'. And fishing is strictly taboo in sacred lakes, such as Lhamo Lhatso, famed for its visions for divining the incarnation of the Dalai Lama.

★★★★★

Yoda is worried: our guide has disappeared. We are due to drive back from Shigatse to Lhasa, but Nima has not shown up. Eventually, Yoda surmises that Nima has been involved in a bar fight overnight, and is probably being held by the police, so we leave Shigatse without him.

Sophie's altitude sickness has become more pronounced. She's having a panic attack. Peter tries to calm her down. This is very frightening. It's frightening to her that she can't breathe properly, and it's frightening to us to have someone aboard who may suddenly turn for the worse in a few hours if we don't do something about it. She's breathless, says she has lost feeling in her legs, has painful hands, stomach cramps. Her face is turning blue. We have to do something – fast – because medical facilities in Tibet are primitive, or non-existent. Hospitals are a joke: medical staff re-use syringes and surgical gloves. When a foreigner comes in, staff blindly subject the patient to a cardiogram, an x-ray, and an intravenous glucose drip, regardless of what illness is presented, and then demand a large amount for these services. Sophie has already seen this in action in the clinic in Gyantse, and she is no better off for the experience. You don't need an x-ray if you're suffering from altitude sickness.

The north route from Shigatse to Lhasa runs through a canyon along the Yarlung Tsangpo River, along precipitous cliff faces, which are none too stable. As we round a corner, the truck in front of us comes to a sudden halt. A slab of the cliff collapses right in front of us and disappears into the river. I have to tell you it is very disconcerting when this happens: what had previously been a road was now a very big crater. And I have to tell you that when this happened, Sophie was becoming quite hysterical. I'm sure she thought it was the end of the world.

For some of us, it nearly was. As we got out and gingerly approached the area of the slide, another section of the roadway cracked and groaned, and decided to break away and join the river, the colour of yak-butter tea, swirling far below. I held my breath. It was like being in the middle of an earthquake. The second slab turned out to be much smaller, but you had no idea what would happen next. Terry, the engineer, summed it up in two words: *bad engineering*. His opinion was that it would take a long time to fix the crater. We had two choices – to go all the way back to Shigatse and take the south route back to Lhasa, which would require several days of detouring, or we could walk around the edge of the 'hole' and try and pick up transport on the other side. With Sophie's condition, we had little choice; we took the faster option.

We persuaded hysterical Sophie to walk around the edge of the crater and found a vehicle on the other side that had come from the direction of Lhasa whose driver had decided to head back. Although we advised them not to, Peter and Sophie decided to get off at the People's Hospital on the outskirts of Lhasa, where they were greeted by an attendant with a blood-smeared apron, smoking a cigarette.

On this one-week Landcruiser trip in central Tibet, only three of us, out of the original contingent of seven, made it back to Snowland Hotel in Lhasa. Two Aliens were at the hospital, the guide was held by Shigatse police, and Yoda and the Landcruiser were stranded at a roadside crater ninety-five miles from Lhasa.

★★★★★

July 15th, back of Everest: the monk's abode is humble, but affords one of the finest views in the world. The stone and wood hut, which he has built himself, looks over Rongbuk Valley with Mount Everest towering at its head, flexing its icy flanks. The monk offers me butter tea, *tsampa* and a whole dried goat leg (with hoof and hair still on it). I offer him a Dalai Lama picture, which he reverently holds to his forehead. He smashes his fist into the palm of his left hand to indicate the desecration of Dalai Lama pictures all over Tibet. And we contemplate the fantastic view at his doorstep.

I am up here to get away from the group on this Landcruiser foray, to get some peace of mind because the last few days have been stressful. The ride is from Lhasa to the Nepalese border at Zhangmu, with two Frenchmen and an Australian couple. The trip started well enough, but developed into a personality clash. Darren and Marge, the Australian couple, are bossy, take-charge types who like to be in control of everything, especially the itinerary. They're not used to anyone challenging their viewpoints: they've spent over a year as foreign experts, working in eastern China, and act like they know everything about the Middle Kingdom. 'Tibet is not China,' I retorted at one point, which ruffled them.

'Of course it is,' hissed Darren.

'You've ruined my holiday!' Marge told me bluntly over dinner one evening – an interesting ploy to try to win an argument.

149

Darren went one better and took a swing at me in Shegar. He missed, but we went at it for a while before Marge managed to call him off. The argument this time was over the timing for dinner. Darren just lost it. He was completely out of breath from his exertions at altitude, but still swearing like a trooper, his face puffed up and red with rage. After that there was a truce, but an uneasy one.

Everest, the number one draw in the climbing world, requires a laborious trekking approach from the Nepalese side, but from the Tibetan side you can drive all the way to base camp. This route, though very rough, was engineered in the 1960s to facilitate Chinese mountaineering attempts on the summit. To the Tibetans, Everest is just another peak. It is sacred, but not highly revered. Tibetans are not interested in summiting peaks, they want to circumambulate them, which in the case of Everest is impractical. Nevertheless, it is held to be the residence of Miyo Langsangma, one of the five goddesses (Five Sisters of Long Life) who dwell on various Himalayan peaks on the southern Tibet border. The most important goddess resides on Gauri Shankar; another lives on Chomolhari, on the Tibet-Bhutan border.

Most tourist literature renders the Tibetan name for Everest as Chomolungma, 'Mother Goddess of the World'. But, in fact, the title comes out as Jolmo (queen or goddess) glangma (on an ox). The mount of the goddess is an ox, though sometimes she is shown astride a tiger. The closest Tibetan phrasing would be Jolmo Miyo Langsangma, which means 'Immovable Goddess Mother of Good Bulls'. Imagine a brochure advertising a tour to 'The Mother of All Bull'.

In the Tibetan scheme of things, Miyo Langsangma is a minor goddess. Wall paintings at Rongbuk show her holding a bowl of roasted barley flour in one hand, and a mongoose spitting jewels in the other. These apparently indicate she bestows food and wealth on those who show devotion to her. Every year in Tengboche, a village on the Nepalese side of the mountain, at the festival of Mani Rimdu, the monks release a yak to wander freely in the mountains as an offering to the goddess. Mountaineers are advised to make some kind of offering before attempting the climb:

if the goddess is not propitiated, she could make the slopes of Everest treacherous. When the British first attempted to climb Everest in the 1920s, the lamas at Rongbuk forecast that the demons of Everest would cast down any man who dared to tread the slopes, and a fresco to this effect shortly appeared on the monastery walls. The monastery and its frescoes were destroyed in the late 1960s and rebuilding is still underway. This accounts for the unusual chorusing to be heard in the prayer hall, where the deep voices of the monks are offset by the higher voices of the nuns. The nuns, who are still waiting for the building of a nunnery up the valley to be completed, come to visit the prayer hall here.

A simple stone building provides rooms for guests at Rongbuk. Inside, beds – if you could call them that – consist of planks of wood raised off bare ground. There's no electricity. You fight for a precious thermos of hot water from the monastery to make soup or hot tea. Rongbuk is 16,500 feet up: to counter the altitude you have to drink plenty of fluids and you dread the resulting midnight trip to the stone outhouse, where it's cold enough to freeze the bollocks off a brass monkey.

★★★★★

In the village of Tingri I stumble across a Tibetan teahouse. In the dim lighting I can make out copper cauldrons hanging off the walls, and some tall wooden cylinders decorated with brass. The cylinders are tea churns, each fitted with a wooden plunger to distribute the yak butter evenly in the tea mix. Yak butter strikes again: the stuff is burned in butter lamps, smeared on the face as a sunblock and to protect against windburn, and consumed medicinally.

Rancid yak butter is the smell of Tibet: the smell of a thousand temples, the smell that scents the woodwork.

I settle on a low bench, covered in carpets bearing auspicious Tibetan symbols. I join four other customers, warming my hands with a cup of butter tea. Tibetans drink enormous quantities of tea – upwards of forty cups a day. Nothing proceeds without the communion of tea. You might not recognise the taste as 'tea' initially, it is more of a salty broth, and with gobs of yak butter floating on the surface, it hardly looks like tea. The black tea content in the churn is actually quite weak – stronger tastes are yak butter and salt. Both have their applications at high altitude: the salt restores electrolyte balance countering dehydration, and the butter, with its high fat element, counters the effects of severe cold.

Three of the customers have red yarn plaited in their hair, and earrings of turquoise. The fourth man miraculously speaks some English, having spent some time in India, so can translate for the owner of the teahouse, Tashi, who struggles with the concept of where I come from. All foreigners, to him, come from the same place, some outer island across the great oceans. He's heard of America, and he once guided an Englishman up to Everest, but he has no idea where England or America are, or how big they are. This leads into a discussion on the world from the Tibetan viewpoint. If you're sitting on the rooftop, how does it look? Tashi explains, through the translator, that the world is flat. He points at the lacquered wooden chest that serves as the tea table. It is square, topped with a circular dragon design in the middle, and knotted patterns at the corners.

'This is the world,' he says, passing his hand over the disk, 'and around it the oceans. And above it the air.'

And I am thinking, he might as well add: *And here be dragons*, the phrase used to explain away the unknown in Mercator's day. *Chinese dragons*. Tashi knows the names of only three nations: China, India and Nepal. And even on these, he is hazy. He can name just four cities in China, one of them being Xiahe, site of a large Tibetan monastery. His concept of geography is vaguely of the land masses of China and India; beyond that lie great oceans.

You have to take into account, however, the vastness of the Tibetan plateau, which appears to be a separate world, a complete world in itself. To Tibetans, the most important features on the mental map are large monasteries, not towns, and the only reasons to travel are pilgrimage or trade. Even the smaller Chinese-designated Tibet Autonomous Region is 425,000 square miles in area, roughly the size of England, France, Germany and Austria combined. With an average elevation of 15,000 feet, Tibet is the highest region on the planet: its southern borders encompass the world's highest peaks; it is the source of virtually all Asia's great rivers, the Indus, Brahmaputra, Mekong and Yangtse among them.

Tingri was once a Tibetan-Nepali trading centre for grain, goods, wool and livestock. This trade largely died out after 1959, although the odd yak caravan still makes the journey over Nangpa La Pass from Nepal. Tingri today is essentially one big army base disguised as a village. Army compounds hidden behind high walls bristle with satellite dishes. The military have electricity via generators; the Tibetans do not – they use kerosene lamps. The compounds at the south end are curious; they first appear to be Tibetan buildings, but on closer inspection turn out to be Chinese-built installations – a new form of military camouflage?

The military tries to keep a low profile, but this is an absurd exercise given the large number of soldiers stationed in Tibet. The main tourist encounter with the military is at checkpoints. On the major routes in Tibet, officers are looking for anti-Chinese literature and Dalai Lama pictures. Major baggage searches take place at the Shegar checkpoint on the road up from Kathmandu (where Dalai Lama pictures are readily available in bookshops). In certain guidebooks, the officers know exactly where the Dalai Lama pictures are, so they simply rip out that exact page and return the book. When the supply truck for a Canadian group tour arrived at a checkpoint to the west of Lhasa and found no one there, the driver proceeded on. A Chinese officer came running out and shot out the back tyre of the truck with his handgun.

★★★★★

The immense Mongolian-style outer walls of the monastery at Sakya dwarf any other structure in the town. There are a few teahouses and shops huddled nearby looking insignificant, and houses with yak dung and brushwood piled high to the rooftops, fuel for the winter months. I make a beeline for the interior of the monastery, the Great Sutra Chanting Hall. The hall is lofty and spacious, hung with huge *tankas* and is remarkable for its massive treetrunk pillars that support the roof. I've been here on two prior occasions, but missed a very well-hidden feature: the library. It takes some coaxing to persuade the monk with the keys (who claimed the library didn't exist) to let me in.

The entrance, a small wooden door that leads to a dark enclosure, is concealed behind a giant Buddhist statue. But I'm ready. My flashlight traces an astonishing contour: the library shelving here is about 180 feet long, 30 feet high and three feet deep. The seven huge shelves are filled with thousands of dusty Buddhist scriptures, many hand-copied by Tibetan calligraphers. Near one corner is a huge manuscript illuminated in gold called the Prajnaparamita Sutra. The book is so large it requires its own special rack: the pages are five feet wide.

The musty atmosphere is evocative of a powerful, ancient world, like the fabled lost library of Alexandria in Egypt. Not such a long shot, either; there were monks from north-west India at Alexandria in its prime, long before the library was destroyed. Credit for the oldest printed books goes not to Europe, nor to Egypt, but to Central Asia around the eighth century. The oldest known *dated* book is a woodblock copy of the Diamond Sutra, printed in Chinese in AD 868, with elaborate illustrations of Buddha and his disciples. This rare tome now rests in the British Library, and is related, content-wise, to the Prajnaparamita Sutra sitting on the shelf at Sakya.

The trouble is that the Tibetans got firmly stuck in the woodblock stage of printing, never advancing beyond that. Their technology became fossilised. Everything was done with woodblock printing: Tibetan postage stamps were printed from woodblocks, all the prayer flags were printed with woodblocks. Still, it was – and is – an enormously complex process to print a Tibetan sacred text from a set of woodblocks. The *Tenjur*, a commentary on Buddha's discourses, requires some 25,000 separate woodblocks to be run off. Then the work has to be sorted, collated and bound in cloth (not glued – all the oblong loose leaves are pressed between two boards and the entire assembly is wrapped in cloth). And then it has to be shipped. There were once three great monastic printing presses in Tibet, at Shol (the Potala), Narthang (outside Shigatse) and Derge (in Kham). Only the latter remains – the other two were razed to the ground by the Chinese during the Cultural Revolution.

*****

A Tibetan car wash: sheets of water cascade over cliffs at intervals as the Landcruiser motors down switchbacks, off the plateau, towards Zhangmu. We punch through minor waterfalls. Like a mechanical car wash, the windscreen is blurred for a few seconds, and the driver has no idea what lies ahead at these points. The roadsides are bathed in greenery; the air is positively balmy and tropical. The scenery has turned moist, leafy and mossy. We have motored right over the Himmies, dropping down a cleft in the plateau towards Nepal.

When you reach Zhangmu, the trading town on the Tibet-Nepal border, technically you're still in Tibet, but in terms of landscape and people, you've definitely left the high plateau. There are Nepali products everywhere, Nepali merchants, and scores of Nepali porters. Nepalis, Tibetans and Chinese unload and reload goods and haggle over currency exchange rates. Otherwise, playing pool, watching action thrillers on video, or drinking beer are the favourite pastimes of porters and drivers in Zhangmu. The town is arrayed along steep switchbacks that snake down to the Chinese customs and immigration post where all the passengers on this trip are deposited for the trip onward to Kathmandu. Except me. I am returning to Lhasa.

Or am I? That night, I start to panic because great torrents of water come crashing down, hammering the rooftop; leaks develop in the flimsy ceiling of the guesthouse. Damn it! The bloody monsoon has hit. And that means the roads could get washed out, and I might not make it back to Lhasa. I will be stuck in godawful Zhangmu indefinitely if a key bridge gets washed away higher up.

But Pingzo, the driver, shows up early next morning. Come hell or high water, we are running the gauntlet to Lhasa. At the top of the hill above Zhangmu, the driver stops at an army base to pick up a new passenger. A Chinese army officer. This is totally unexpected, and I am slow to react. An ominous amount of luggage is loaded – boxes of goods – and when I get out to look around the base, the officer slips into my front seat position and indicates that I should sit in the back, which proves a disaster because he is fond of spitting and I have to keep the windows closed in case I get hit by the fall-out. To make matters worse, he smokes like a chimney.

Pretty soon, both he and the driver are smoking up a storm, fogging up the interior, but I can't open the back window because of the flying spittle and the rain that's pouring down. *The forecast: heavy spittle, easing to light dribble, with a high chance of fog and tobacco haze overnight.* Torrential rain is crashing down around our heads; there are fresh landslides to skirt around, with big rocks littering the road. The ride is a blur. For some reason, the officer is in a rush and the driver is attempting suicidal manoeuvres in the rain, with fogged windows and half-hearted wipers.

The officer acts like I am not there at all. He does not bother to introduce himself , so I do not know his name. He barely acknowledges my presence, even though I am paying for the vehicle. He spends all his time talking to Pingzo in high-volume Chinese. I am getting a taste of life from a Tibetan's point-of-view, as a tenth-class citizen. The officer has taken over the vehicle and is giving all the orders. But I am determined not to let him get away with this bravado. At Nyalam, in a roadside teahouse, I meet a Tibetan guide, Nawang, who is looking for a ride as far as Lhatse. So I invite him along. For the first time, the officer actually looks at me – weirdly – but there's nothing he can do. I talk with the Tibetan guide in English as loudly as I can in the back seat; Nawang is enjoying this situation immensely.

The one plus of having 'the general' aboard is that we fly through the checkpoints. Those manning the checkpoint take one look at the front seat, spot the olive-green uniform, and wave us through. There's something else I notice too. The hordes of grubby children that usually descend on a Landcruiser when it stops, holding the passengers to ransom for pens and gifts, stay well away from this one. As soon as they see the man in green, they back right off. Adult Tibetans stare at me strangely as if I'm in cahoots with the Chinese military or am being escorted under arrest. Nawang can break the ice in these situations, so I am sorry to see him go in Lhatse.

Crashing rain, thunder: at one point I'm jolted awake when Pingzo hits a rut. I wonder if I am dreaming or sleeping as a bolt of lightning pierces the darkness. This is like racing a horse over a field of gopher holes; it is miraculous that the Landcruiser is still in one piece. At Shigatse, around midnight, the officer takes us on a Fellini-esque tour of the karaoke bars and girlie bars, apparently looking for his contact. He eventually finds a man in a grey suit who looks peeved to be torn away from his temporary paramour, but guides us to the final destination, where the officer unloads all his goods, thank God, and slams the door. The driver is exhausted – he has been at the wheel for over sixteen hours. He pulls into a guesthouse, finds a dormitory bed, and is instantly asleep.

The next day we tackle the last leg, the road to Lhasa. Fifteen miles from Lhasa, I request a stop at tiny Drolma Lakhang, dedicated to the goddess Tara. This exquisite temple has a sutra-chanting hall lined with life-size bronze images of Tara. The micro-temple is like a jewel: it is tiny, housing only twenty-five monks, but everything is here – library, meditation rooms, beautiful chapel. Five monks are chanting; I take a seat and listen. The temple is my touchstone. I have stopped at it on a number of trips out of Lhasa. I have come to give thanks for deliverance from the monsoon rains, for safe passage back to Lhasa. I am here to press the reset button, go back to ground zero. Central Tibet is beyond the Himalayan rain shadow and experiences only mild rains. But I later learned a key bridge was washed away above Zhangmu: my premonitions had been correct.

★★★★★

August 19th, Namtso Lake: giggling nuns are selling beer to backpackers. Attached to the cave-like nunnery is a simple wooden structure where everyone sleeps on the floor. It's a case of rival Landcruiser passengers jockeying for floor space with their sleeping bags – a kind of backpackers' pyjama party. All very homey. My Landcruiser crew on this northern trip is great: Thysje from Belgium, Johanna from Sweden, Tess from England – a lively lot.

Namtso is a sacred lake of beautiful turquoise hues, with a string of snowcaps backing it. Everything here is on a vast scale, and the sweeping sense of space takes your breath away. Surrounding the lake is a high grassland valley dotted with nomad encampments: yak-hair tents, and herds of grazing yaks, sheep and goats. Several times we pass caravans of yaks loaded with saddlebags. The yak is the lifeline of the nomad, supplying milk, butter, cheese, curd and dung for fuel; it supplies the principal source of meat, and its hair and hide are used for making tents, ropes, clothing and boots.

You would be hard-put to find a tougher human being than a Tibetan nomad. Among the last nomads of Asia, they endure incredible hardships, particularly in the winter months, with long snowfalls, temperatures that dip well below freezing and howling winds. The high-altitude sun also takes its toll: many nomads do not use sunglasses. Constant exposure can lead to cataracts and blindness in old age, while the skin becomes incredibly wrinkled.

I remember once showing off the local mountains to a Tibetan friend, Gerry, on the Canadian west coast. He was stunned to learn there were such things as snowshoes to make passage across snow easier. The idea that snow could be fun was a completely alien concept to him, but Gerry quickly caught on and found it exhilarating to go tubing – to be sent spinning down a snow-covered hill at breakneck speed in an inner tube. How useful snowshoes would be in Tibet, he told me. Nobody had ever seen anything like them. He was thinking how Canadians had not only snowshoes, they had skis, snowboards, toboggans, snowmobiles and trail-clearing machines. The Tibetans had seen none of these devices.

At Damxung, we chance across a grasslands fair, a combination of horse racing, other competitions, and impromptu tent shops and teahouses. Obviously, too, matchmaking is a key element: nomad women come dressed in their finest, in ornate *chubas* (cloaks) trimmed in sealskin, with elaborate silver and turquoise jewellery and stylish fur hats.

The last stop on this trip is a bone-jarring ride up a dirt track to Tsurphu, about forty-five miles from Lhasa. By Tibetan standards, Tsurphu Monastery is modest in size. It's remarkable that it exists at all: the place was razed during the Cultural Revolution and completely rebuilt, beam by beam, in the interests of tourism. But Tsurphu is no ordinary Buddhist showcase. What immediately catches my attention is the flag mounted high at the front. The monastery flies its own blue and yellow ensign, a dharma wave design or 'wisdom flag' that is said to have appeared in a dream to the sixteenth Karmapa. The flag is the special logo of Tsurphu. Flying such a flag alone is extraordinary, given the extreme Chinese aversion to the display of flags other than their own (the penalty for displaying the outlawed snow lion flag in Lhasa can be a bullet in the head).

Tsurphu's *gonkhang*, or protector chapel, qualifies as one of the most bizarre in Tibet. Offerings by the faithful here are in the form of stuffed animals, a collection by no means limited to Tibetan fauna. One of the specimens is a stuffed kangaroo (from an Australian devotee?). An enormous stuffed yak hangs from the rafters, and birds of prey – eagles, vultures, owls – glare down in stuffed majesty.

Tsurphu is special because it is the traditional seat of the Karma Kagyu, one of the four great religious sects in Tibet. Until 1959, the leader of the Kagyu, the sixteenth Karmapa, lived at Tsurphu. Like many other religious leaders at the time, he fled for India, where he established a lavish new base at Rumtek Monastery in Sikkim. Under the sixteenth Karmapa, the Kagyu sect flourished in the West, with centres established in many countries, and an estimated five million followers.

When he passed away in Chicago in 1981, the sixteenth Karmapa left no obvious clues about where to find his successor.

The matter was in the hands of four regents at Rumtek. After mulling it over for a decade, two regents found a seven-year-old boy, Ugyen Trinley Dorje, in eastern Tibet, but a third regent backed a rival candidate, Thaye Dorje, also discovered in Tibet.

In 1992, for the first time, the Dalai Lama and the Chinese government arrived at a consensus over the choice of the seventeenth Karmapa, enthroning Ugyen Trinley Dorje in an elaborate ceremony at Tsurphu. Actually, the Dalai Lama has no jurisdiction over the Kagyu lineage holders, but his blessing is important to world opinion. The business of selecting incarnates was previously scoffed at by the Chinese, but now the selection was viewed as a matter of patriotic politics. The seventeenth Karmapa was the first incarnate recognised by the Chinese since 1959: he was obviously being carefully groomed as a patriotic alternative to the Dalai Lama.

The courtyard at Tsurphu is thronged with dishevelled pilgrims in a high state of excitement. We have arrived to witness the mid-day blessing by the 11-year-old Living Buddha. Bearing *khatas*, we file into the main prayer hall, where the Karmapa sits on a throne, surrounded by monk-attendants. The pilgrims each present a *khata*, and he touches them on the head with a sceptre. Every so often, he reaches out to drink from a can of Coke. My turn comes up. I present a *khata* and come under the scrutiny of the Karmapa's mesmerising gaze. The eyes seem to bore right through you, with a mixture of arrogance, ennui and tension. The look is hard to read. What lies behind it?

6

RED RIVER VALLEY

Travelling through time in Gyantse

There are times, travelling, when you fall into extraordinary circumstances doing things you couldn't ever imagine. Like right now, standing in a monastery courtyard, adjusting my sword and pith helmet, with a make-up artist streaking dirt and blood stains on my face.

When three buses disgorge their loads of People's Liberation Army soldiers at the monastery, we know we're onto something big. Why so many soldiers? For security? For an execution? The fresh-faced recruits stand at attention while a commander barks at them. Then one platoon proceeds to remove their camouflage fatigues and ... put on khaki uniforms – and wigs, moustaches, sideburns and pith helmets. One of them picks up a pole with a ragged Union Jack mounted on it and waves it around. They are the British Army!

'Stiff upper lip, lads – hold the flag high!' shouts Nick, a Hollywood actor. We're in the courtyard of Nenying Gompa, a monastery south of Gyantse in central Tibet. The massive fort at Gyantse was the last major barrier on the road to Lhasa when the British invaded Tibet in 1903–1904, forcibly seeking to open it to trade, and to flush out any Russian agents lurking in Lhasa. We're dressed as British officers; in real life, five travellers recruited in Lhasa as extras in the Chinese film, *Red River Valley*, a fictionalised account of the British invasion.

Having heard about the film, I jumped at the chance to be on the inside of the film-making process, to see how the director would handle political correctness with such a hot potato as Tibet. Getting into the film is a matter of luck and timing: I happened to be sitting in the right café in Lhasa when the recruiters went about their talent quest. A rum bunch they rounded up: two Americans, a German, a Spaniard and myself. Actually, our main qualifications for the role are our big noses and round eyes. A wardrobe assistant shows me how to wrap leggings, and thrusts a .303 rifle in my hands.

There are two Hollywood actors on the set, Paul Kersey, a soap opera star, and Nick Love, from Los Angeles. Nick enlightens us on the storyline: 'All you have to know about the script is that everybody dies at the end. The heroines are blown up, the Tibetans are all blown away, a lot of Brits die – even I die a few pages before the end. After that, I can go home, thank God.'

Nick plays Colonel Rockman, and bears an uncanny resemblance – with scruffy goatee – to the real British commander, Colonel Younghusband. However, he has seen fit to affect a Scottish brogue (in keeping with the script), oblivious to the fact that Younghusband was definitely not a Scot. Off-camera, he reverts to his regular English accent. Kersey, who is supposed to play a British reporter, sometimes comes up with a London accent and other times lapses into a Los Angeles lilt.

To see history spring to life is magical for me, having researched this era. In the real invasion, Younghusband didn't die, he thrived. Fewer than forty British soldiers died in battle, compared with some 2,700 Tibetan soldiers. Everything in Tibet is medieval – and that includes weapons. Tibetan muskets and swords were no match for British weaponry: in one engagement, six hundred Tibetans, believing their amulets would protect them from bullets, were mowed down by Maxim machine guns. The amulet-makers later claimed that the amulets were only good against *copper* bullets, and obviously the British had used another metal. The British stayed two months in Lhasa, failed to find any Russian agents, negotiated a useless treaty with some head lamas, then withdrew, leaving behind a telegraph line and a couple of trade agents. The Chinese director's problem is how to rewrite history to suit the theme of heroic Tibetan resistance to the British barbarians, who also happen to be the military victors.

Camera, horses, action: pretty soon we're in the thick of things, among droves of neighing, farting horses with jingling bells mounted by nervous PLA-Brit riders. The energetic director, Feng Xiaoning, seems to be in a dozen places at once in his roles as scriptwriter, director, cinematographer and chief PLA consultant. He signals the start of a scene where the British Army files slowly past some Tibetans on pilgrimage. Paul Kersey is grovelling on the ground, trying to get into character. He plays Lieutenant Jones, a sensitive British war reporter who sympathises with the Tibetans and falls in love with a beautiful Tibetan woman (well, actually, a Chinese actress dressed in Tibetan robes). The interpreter wants to know if Paul has read up on this scene. 'Of course I've read the fucking script,' he tells her sharply. Our job is to march past the camera in close-ups; behind us – slightly out of focus – are scores of PLA-Brit soldiers.

The eerie thing is that if you ignore the film crew, the illusion of being with the British expeditionary force of 1903 is complete. Long lines of horses and riders saunter through desert terrain under cobalt-blue skies; in the background the imposing ruins of a Tibetan fort command a hillside. Adding battle atmosphere, an assistant runs amok with a sizzling censer that billows black smoke everywhere. This device makes the horses skittish, and one bolts through the ranks with a novice PLA rider dangling off the saddle. In my rush to get out of the way, I trip over my sword. The PLA commander bawls the PLA rider out; the Tibetan horse handler changes mounts. We do the scene again. And again. About ten times altogether, I think.

The PLA men are total klutzes, and very dangerous when handling rifles with blanks and fixed bayonets. During an infantry charge a PLA-Brit soldier stumbles and nicks Markus, the German extra, in the back with a bayonet. Only his leather bandolier saves him. Even more hazardous are blank bullets – life-threatening if fired too close. Comically, the PLA men have great trouble with timing. In one scene, the director shrieks *Cut!* when a soldier prematurely fires a blank. When a second recruit misfires, his PLA commander goes ballistic – he wades in there, grabs him by the ear and drags him howling off the set.

In the background is Nick, riding a black stallion, which has been specially imported; it towers over the Tibetan horses. Nick gets his kicks from shouting orders at the PLA-Brits like: *You silly blighter! Get out of the way*! or *Steady lads, hold your fire!* – none of which the recruits understand. Nick is the best-dressed actor: he carries a revolver, sports a set of field-glasses, and wipes his brow with a white handkerchief. He also flips the handkerchief forward when signalling the start of an all-out attack; it is his favourite theatrical prop.

Our least favourite prop is the sword. It is a very awkward attachment and can get stuck between your legs when running, which means you trip over the damn thing. If you run, you have to hold it, but then you can't operate a rifle, which requires both hands. Discreetly, we're all trying to offload our swords. Ridiculous, too, are the vintage backpacks supplied, made of some moth-eaten animal skins. They're useless for carrying anything and heat your back up, though they make good cushions for sitting on between takes.

The last scene of the day calls for charging into Nenying Gompa courtyard and firing away with blanks at unarmed monks. 'I can't shoot a lama,' protests Keith, the American extra. A pause here while fellow American Tom convinces Keith that he is actually only shooting shaven-headed PLA soldiers dressed up as monks. 'Oh, that's OK, I can do that!' says Keith. In the background, crowds of curious Tibetan villagers – and real Tibetan monks from Nenying Gompa – watch the filming in progress. A day in the life of a motion picture extra: we rush into the courtyard, fire away at monks, scale the steps of the monastery. Smoke billows over the courtyard (smoke appears to be the special signature of this director – we are never without smoke), dead bodies litter the place.

In early 1904, British troops partially destroyed Nenying Gompa, killing the armed monks who defended it. British reporters glossed over this, unaware of the temple's sacred significance, but Chinese chroniclers single out the desecration as evidence of British barbarism: one source claims the temple courtyard was 'a lake of blood'. Ironically, Nenying Gompa was rebuilt after the British departed only to be destroyed again by the Chinese during the Cultural Revolution (it was then rebuilt again). It has probably never occurred to the Chinese that they might be guilty of the same thing as the British, albeit on a much grander scale. The Chinese have occupied Tibet by force for over forty-five years. The death toll of Tibetans under occupation is estimated to exceed a million; scores of monasteries have been reduced to rubble.

Cut to: Nenying Gompa, upper floor. After the shooting scene we set about emptying the monastery of paintings, statuary and other treasures. We file past the camera in the background, loaded with booty. In the foreground, Jones argues with Rockman, debating the finer points of imperialism (Rockman sounding off in a thick Scottish accent):

Jones: But we're destroying their priceless cultural heritage.

Rockman: It is exactly because they are priceless that we must act as proper stewards. We have an imperial and scientific responsibility.

Oh yeah – great! We'll take all this stuff in the name of science! Lieutenant Jones, the pacifist, sees a kind of innocence, unchained freedom, and harmony between man and nature in Tibet. Colonel Rockman, the boorish imperial warmonger, sees a medieval world, and the British Empire bringing science and civilisation (and toilets!) to the heathens, for which they should be bloody grateful. Looting is a hotly disputed facet of the British invasion; it went on largely because British soldiers wanted souvenir trinkets from the campaign.

It is during the shooting of this scene that I solve the Mystery of the Dogs. When I visited this monastery ten years earlier on a bicycle trip through Tibet, the most vivid image that stayed with me was the scores of dogs lying around the courtyard; you had to tread warily in case they decided to wake up, gang up and shred your ankles. But I haven't seen a single dog this time, so I'm wondering if my memory is playing tricks on me and this is a different monastery. Until the looting scene. As we venture deeper into the monastery, we pass an alcove where there are … scores of dogs huddled together, all curled up. They most likely bolted at the first sound of gunfire. They will obviously be sitting this one out.

Back to the film: I'm trying to find out more about it, but I must be discreet. I can't openly interview the director, but I manage to ask the odd question. According to the director, *Red River Valley* is the first full-length film ever shot in Tibet, and the highest-budget film (at US$1.8 million) made by the prestigious Shanghai Film Studios. Filming takes place at half a dozen Tibetan locations – one on a glacier at over 18,000 feet – and several more in western China.

One small oversight: there are very few Tibetans in the film. The plum roles are played by Mandarin-speaking actors and actresses from Shanghai or Beijing (the film will later be dubbed in Tibetan). The 'Tibetan' hero is a Chinese actor who struts around the set shirtless, with a red headband, looking like Rambo. Everyone speaks Mandarin and the only Tibetan actor we've seen mumbles mantras. The two heroines are name-brand Chinese actresses decked out in Tibetan jewellery. One of them is the beautiful Ning Jing, a woman with a Sharon Stone gaze – and figure – who has starred in a number of top films. The director has custom-built this role for her, 'imported' her into the story. At the start of the script, in western China, beautiful young Xue Er is about to be sacrificed to the river gods by a band of peasants. Her brother saves her, and while fleeing villagers, she is rescued by a Tibetan nomad family, and thus takes on Tibetan dress. She, in turn, helps rescue the two British characters from an avalanche.

Tibetans have higher cheekbones and bigger noses than Han Chinese, yet all the monks are played by PLA troops, as are the Tibetan soldiers and British troops. Maybe real Tibetans with real weapons pose a real problem: they might get carried away when fighting PLA soldiers dressed as British troops. *Red River Valley* could well be called 'the Red Army film'; the PLA provides all the extras, the explosives and the special effects. Despite this, the film is a fascinating departure from the usual dreary Chinese propaganda spiels – it's a shoot-em-up action film, more in the style of Hollywood epics like *The Man Who Would Be King*.

But make no mistake: film-making in China that is funded by the state is a species of propaganda, whether blatant or refined. Timing is everything here; the handover of Hong Kong is coming up, the British will be booted out, and China's opium-induced humiliation at the hand of the British will be revenged. So, I calculate – yes, the timing of *Red River Valley* is right on the nose – ready for mid-1997, for the big handover, swelling the great wave of patriotism in true PLA entertainment style. In Hong Kong, members of the PLA Song and Dance Troupe will be rehearsing for the big day, performing bumps and grinds and high-kicks and acrobatics – all in uniform. I am convinced that watching PLA choreography is where Mel Brooks got his idea for the film, *The Producers*, with high-stepping Nazi dance numbers and songs like *Springtime for Hitler and Germany*.

On the set of *Red River Valley*, the PLA provides all the military extras and – double bonus – arranges all the blowing up that needs to be done. And I am on the inside of this Chinese film propaganda machine. I am undercover. I have never felt more like a spy in my life. This is great! Never, ever, invite a writer along as an extra on a film shoot; they come up with their own script on the proceedings. If Nick or Paul found out I was a writer, I'd be out on my ear. Or up against the wall for execution by PLA extras.

★★★★★

Day two on the set: several PLA men show up with wigs and moustaches that make them look like Wild Bill Hickok. They point at Jorge, who finds this all hysterically funny. Jorge is the Spanish backpacker with beard and shoulder-length hair. On arrival, he asked if he should cut his hair: the answer was negative. Instead, the director has decided to copy the hairstyle with a few of the PLA extras, though this is extremely dubious, historically. The only long-haired possibilities on the Younghusband expedition would have been members of the press. Jorge is putting in some sterling performances. He tries to hog the zone facing the camera; he is convinced that the film will be shown at Cannes.

Back to the day's shooting: we spend a lot of time charging through breaches in walls, shooting at anything that moves. Ever tried sprinting up a hill at 13,000 feet? You're out of breath in a flash. And it doesn't help to yell – at the top of your lungs –

167

Chaaarge! or *At them!* or *Aaaiieeyyy!* After each take, all you can do is collapse and catch your breath.

The interpreter primes us for the next scene: 'Wait for the third explosion, then run through the hole in the wall and start shooting.' On the other side are wild-looking PLA-Tibetan troops armed with swords, blunderbusses and rattan shields. We wait, we count, we charge. *Bastarrrrdos!* yells Jorge. Just as I race through the breach, a fourth explosion goes off. Then a fifth. Then a sixth. Dust is flying everywhere. This isn't acting anymore – it's sheer terror. All of a sudden, a wall of flame shoots up, engulfing Jorge. Scene over, we rush to see what happened. Jorge's fine, if a tad shell-shocked. The flame was faked: by staging surprises, the crafty director has elicited looks of real horror from his novice actors. But you couldn't have got Jorge to repeat that scene, not for all the tea in the PRC. Later that day a Chinese heroine is hurled sideways by a mis-cued bomb blast and showered with dirt. The wardrobe seamstress rushes in to dust her off and give her bruised back a massage. The seamstress! She probably sews you up if you get skewered by a bayonet too.

In the afternoon, more killing of unarmed monks (well, actually, they're armed with wooden planks this time). Mercifully, we do not have to participate: for hand-to-hand combat, the PLA-British clones do the job – rather efficiently, I might add.

It's been a long day, and we're exhausted. Back at the hotel in Gyantse, a look of horror from the woman at the reception desk – I've forgotten to remove my bloody make-up. A kind of battle is still on, anyway: after an unsuccessful attempt the previous night, we rally our forces to crash the hotel's evening buffet, which is a big step up from the film crew rice-slop that masquerades as food. We gleefully make off with our trophies: plates piled high with vegetables and meat. The British troops are hungry.

★★★★★

Day three: I feel like I've been in the British Army for a year now – too many bombs and bayonets. We've come to the stark conclusion that there are no stuntmen on the set. After almost getting our bollocks blown off the day before, we wise up and ask for a script preview.

This morning starts with page 75: a British officer is shot from behind a large Buddha statue (awfully bad karma). *A battle of Tibetan swords and spears against British bayonets. Outside the castle, a wall is blown open with a cannon and bodies shoot into the air. Followed by the rattling of machine guns.*

Sounds like a whole lot of stones, arrows, spears and bullets – it will be a miracle if we survive today's shooting. Actually, we don't. The director decides to kill us off by sundown. Keith is decapitated with a broadsword by the Chinese Rambo actor. An extra-special fate, only possible in Tibet, is in store for Tom. Confronted by a mad white yak, he fails to reload his rifle in time and is pinned to a wall by the beast's gigantic horns. His last words are: *No! No! Noooo! Arrgggh! Oh my Gaawwd!* as he is gored and re-gored. The air hisses out of his stomach and his head clicks sideways as blood runs out of his mouth. The film crew pack away the stuffed yak, and that wraps up our bizarre couple of days on the set. Director Feng Xiaoning wishes us well, and leaves us with this startling thought about *Red River Valley*: 'It's an anti-war film,' he deadpans. 'Shows the futility of war.'

★★★★★

Back in Lhasa, in a Xinhua Bookshop, I come across a Chinese war comic that shows the Tibetan struggle against the British marauders to defend the 'Chinese Motherland'. Obviously a popular theme in Chinese-produced books – patriotism versus pith helmets. It's all there, dead monks, evil Brits, handy Chinese advisers and a caricature of Younghusband. Just like us, but add the PLA platoons. Historically, however, there were no Chinese advisers or military officers helping the Tibetans as *Red River Valley* claims.

★★★★★

Fast forward to mid-1997: *Red River Valley* is released across China, causing 'a patriotic sensation' according to Xinhua news service in Beijing. More than this, it is the patriotic duty of government employees to see the film. In numerous cities, including Lhasa, workers are handed free tickets (compulsory viewing). Blame it on the British: the film is released in time for the British handover of Hong Kong to the Chinese, along with another epic film, *The Opium Wars*, making a double round of Brit-bashing.

Although *Red River Valley* flops in Hong Kong itself, the Chinese think highly enough of the film to nominate it for the Gold Wine Cup Award at the Shanghai Film Festival. Paul Kersey and Nick Love return to China for a ten-day publicity tour as the film premieres. Paul apparently has conducted an off-screen romance with his on-screen lover: he marries the female lead of the film, Ning Jing. Their son is born in Los Angeles a few months after the film's launch.

I finally get my paws on a video copy of *Red River Valley*. Here the full script is revealed: a number of other Western extras appear as British soldiers in a different location. The dialogue is all in Mandarin, but when the British speak, they do so directly in English, with Mandarin subtitles. This results in classic one-liners such as: 'Perhaps it is a blood-red sun that never sets on the British Empire.' Also revealed is why Rockman adopts a thick Scottish accent. Feng Xiaoning is a crafty director indeed. In one scene, an English-speaking Chinese military commander confronts Rockman with the fact that Scotland is part of England, yet Scotland wants to separate, and argues that, in similar fashion, Tibet is an inseparable part of China.

7

IN THE LOST KINGDOM OF GUGE

A wild ride to western Tibet

You have to get your timing right if you travel to western Tibet. The window for possible travel is small. It's snowed in for much of the year: snowbound passes lock the 'doors'. Late June and the month of July are good times to visit. August is terrible as monsoon rains can wash away roads and bridges leading in. September, the month of our intended journey, is possible, but unpredictable. So as preparations are getting finalised – food and drink and transport coming together – there's one very important thing to do: consult the Weather Oracle. If the rains are still really coming down, the road will be cut in several places.

The Weather Oracle was out at the Holiday Inn in Lhasa, in a tiny bar. My oracle was CNN; the telly was hooked up to a satellite dish. After the news was a world weather report, which, if you paid careful attention, showed rain formations all over South Asia, including the Tibetan plateau. The woman who gave the weather reports never actually spoke about Tibet (how many viewers would be following the weather report for Tibet?) but the information on the map behind her was enough for me. Except that she often got in the way of that part of the map to point out something else in China.

The news was over. The weather was up next. I craned forward, scanning the map. The weather announcer moved in front of the Tibetan plateau. Damn her! Then she moved left, and I got a clear view of the raincloud symbols. To my great relief, the situation looked OK. The rains were moving on into India.

All you needed to justify watching CNN for an hour at the Holiday Inn was to buy a Coke and some peanuts, and treat the Tibetan staff well. Looking at the bar menu, I noticed something peculiar. The menu said *Tintin Bar*. But outside, in the hallway, it said *Chang Bar*. Hmmm. Curious. As it happens, the murals in this tiny bar are taken from *Tintin in Tibet*. This is one of Belgian creator Hergé's bestsellers, translated into dozens of languages, including Tibetan. The comic-book was on sale in the lobby of the Holiday Inn, along with *Tintin in Tibet* T-shirts.

Tintin is tolerated in Tibet because he is harmless; the comic was drawn in the late 1950s, before the Lhasa Uprising, and there's not a single Chinese soldier in the story. Furthermore, the sympathetic Chinese character of Chang is the main focus of the story. Tintin goes to Tibet on the noble mission of rescuing his friend Chang, who disappeared after a plane crash (it turns out Chang was taken from the plane wreckage by a yeti). Looking more closely at the murals, I discovered I could not find Tintin at all. Tintin had been *purged!* Mrs Hergé, wife of the comic-strip creator and an avid traveller, had dropped by, discovered the bar, and demanded Tintin's image be removed as the Hergé Foundation did not like associations with smoking or alcohol. So the name was changed to Chang Bar (*chang* with a double-meaning could mean Tibetan barley beer), and Tintin was replaced in the mural with the figure of Chang, the Chinese character. Tintin, in any case, is a reporter – and reporters are not welcome in Tibet.

Especially not reporters from the BBC. The naughty BBC news has been 'purged' in China. In 1994, Rupert Murdoch, chairman of News Corporation (which owns Hong Kong-based StarTV), removed the BBC news from his satellite services to China to calm tense relations with Chinese officials who complained about a profile of Mao Zedong and objected to coverage of Chinese dissidents. Murdoch's reason for doing this was clearly money; he has extensive holdings in China and ambitious plans to expand them. In 1997 the BBC again incurred the wrath of the Middle Kingdom: the Chinese went ballistic over the airing of a programme on the disappearance of the eleventh Panchen Lama.

★★★★★

Fast forward to a year after my visit: in 1997, the Holiday Inn itself was 'purged' and its name reverted to Lhasa Hotel. The Holiday Inn management group announced it would not renew its contract for running the Lhasa branch, the only luxury hotel in Tibet. It would turn the management of the joint venture over to the Chinese government. No reason was given, and the international hotel chain continues to run its numerous other branches around China. Victory was claimed by various campaign groups in the West, particularly the Free Tibet Campaign in England, which had launched a boycott of Holiday Inn operations and those of its British parent company, Bass. The objection of the protesters was that the Holiday Inn's Chinese management was in cahoots with Chinese security forces. Several guests had been arrested for attempting to send out faxes that were deemed critical of China or a breach of security. A brand name like the Holiday Inn brought a certain amount of prestige, a veneer of respectability, and a seal of approval for Chinese operations in Tibet. There were even Miss Tibet contests, conducted in 1992 to attract tourism during the slack winter months.

★★★★★

In Thailand, I once went to Ripley's Motion Master Theatre, an innovative theatre that utilises, apart from big-screen cinemascope, the added sense of motion. Your seat is rigged up with hi-tech hydraulic gear; you're strapped in with a full lap-and-shoulder seatbelt. You watch a *RoboCop* motorcycle chase or a high-speed spaceship pursuit; synchronised with the action, you are hurled to the left, right, upwards, downwards, sideways – hydraulically, of course – as you hang on for dear life with hand grips. The show lasted just seven minutes as the expensive technology couldn't be sustained any longer.

The Landcruiser to western Tibet was just like that except there were no handgrips, no seatbelts and the show went on for five days. Five days of being banged around from tea kettle to breakfast time to get to a town called Zanda. Our target was the site of the

ancient kingdom of Guge (pronounced *Goo-gay*), whose ruins
are scattered in valleys around Zanda. It required a stack of permits
– town permits, military permits, cultural relics bureau permits –
you name it. We had enough paperwork to open an origami salon.
But eventually we edged closer to our target.

Perhaps 'edged' is not the word I'm looking for here. There was
virtually no suspension in our Landcruiser – the shocks were
shot. If you were in the back seat and the driver hit a rut, you
would fly up and bang your head on the roof, then be thumped
down hard on your arse and get the stuffing knocked out of you.
There were hardly any springs left in the seats either, and you'd
get showered in dust. At times it got so bad you had to wear a silk
scarf over your face to filter the dust out of your breathing
apparatus. And you might – as I did – take to wearing a wool hat
to soften the blow of the interior roof.

Actually, it was more comfortable in the front cabin of the truck.
We'd hired two vehicles, a Landcruiser and a Dongfeng truck.
The latter acted as a tow truck should the Landcruiser ride too
deep on a stream crossing, which at one point ours did. Coming
round a bend in the truck, I got to witness the spectacle of four
bedraggled foreigners struggling to get out of a river away from
their Landcruiser, which had water swirling over the tyres. The
driver, Speedy, had seriously misjudged the depth of a stream
crossing. Fortunately, the Landcruiser started up first time after
being hauled out (I've heard of other Landcruisers that never
started again).

Our team of backpackers clubbed together in Lhasa to split
expenses on this epic 4WD tour of far western Tibet, a round trip
of some 2,000 miles, taking twenty-five days to complete. Our
main targets were the ruins of the Guge Kingdom and the hike
around sacred Mount Kailash.

It was a motley crew of riders: ages varied considerably. Pema
was only twenty-one. She was given her Tibetan name by her
Swiss father, who used to work in Nepal and who had encouraged
her to come back and see the Himalayas. At the other end of the
spectrum was Diane from Belgium, in her forties – a latecomer to
trekking. Her role model was Alexandra David-Néel – the famed

French explorer who travelled extensively in her fifties, carrying a revolver to protect herself. Like her mentor, Diane was obstinate, moody and cantankerous by turns – and bossy. Others in the group were Verena, from Austria; Kozo, a young Japanese man; and Barbara, a Filipina photographer based in Hong Kong.

The Tibetan crew consisted of Doko, the young guide; 'Speedy', the Landcruiser driver; and Tenzin, the Khampa truck driver who seemed to have a woman in every major town along the route. Speedy was inseparable from his Chicago Bulls cap; the NBA is big in Amdo, where he was from. Speedy was so nicknamed because of his terrifying shortcuts – he liked driving straight down sand-dunes, instead of using the switchbacks provided. Moody Doko would cheer him on, while the rest of us gritted our teeth. It was much more relaxing in the cabin of the truck, if only because Tenzin loved to sing and had a great voice, and an endless repertoire of nomad folk songs, which he was keen to expand on; this Tibetan bard hounded us to sing in English or in French.

The hardship of the trip was counterbalanced by the stunning scenery en route. We planned to take the north route to Ali, and from there dip south to Guge and Kailash, and return to Lhasa on the south route. The initial route took us on a great loop through Chang Thang, the vast desert and grassland region of northern Tibet. We passed nights in no-name inns at horrible, polluted truck-stop towns along the way, but otherwise it was pristine terrain, and we spotted Tibet's rare wildlife – wild asses, black-necked cranes, the odd antelope. We'd see groups of four or five *kiang* (wild asses) – not the great herds that used to roam these high grasslands. The once-abundant wildlife has been machine-gunned into oblivion by Chinese settlers and the military, both for food and for sport.

Speaking of food: the back of the truck was stacked with barrels of fuel. Fuel depots are few and far between out this way, and more designed for the Chinese military. Besides, any fuel out west is way more expensive than it is in Lhasa. Over and around the barrels were burlap bags and cardboard boxes packed with food – potatoes, carrots, bottled water, 761 army ration biscuits, and other essentials that we'd salvaged at Lhasa's main market. Trouble was, the two elements – food and fuel – got mixed together a few days' ride out of Lhasa. A barrel sprang a leak somewhere, but the driver couldn't determine which it was, and didn't care to empty the entire cargo to find out, so we had potatoes that reeked of petrol. This was quite dangerous because the method of cooking was a miniature flamethrower – the same device used to heat up the engine when frozen (the Tibetan version of antifreeze). You'd aim this gadget side-on at an elevated pot, and a great flame would shoot out and nuke the food.

The tough-as-nails Tibetan crew turned their nose up at our fuel-scented food. They had their own hessian bags filled with dried carcass of goat or rock-hard yak cheese – things like that. At picnic stops, they'd exhume the carcass of the day and resume work on it, carving off great hunks of dried meat with their knives. A bit like beef jerky in texture. That's all I want to say about the food. It makes my stomach churn if I write any more.

★★★★★

At the PSB office in Ali, Doko got bored with the permit procedures, which were taking forever. I was scribbling some notes, and he looked over my shoulder.

'So how's the book?' he asked.

I could've strangled him right then and there, but fortunately the PSB woman didn't tune into the conversation. She was too preoccupied with the problem of Belgium. Belgium was one of the nations listed for our permit. But what exactly was Belgium? She's never heard of Belgium. We sorted this one out by indicating Belgium was sandwiched between England and France.

'How many books have you written?' piped up Doko again.

'Listen Doko, I don't write any fucking books, OK?' I shot back.

'OK!' he laughed. It was a knowing laugh because he had recognised my face in the author credit page of the Lonely Planet guide to China.

We had no desire to stay in Ali, but permits had to be checked, validated, re-checked and stamped again. Ali is an architect's nightmare – concrete blockhouses, kiosks, rubbish strewn all over. And at night, tuneless wailing from karaoke bars. This is Karaokeville, full of Chinese army officers and girls in private karaoke booths, in the middle of the desert, in the middle of nowhere, in western Tibet.

★★★★★

So you're driving along one day, and suddenly you forget where you are, or where you are going, or what you're doing, or why. Ever experienced that feeling? It happened to me in the cabin of the truck; I'd been dozing off, in some distant dreamworld, and woke up when the engine started wheezing and spluttering. I wearily opened my eyes – and my jaw dropped. There was snow everywhere. There were great peaks all around, with yaks cavorting in the background. I thought I must be hallucinating from the altitude; my eyes grew wider as we crested a pass that registered 17,400 feet on my altimeter. 'How high?' asked my fellow trucker. 'Um, fairly high,' I hedged, gasping from the thin air. We were driving over an entire frigging mountain range! And if my sources were correct (putting Zanda at 12,000 feet), that meant an astonishing drop of 5,400 feet on the other side of the pass.

It was indeed a long drop down. At dusk we levelled out, hitting a canyon and following a riverbed. This turned out to be a phantasmagoric canyon: a sorcerer's creation of mud and clay, sculpted into surreal shapes. And it went on and on … for over an hour. It was thoroughly entrancing. 'It is very shapeful,' said Doko. 'The rocks have shapes like *chortens* or castles.' He pointed out a huge rock resembling a seated Buddha, and another that looked like an old man with a wispy beard. The imagination could run riot here. Phantoms appeared everywhere – warriors, kings, queens, monks. They all seemed to jump out of the clay, silent sentinels guarding the approach route.

In one day I'd absorbed enough new landscape to last the brain several months to process. Finally, in the distance, rays of light lit up Zanda on an outcrop. Set in barren desert terrain, Zanda is unmistakable; it is an oasis with poplar trees. The Sutlej River lay in our path, and it required another six miles of detouring to gain a bridge across the river. At one corner, Speedy almost lost it on a piece of loose gravel. He could have sent us plunging into an abyss but at the last minute the Landcruiser corrected itself, and we all breathed easier. Speedy, of course, would not acknowledge that he'd almost killed us all. He laughed it all off. But you could tell it was a nervous laugh.

That said, the trip to Guge was a hell of a lot easier than it used to be. The earliest Western accounts of this hidden valley, the Guge Kingdom, were by Jesuits, who'd heard rumours of a lost Christian-like sect. In March 1624, two Portuguese Jesuits, Father Marques and Father Andrade, set out from India disguised as Hindu pilgrims. They were on foot with pack animals, crossing passes that were probably 18,000 feet or more. At times, they sank into snow up to their chests. They complained of frozen feet, of blindness and of suffocating 'poisonous vapours', probably the first Western accounts of altitude sickness by the first Europeans known to have entered Tibet. Their round trip from India took over eight months.

Arriving in Tsaparang, the centre of the Guge Kingdom, the Jesuits were surprised to be warmly received. They puzzled over how people in such a barren wasteland could survive – all the food had to be imported from fertile valleys that were two weeks away on foot. But part of the jigsaw fell into place when they witnessed a caravan of two hundred Chinese traders passing through, carrying silk and porcelain. Tsaparang was an important trading centre, and flocks of goats and sheep kept the royal court supplied with basics.

Father Andrade wrote of being invited by the king to Toling Gompa, to celebrate a special occasion. There were over 2,000 monks in attendance. The Jesuits found that the temple rituals bore superficial similarities to Christian ones – monks in robes spent hours chanting – but drinking from human skull-cap vessels and playing trumpets fashioned from human thighbones were definitely a little different. Andrade was the first to publish to the world the sacred chanting mantra *Om Mani Padme Hum*, but could not determine its meaning (which experts still debate today).

Andrade returned to Tsaparang in 1625 with fellow missionaries, and the Jesuits eventually built a small church there. Andrade died in India in 1634, poisoned by a colleague who evidently didn't share his enthusiasm for the Inquisition.

But back to the religion of Guge. It was actually quite special. In the ninth century Buddhism was snuffed out in central Tibet by King Langdarma, a staunch supporter of the rival Bon faith. Upon the assassination of Langdarma, Tibet was broken up into lay and monastic pockets of influence. The Guge Kingdom became an enclave that was vital for the survival of Buddhism. The king of Guge promoted cultural exchanges with Indian Buddhists, and Guge became an important centre of Buddhist studies, a reputation that grew with the arrival of the famous eleventh-century scholar Atisha, from India.

The Guge Kingdom probably lasted over five hundred years. In several sources it has been described as a cultural Mecca, a citadel greater than Lhasa at the time. But around 1650 (some sources give 1630), Tsaparang was suddenly abandoned. It is said that the king angered his lamas by favouring Father Andrade and that factional fighting ensued, tearing the kingdom apart.

Other sources claim that a two-year siege by Ladakhis led to the fall of Guge. The reason: the king rejected a bride who happened to be the sister of the king of Ladakh, who was supremely insulted. Although well entrenched in his citadel, the king of Guge decided to cut a deal and surrender, according to one source, but this backfired because the treacherous Ladakhis had no intention of honouring the deal. The king and royal family were carried off into exile, and his followers reduced to slavery (another source claims the king and his courtiers were killed on the spot). Guge fell into obscurity – and ruins. Not only that: successive waves of invaders went to great lengths to wipe out all traces of the kings of Guge, making it near-impossible to recount the history of the place.

As I trace a mandalic mural in the Red Temple at Tsaparang with my flashlight, I am convinced of one thing: this must have been a brilliant culture. We'd arrived by Landcruiser on the short commute from Zanda, only sixteen miles distant, but it seemed to be light years away. To enter the temples at Tsaparang is to venture into a different world, to be in the presence of master artisans. The murals resonate their power and that of their patrons: they are mute testimony to the brilliance of the Guge Kingdom. They speak of a culture that is at once alien yet highly imaginative, with bold design and vibrant use of colour.

Eerily illuminated by flashlight are huge, beautiful Tara frescos, white and green wrathful manifestations, and other icons from the Tibetan Buddhist pantheon. There are fantastic creatures, half-beast, half-human. And then the flashlight picks up some detail that turns out to be a stunning miniature, an entire work of art in itself. The murals are breathtaking and offer some clues about dress and customs in the long-lost kingdom of Guge, because not everything portrayed is mythical. They really bring Guge to life. One depicts courtiers welcoming an important envoy, arriving by donkey. Another fresco shows a high lama giving teachings. Moving along to the Yamantaka Chapel, once dedicated to tantric deity Dorje Jigje, the walls bear a quite different kind of ancient mural: sumptuous paintings of Tibetan tantric deities tangled in *yabyum* embraces with their consorts. *Yabyum* is the tantric sexual pose of deity and consort, symbolising fusion of opposites.

The murals date from the sixteenth and seventeenth centuries, before the fall of Guge. We will probably never know the identity of the artists; in the tradition of Tibetan Buddhism, this kind of art springs from an anonymous well. We do know that the king of Guge was wealthy enough to be able to import artisans from regions like Kashmir. But while the style may be Kashmiri, it is also distinctly Tibetan. Visiting in 1933, Italian scholar Guiseppe Tucci noted 'an art peculiar to Guge, distinctive in itself and independent of the art movements in other parts of Tibet'.

Tucci was among the handful of privileged Westerners to see the site in its pre-Chinese days. He left a detailed description of the artwork in its more intact state, particularly the statuary. Guge seems to have escaped plundering by Western treasure-seekers and museum collectors, but not the Chinese. In the mid-1960s Red Guards ran amok and trashed the temples of Guge, smashing precious statuary, but miraculously the murals were left largely unscathed. The temples suffered some water damage, but since this is a desert area things are kept freeze-dried naturally. It's an odd juxtaposition of clay ruins, destroyed statuary and intact murals on the temple walls.

Having nearly destroyed the place, the Chinese now see fit to be overly protective of it. The Chinese appear to have a monopoly on Guge Kingdom photography. In addition to the reams of paperwork we have already acquired, we discover that if you want to photograph interiors at Guge, you need a special permit from Beijing. A little inconvenient at this point to arrange that, and it is most likely exorbitant and time-consuming to procure, so we employ a shortcut. Doko and Tenzin will keep the Tibetan caretaker busy with a flask of *chang*, while Speedy brings along all the keys to the chapels. There is nobody else around except us – nobody will notice the odd photo-taking episode. A second photography problem: there is hardly any light to work with. The chapels are dim, and even when electric light switches are found, the murals are dark. Fortunately for me, Barbara has a whole bag full of photo gear, and I borrow a flash unit, hoping it will communicate with my camera and synchronise to take the right exposures.

We are still at the lower extremities of Tsaparang: the site is a great peak made of clay. Winding upwards from the lower temples, we walk past a series of 'cave-condos' fashioned from clay, and small fort-like structures with watchtowers poking up. To withstand siege, Tsaparang Citadel has an ingenious system of tunnelling to internal springs deep in the mountain. Other tunnels had served as escape routes. We could not see these, but to reach the top of Tsaparang Citadel, you must scramble through a long spiralling tunnel that is bored out of clay, with steps cut out. This tunnel could be completely sealed in times of siege.

At the uppermost reaches, crowning this mountain of clay, is Tsaparang Dzong, with various structures thought to serve as palaces for the king, queen and high officials. The finest artwork at Tsaparang is to be found in a tiny building here, thought to be the *gonkhang*, the site of special initiation rites. Centrepiece of the *gonkhang* is a large 3-D mandala that now lies in ruins, smashed to pieces by Red Guards. However, exquisite miniature murals still grace the walls: depicted are rows of voluptuous dancing *dakinis*, who personify the wisdom of enlightenment. Apart from their elaborate jewellery, they are naked, representing the uninhibited dance of awareness. In Tibetan lore, *dakinis* live in hidden heavenly paradises and, like personal guardian angels, appear mysteriously to practitioners when they face great trouble to provide motivation when the chips are down. Below the *dakinis* are gory scenes of disembodiment from hell realms. The chapel is dedicated to protector deity Demchok, shown in murals with his consort Dorje Phagmo. Together they symbolise the union of bliss and emptiness.

The view from the top of the citadel is phenomenal; on this crystal-clear day, dramatic desert landscapes stretch to the far horizon. 'Desolate' and 'barren' are two adjectives that spring to mind, but somehow seem sadly inadequate to convey the immensity of space and the stillness that envelops it. Standing there, some lines from the poet Percy Bysshe Shelley popped into my head, lines I'd learned by heart long ago, about an Egyptian king:

My name is Ozymandias, king of kings:
Look upon my works, ye mighty, and despair!
Nothing beside remains. Round the decay
Of that colossal wreck, boundless and bare,
The lone and level sands stretch far away.

★★★★★

Back in our base in Zanda, there were more glorious murals to be viewed at Toling Gompa – but at a price. The monk-caretaker who held the keys to the different chapels was a highly skilled extortionist. Every step of the way, every new door, required more cash donations and it got to the point where some among us just said no (or used stronger language). But I persisted, because at this point the money wasn't going to stymie my thirst for such original artwork.

Scattered through the valleys around Zanda are numerous meditation caves, some lined with murals. More are waiting to be discovered. Incredibly, I found that the concept of a citadel topping a mountain of clay was not limited to Tsaparang. Just outside Zanda is a similarly sited citadel, with access through a huge tunnel carved into the side of the clay mountain. This is the weirdest hiking I've ever done. Once through the tunnel, you reach an upper plateau with scores of former cave-dwellings and dangerous crevasses of clay, and majestic views of the valley where Zanda lies.

From this aerial perch, Zanda seems like a fantastic, mythical place. It has that touch of Shangri-La – a remote valley, an oasis of poplar trees, an ancient ruined temple and snowy peaks in the distance. But my idea of Shangri-La is not a Chinese army base and Chinese restaurants, which, essentially, is what Zanda is. Although there is a Tibetan quarter near the monastery, Zanda is not a Tibetan town any more, it's a Chinese garrison town: little more than a main drag lined with concrete blockhouses. Most large towns in Tibet have an obvious military presence, but it is more pronounced here because of an ongoing territorial dispute between India and China. Zanda lies close to the border with Ladakh.

In our final hours in Zanda, before our Landcruiser headed south, I went about some mundane chores. One of these was to visit the tiny post office. I bought some postcards of the Guge ruins in Lhasa and wanted to post them from Zanda (where no postcards were on sale, naturally). I always do this from really remote places, just to see if the post actually works.

Feiji! I said to the woman at the post office hopefully, slapping my right hand off the palm of my left, imitating a plane taking off. At this, she let out a high-pitched cackle. *Airmail!* Airmail from Zanda! She rushed to tell her co-workers. Pretty soon there were guffaws coming from all directions. *Airmail!*

8

JOURNEY TO THE CENTRE OF THE UNIVERSE

Powering up at Kailash

Not much has been said about group dynamics on this excursion. In fact, not much has been said about the passengers on the trip at all. But you can be certain that by the time we reach Darchen we have spent considerable time at close quarters and tempers have frayed somewhat. Darchen is a godawful place with a few huts, tents and concrete hutches. This encampment serves as the base for the Mount Kailash trek: pilgrims pick up supplies here.

We have split into two parties, along lines of compatibility. I call one group 'the strong-headed European women' – Diane, Verena and Pema; and the other, 'the black sheep' – myself, Kozo and Barbara. Which suits me fine, because I don't want to do the circuit in a pack of six people. This way, we will get a break from each other for a few days.

★★★★★

Call me superstitious, but before I set off around Tibet's holiest mountain, I do some shopping. I stock up on essential supplies, just like the other pilgrims. I stop at a tent in Darchen to purchase prayer flags (to drape at the passes), small squares of paper embossed with windhorses (to fling around at the passes), and, for good measure, a set of prayer beads to sling around my neck (to assist when mumbling mantras to get over the passes). There are, after all, no helicopters to come and pluck you off the mountainside if you collapse at Kailash. So you need all the insurance – and assurance – you can lay your hands on. The windhorse, featured on both the paper squares and the prayer flags, is the beautiful steed that brings good fortune, symbolised by the jewel on its back. Wind sets the horse in motion, carrying good fortune in all directions.

My impromptu guide in all this is a middle-aged Tibetan nun who's been educated in India and speaks quite good English. She thinks the whole thing is pretty funny – a Westerner decked out in prayer beads.

'Are you a Buddhist?' she giggles.

'Sometimes,' I tell her with a grin. The brand is probably better termed White Buddhism or McBuddhism – an amateur Western attempt to come to grips with the faith. Someone like me can only hope to scratch the surface. Meanwhile, you can conveniently believe anything you want, a sophisticated form of agnosticism, if you like. Convenient for keeping door-banging evangelists at bay, anyhow.

*****

Kailash is the centre of the universe. Well, the Tibetan Buddhist universe. On the mandalic 'map', at the cosmic axis of the Tibetan universe lies Mount Meru, the abode of the gods. Mount Kailash is thought to be the earthly embodiment of the mythical Meru. On its summit is the celestial city of Sudarsana, with a palace at its centre being home to the leader of the thirty-three chief gods who govern this realm. Above Meru float twenty-five more heavens of the gods, while under the mountain lie the hell-realms – the searing-hot hells, the freezing hells, the forest of razors.

If that sounds very Dantesque in conception, it's because the source of inspiration – as with most things in Tibet – is spiritual. The Tibetan cosmos is highly eccentric. Mount Meru is surrounded by seven rings of golden mountains and seven oceans. At the outer edge of a flat circular disk, across the outer ocean from Meru, are a few spin-off worlds, like the one we're on. This is identified as the continent of Jambudvipa, trapezoidal in shape, where inhabitants live for a century, and where the dharma flourishes. East of Meru lies the continent of Videha, which is white and half-moon shaped, with inhabitants whose faces resemble half moons – they are said to be twice as tall as humans and live up to five hundred years. Videha's mountains are made

185

of diamonds, sapphires, pearls and crystal. North of Meru is Uttarakuru, a square continent where giants with squarish horse-shaped faces live for a thousand years without worry or effort. West of Meru is Godaniya, ruby red and circular in shape. Godaniyans are thought to have round faces, are four times taller than humans, and live five times longer. Beyond all this are the paths of planets and the massive rings of fire that enclose the mandalic model.

Tibetan Buddhists have had to seriously reconsider their traditional cosmology model in the light of modern discoveries. Some Tibetans cling to the literal truth; others claim that Meru is symbolic. There is obviously no huge mountain at the navel of the world, there is no city on the top of that mountain, and there is no continent of lanky giants with half-moon faces to the east either. Kailash, at around 22,000 feet, is modest by Himalayan standards.

But Kailash has foxed Western geographers too. In the late nineteenth and early twentieth century, the mountain assumed mythical dimensions among Western geographers and explorers. For the longest time there was reputed to be a peak in western Tibet that was the source of the great rivers of India. But Tibet was inaccessible, so geographers were unsure if this was myth or fact. Finding the source of India's great rivers was a prime geographer's puzzle, on a par with finding the source of the Nile. The British employed Indian pundits with codenames. Disguised as pilgrims, they measured distances with prayer beads, and tossed marked logs into rivers to find out where they would pop up further down the line in India.

Eventually it was discovered that the headwaters of four of Asia's mightiest rivers lay within sixty miles of Kailash: the Indus, the Yarlung Tsangpo, the Karnali and the Sutlej. Remarkably, the mouths of the same rivers end up as far as 1,800 miles apart. The Tibetans know the rivers by more prosaic names, identified with the four cardinal directions and four legendary animals. The Indus is Sengghe Khambab (River issuing from the Lion's Mouth, to the north); the Yarlung Tsangpo is Tamchok Khambab (from the Horse's Mouth, to the east); the Karnali – Mabchu Khambab (from the Peacock's Mouth, to the south); and the Sutlej is Langchan Khambab (River issuing from the Elephant's Mouth, situated in the west). So in some ways, Kailash is the centre of things.

In their lifetime, Tibetans aspire to make a *kora*, a full walking circuit, of Kailash as a way of accruing merit. Many Buddhists believe that they may have inherited some bad karma from previous lives, a situation that must be corrected by doing good deeds in the present life, or by performing other meritorious tasks. On a sliding karmic scale, the greater the suffering involved at Kailash, the greater the merit earned. It's a bit like clocking up airmiles with shopping purchases. Get enough miles in and you get on a plane – or, as the Tibetans might see it, an altered plane. To speed things up, some attempt not one circuit of Kailash, but thirteen, or even one hundred and eight circuits (spread over a period of several years). Others cheat a bit, by hiring hikers to do the circuit for them.

And then, incredibly, there are die-hards who perform body-length prostrations right the way round the mountain, a distance of thirty-two miles. They throw themselves forward on the ground, pick themselves up, and resume this inchworming motion through mud, snow, rain, hail, or whatever else gets in the way. A *kora* like this can take fifteen to twenty-five days to complete: the only ones strong enough to survive the rigours are very fit young men.

The peak is sacred not only to Tibetan Buddhists, but to Bon adherents, who hold Kailash is the centre of the ancient Shangshung Kingdom. There is an ancient tale about Bon and Tibetan Buddhist sorcerers fighting over who should occupy the peak of Kailash: the Buddhists prevailed, but the Bon deity shifted to a nearby peak. Tibetan Buddhists believe the deity Demchok occupies the top of Kailash and his consort, Dorje Phagmo, lives on a sister peak. Kailash is also sacred to the Jains and Hindus of India; the Hindus claim the mountain is the celestial home of Shiva and his consort Parvati.

The Indian pilgrims come as part of a lottery system run from Delhi since the 1980s. Each year, up to 10,000 Hindus from all parts of India apply. Some seven hundred finalists are chosen; after fitness tests, this number is whittled down to around four hundred. Hindu pilgrims are allowed ten days in Tibet. The lucky lottery winners mass at the Indian-Tibetan border, and then, travelling in groups of thirty-five or so, they pour across Lipu Lek Pass, where they are met by a Chinese entourage, and the sacred circuit of their dreams gets under way.

There used to be fourteen monasteries around Kailash to assist pilgrims in their contemplative tasks. Most were destroyed by the Chinese during the Cultural Revolution, but a few have been resurrected. There are basic guesthouses attached to these – it is here we plan to pass the nights.

Trekking around Kailash is hard work. The terrain is high altitude, cold, rugged, and sometimes hallucinatory. Turn the first corner west of Darchen and you come across a prayer flag cairn with some unusual decorations – old socks, Chinese longjohns, sheepskin jackets, tattered shirts, sweaters, head of a yak, horns of a goat, hats, pairs of old trainers. The pilgrim offering here is discarded clothing, left as proof they've been on the holy circuit. The clothing is full of holes or shredded, though whether this was caused by the elements or not, it's hard to tell.

It looks like rubbish to my eye. Here's a conundrum: the clothing is discarded as part of a spiritual journey to visit pristine peaks and lakes. Tibetans may have little concept of rubbish disposal, sewage systems or personal hygiene, but they were light years ahead of the West when it came to preserving the environment. Long before the concept of national parks was developed in the West, Tibetan Buddhists held certain lakes, peaks and high passes to be sacred. These were left totally untouched, and mining was rare. With its harsh environment, Tibet has a delicate ecological balance, one which the Chinese are interfering with. All of the Chinese-built truck-stop towns we have stopped in thus far in western Tibet have glass from broken bottles scattered around and big mounds of rubbish lying in the open air.

The Buddhist compassion for all life – human, animal or insect – protected Tibet's wildlife and, in a sense, made Tibet one great wildlife preserve. Because Tibet was so isolated, it sheltered rare species; even in the 1990s, species long thought extinct were discovered, including a breed of forest pony, found in Kham. If animals were culled, the Tibetans took only what they needed, so the impact on wildlife was minimal. After the coming of the Chinese, Tibet's once-plentiful wildlife now faces extinction: in the last forty years large mammals have gone the way of the bison in North America. Apart from supplying China with meat, there is a demand for rare animals in Chinese restaurants and traditional medicine. This has decimated the numbers of the snow leopard, for instance.

★★★★★

A little further along the Kailash circuit lies a pilgrim camp. Trucks arriving from central Tibet unload here. Dangling off the sides of the open-backed trucks are scores of woven yak-hair bags, the filing system of the humble nomad, used for holding food and clothing. The first major pilgrim stop is Choku Gompa, a small monastery clinging to a cliff face. Wild-looking pilgrims crowd the inner sanctum of this *gompa*, which is illuminated by hundreds of yak-butter lamps, to touch a revered silver-coated conch shell, said to have belonged to the great sage Milarepa. The second treasure is a statue of the Buddha Opame, highly unusual because it is made of some sort of white stone, like marble.

The pilgrims are so entranced that they fail to even notice a foreigner or two in their midst. In this dim light I can blend right in, rub shoulders. Because Kailash draws pilgrims from all over Tibet – and beyond – there are nomad groups whose flamboyant dress I have trouble identifying. I notice some pilgrims are not only shiny-eyed, they have green faces. I figure I must be hallucinating from the altitude, but no – the women's faces *are* green. I later discover that this green 'make-up' is made from concentrated buttermilk or roots. It functions as a cross between a cosmetic and a sunblock, and is applied to ward off the high-altitude sun and counter skin dryness.

Back on the circuit, yaks with booming bells pass us. This yak caravan is ferrying camping gear ahead for a group tour. Then the yaks disappear in a sudden snowfall, and we find a rock shelter. Looking out, I see a ghostly figure performing full-body prostrations through the biting snow. Suddenly I don't feel so cold. We carry on towards Drira Phuk Gompa, where a monastery guesthouse awaits.

Early European visitors to Kailash had to brave more than the elements – there was the added danger of bandits, who set upon hapless pilgrims. And since the Tibetans were not keen on foreigners at sacred sites, use of a disguise was also called for. The first outsider to complete the *kora* was Japanese monk Ekai Kawaguchi, who disguised himself as a Chinese lama. In 1907 Swedish explorer Sven Hedin became the first Westerner to complete the circuit. Italian Tibetologist Guiseppe Tucci and his colleagues made the pilgrimage in 1935. Under threat of bandit attack, they simply shot the brigands. On film, that is. The Italians bluffed their way out of trouble by pointing a tripod-mounted cine-camera at the bandits.

*****

The second day dawns crystal clear. We're taking a rest day here to explore. I step outside the monastery guesthouse and am stunned to see, looming right in front of me, the north face of Kailash, which up to now has been shrouded in mist. The dome-shaped peak glistens with icy walls, bewitching, hypnotising, powerful. Now I know why the Tibetans call the mountain Kang Rinpoche – Jewel of the Snows. The symmetrical dome looks like an uncut diamond. I set off with Kozo to visit the toe of the glacier at the north side. For here, it is said, any wishes made will definitely come true, and I certainly have a few to make.

On the way back to the guesthouse, we come across the same prostrator we saw the previous day. We examine his gear close up – leather apron, rubber kneepads, mittens cut out of old tyres and a pair of old running shoes. I donate a chocolate bar, which he gratefully pockets (if I were in his shoes, I would've wolfed that bar down). But where is his gear and his food? He manages to get across the information that he has to get up early and deposit his gear at his projected end point for the day. So he not only prostrates around Kailash, he ends up walking the distance a few times too. But without a water bottle? This is hard to fathom.

While we huff and puff our way round Kailash in four days, the Tibetans polish it off in one long day, pausing only for a picnic lunch. Of course, they don't stop to admire the scenery or take photos, I reason, but still, the idea of being lapped by a sturdy grandmother somehow bothers me.

The next day that's exactly what Tenzin, our truck driver, does – he overtakes me near the crest of Drolma Pass, at 18,400 feet, the highest point on the circuit. It is the focus of the entire *kora*: a large boulder, carved with an image of Tara, is festooned with prayer flags. Tenzin is on his second circuit in as many days. And he's got a girlfriend who keeps him busy back in Darchen as well. The man is indefatigable. He instructs me on where to tie up prayer flags and how to cast my windhorse squares to the heavens. We shout *Tso-tso-tso-tso! Lha Gyalo!* (Victory to the Gods) which is what all Tibetan pilgrims yell when they power over a high pass, as protection from evil. Apart from windhorse squares and prayer flags, pilgrims leave coins, paper bills, locks of hair, photos of themselves or other mementoes of their passage.

Then the driver marches off at a blistering pace, and I start to feel woozy. An altitude of 18,400 feet is uncharted territory as far as my bloodstream is concerned. I am really torn. Torn between staying and drinking in the majesty of it all, or making a quick descent to keep the demons of altitude at bay. Over the ridge is a greenish tarn, a tiny lake where Hindu pilgrims are supposed to bathe. Ice-skating might be more appropriate right now – it is frozen over. I'm entranced by the frozen lake, the clouds, the yaks, but I must push on down; the demons of altitude are gathering in my brain – dark clouds.

I end up doing a bit of prostrating myself on the downhill run: I drop to my knees, throw up, stand up, stumble on, drop to my knees again, throw up. Moving down, down, down to where my head finally stops spinning from the altitude. Now the problem has shifted to the knees – the old shock-absorbers have taken a terrible pounding. I stop by a stream to watch the lines of pilgrims striding past, muttering mantras, spinning prayer wheels. They are two-thirds the way through their one-day circuit. Grandmothers are overtaking me again. *Howdy pilgrim! You got bad legs or something? Move over, sonny!* How do they do it? Grandmothers! I stagger into Zutrul Puk Gompa guesthouse at dusk, feeling totally knackered. I hit the bed, which, though it is rock hard, feels absolutely blissful, and crawl into my sleeping bag with my mind on a short nap before dining on soup.

When I wake up, I feel a lot better. I put a hand out of the cocoon of my sleeping bag. The exterior of the bag is freezing; the interior is toasty – those goose-down feathers provide remarkable insulation. I glance at my watch, puzzled. It says six o'clock, but I crawled into the bag later than that. It is morning: I have been out for almost twelve hours. I discover that the others in our 'caravan' have trickled in, including Kozo and Barbara. Barbara collapsed a few miles short of the guesthouse and was picked up by two Tibetan pilgrims, who carried her in on their shoulders and dumped her on a bed like a sack of potatoes.

★★★★★

Tibetan sage Milarepa is credited with these words: 'All worldly pursuits have but one unavoidable and inevitable end, which is sorrow: acquisitions end in dispersion; buildings, in destruction; meetings in separation; births, in death. Knowing this, one should, from the very first, renounce acquisitions and heaping up, and building, and meeting, and … set about realising the truth.'

Easy for Milarepa to say: he dined on nettle soup, lived in caves and sat on an antelope skin, composing songs all day. And in the twelfth century, when Milarepa was around, there weren't a whole lot of possessions to get attached to anyway. Those were the days long before the invention of the sleeping bag, the ballpoint pen or the chocolate bar. But for me, there's a certain resonance to his philosophy: in the West, mindless consumerism is a distraction from living, from seeking real experience. The Tibetan's view life from a very different perspective: the attainment of spiritual well-being is a prime priority. The Kailash *kora* is one of those raw experiences that Tibetans thrive on: pilgrimage as a kind of truth-seeking, a source of inner strength.

Around the Kailash *kora* are relics left by Milarepa, founder of the Kagyu sect, who engaged in fierce competition with Bon sorcerer Naro Bonchung. At Zutrul Puk Gompa, the reconstructed monastery encloses a cave that Milarcpa is rumoured to have fashioned with his bare hands, and there's a statue of him within. The legendary showdown between Milarepa and Naro Bonchung took place on the peak of Kailash. Milarepa reached the peak through his magical power of alighting sunbeams. In the ensuing duel, Naro Bonchung fell and, in so doing, is said to have carved a long vertical cleft in the mountain's south face. The duel established the supremacy of Tibetan Buddhism at Kailash. The monasteries around Kailash are mostly associated with the Drukpa Kagyu sect, but Milarepa allowed Bon adherents to continue circumambulating the peak in anticlockwise circuits.

★★★★★

The hard hiking is over. The final walk into Darchen is a piece of cake – all downhill or flat. My knees have recovered enough to dribble back into town. I have come full circle. On the spiritual score, I've accrued enough merit, and I'm not about to set off for another circuit of the sacred peak. Not for a few years, anyway. My brain is fixated on accruing some lost weight, as in food: after consuming only packets of soup on the circuit around Kailash, the noodle houses in Darchen look positively paradisaical.

Aching limbs are revived at Chiu Gompa in sulphurous hot springs channelled into a small pool. Here you can experience the heavenly luxury of hot water – natural plumbing for the great unwashed. Tibetans do not bathe very often because river water is freezing, and because caked dirt provides a layer of insulation against intense UV rays. Washing accumulated Landcruiser dust out of my hair is sheer bliss, even though these ablutions are a temporary respite. After soaking in the 'pool' I somehow manage to find the energy to mount the stairs of the top chapel at Chiu Gompa, affording a grand panorama of the entire area. In the distance, the striking dome of Kailash looms, gateway to the realm of the gods, object of veneration for legions of pilgrims over the centuries. When you stand here, you can feel that sense of sacred earth, feel that energy charging the air.

If you're still feeling perky after the Kailash *kora*, you can set off for a five-day circumambulation of Lake Manasarovar to the south. That's next on the Tibetan pilgrim's list. Raksas Tal, the second lake down this way, is thought to have poisonous waters, as opposed to the healing waters of Manasarovar, so even though the water is fine, Raksas Tal is shunned by pilgrims. Manasarovar is of particular interest to Hindus, who come for ritual bathing in its icy waters, and to pick up pebbles and fill containers with holy water – both are prized gifts on their return to India. In 1948 a portion of the ashes of Mahatma Gandhi were scattered into the lake.

Cutting past in the Landcruiser, we sight Kailash off in the distance, floating above the lake – a thrilling perspective. And then another beautiful peak pops up to the south, a colossus called Gurla Mandhata. We're headed for the old caravan stop of Burang, right on the Nepalese border. Along the route are the pretty Tibetan villages of Garu and Topa, with hand-built houses. Burang, on the banks of the Karnali River, used to be a major centre of the wool trade, of which traces remain. At the Nepalese bazaar, goods from Nepal – everything from biscuits to batteries – are sold in exchange for Tibetan wool, which is rolled into huge balls. Today Burang functions as a military outpost, with lots of men in green running around. The town is a strange mix of ancient and modern. There are herds of sheep coursing through town, and satellite dishes and solar panels sprouting on the rooftops of concrete Chinese buildings.

Burang is the end of the road on this trip: the Landcruiser and the Dongfeng truck turn back north to Manasarovar, swing east and head for Lhasa. And all these fantastical places we have seen become memories.

*****

Why The Chopper Wouldn't Come

In Nepal, if a trekker breaks a leg or suffers from advanced altitude sickness, whatever, someone will radio for a helicopter – on guarantee of a US$2,000 payment. The helicopter cruises in and picks the trekker up and whisks him or her back to civilisation, and specialised medical care, in Kathmandu. In Tibet, no such whirlybird. The terrain, to begin with, is at a much higher altitude than in Nepal. The air is so thin that helicopter rotors have nothing to cut into.

There are US-made high-altitude Sikorsky and Boeing CH-47 choppers in Tibet, but these are solely for military use, as are the military airfields scattered around Tibet. In any case, the Chinese don't give a fig about sick or dying tourists. In Nepal there are special facilities to treat altitude sickness, some staffed by volunteer Western doctors. In Tibet, nothing even remotely close to this concept exists.

On the way back to Lhasa, in the village of Huore, we ran into Gary McCue and his partner Kathy Butler, who told us a sad story about a traveller who didn't make it. We'd last seen Gary and Cathy back in Zanda. As we were about to leave Zanda, two Landcruisers of German tourists pulled in. Gary went on to tell what transpired.

A 73-year-old German woman on the group tour had a stroke. A German doctor in the group mistook her condition for a mild case of altitude sickness, and recommended she stay in lower altitude Zanda. Inexplicably, the group – and the German doctor – decided to leave the woman behind in Zanda, in the care of Nepalese Sherpas. The group left in the Landcruisers, and continued on with their tour. The woman's condition quickly deteriorated, and she was taken to Zanda's only clinic – a tiny place for the military.

When Gary and Kathy went to visit the woman, they were shocked by what they saw: the clinic was filthy, there was human waste all over the place, and the woman was on an unsterile IV drip. They cleaned up, and changed the woman's clothing as best they could; the terrified woman was calmed by seeing Western faces.

The Chinese doctor was doing his best with the limited equipment at his disposal, but Gary and Kathy realised that if the woman didn't make it to Nepal, she wouldn't pull through. There was, however, no way she could survive an 'ambulance'. Failing helicopter rescue, the last resort in Tibet is to use a Landcruiser as an ambulance: put the patient in the back seat and head down to Kathmandu as fast as possible. But that may not be fast enough: full throttle from Zanda down to Kathmandu might take three days, and in this case the patient was in no condition to be thrown around in the back of a vehicle.

Gary and Kathy managed to contact the German Embassy in Kathmandu by phone and tried to arrange for a Nepalese helicopter to fly into Zanda. Obviously, the Chinese military would not be keen on the idea of a Nepalese chopper flying by sight over Tibetan terrain and landing at a Chinese military base. Because the Chinese objected to the hosting of a Tibetan conference being held in Germany at the time, communication lines between the German and Chinese embassies in Kathmandu were slow. By the time the Nepalese helicopter was approved to make the rescue, five days had passed. The woman's condition had seriously deteriorated, and she died. Gary said it was not all as bad as it sounded: although afraid, the woman told them she had fulfilled the trip of her dreams; she had trekked around Mount Kailash and she felt at peace.

PART THREE

TALES FROM TINY KINGDOMS

9

TEA WITH THE KING

The news from Mustang

As we march up the stony gorge it suddenly occurs to me what all this reminds me of. The steep canyon walls, the packhorses and mules stirring up the dust, horsemen urging them on and the sun beating down: it could be the set of a Western, circa 1890. But we're high in the Himalayas, and the horsemen are shouting in Tibetan – and we're going much further back in time than 1890.

We're on our way to the kingdom of Lo Monthang in Upper Mustang. It's the same kind of terrain I witnessed a few weeks earlier in the far west of Tibet, but now I'm on the other side of the Himalayas, in Nepal. Mustang (pronounced 'Moose-tang') is not related to the English word for horse, but is a Nepalese mispronunciation of 'Lo Monthang', meaning 'abundant fields'. By sheer coincidence, the horse rules here; it is the only 'automobile' into, out of, and around the kingdom, and wealth is measured by the number of horses owned.

Mustang traffic consists exclusively of bipeds or quadrupeds – horses, mules, sheep, goats, yak crossbreeds. All supplies come in this way: packhorse caravans moving north bear sacks of rice, crates of beer, wicker panniers of apples. Trekking groups entering Mustang must also move all food and camping supplies by packhorse or mule.

Although we travel in separate units, our full caravan consists of nine mules bearing duffle bags, two riding horses, two Mustang horsemen, nine Nepalese crew, a liaison officer, and eight Canadian trekkers with Canadian flags emblazoned on their day packs. The two horses that accompany us are, in fact, the Mustang version of an ambulance. If a trekker gets tired or sick, the horse will carry him or her onward, or back out if need be. We are under the watchful eyes of 'Canada boss', Gary Coopland, and 'Nepali boss', Rinzin Sherpa. When Gary insists that the Sherpas do not call him boss, Rinzin Sherpa nods and says, 'Yes, Gary boss.' Our Nepalese 'liaison officer' is a giggly woman called Ambeka. She's related to the outfitter's director, who casually asked if she'd like to step out for a short walk.

With our colour-coded bags and Canadian flags, we look like a mini invasion force. The average age among the clients is fifty-eight, an age, it seems, when there is sufficient booty in the bank to indulge in high-priced treks like this. Leading the way are Bob and Bob. The first Bob is an investment banker; he's along with his wife, Audrey. The second Bob is a pharmacist; he's along with his stepdaughter, Leanne. Making matters doubly confusing in the name department are Gwendda and Glenda. Gwendda is Gary's wife, and Glenda is a retired teacher who always dreamed of hiking in the Himalayas, but never got round to it. But she's finally made it, setting those dreams in motion.

On a trek like this you burn up energy. To keep going, you have to consume lots of carbohydrates. Next to Rinzin, the most important crew member is Maila, the cook. He and the Sherpa servers spoil us rotten with hearty food. Maila is a genius with subtle sauces and flavouring. His mobile kitchen can dish up five kinds of flatbread – chapatti, *puri*, cheesebread, pancake and poppadom. The food is an eye-popper for me, I'm more used to chewing on a power-bar of some kind during the day. We stop for morning tea – and lunch, and afternoon tea. In the morning, 'bed tea' is served at the door of your tent, a relic from British days.

This trek was arranged well in advance, nine months in fact. I flew in from Tibet, helicoptered into Jomosom from Kathmandu, and met the group on the eve of the departure date. Meeting halfway around the globe has been accomplished with no more trouble than getting together with a friend for a weekend camping trip.

Mustang is a highly restricted area: the Nepalese government charges a hefty fee to enter and restricts access to trek tours that pack their supplies in and out. Until the early 1990s Mustang was forbidden to foreigners because of previous problems with Tibetan guerrillas, the Khampas, who used the region as an operations base. In 1992 the Nepalese government opened the door to Mustang a crack, permitting entry to a small number of trekkers each year.

The trek into Mustang is an expensive proposition. I have worked out a deal with the trip outfitter, Everest Trekking, to pay a reduced fee in exchange for writing a newspaper article on the kingdom. So I make news out of Mustang. I am selling the news to make my trip possible.

In my bags, strange cargo: a bottle of Scotch for the king of Mustang, and in my pocket, a saligram, a marine shell fossil, reputed to be a talisman against the wrath of Kali, the goddess after whom this valley and river are named, the Kali Gandaki.

Here we get off to a dawn start because as the sun warms the valley up, the goddess turns nasty. By late morning, a fierce wind blasts through the gorge, sending up great plumes of dust. The wind has, over the millennia, sculpted the canyon walls into surreal shapes – organ-pipe cliffs, fluted pillars, rock spires. Striking bands of colour appear in the hills: blue, grey, rust and green tones. High overhead a Golden Eagle soars the thermals on giant wings, looking for lunch – a tasty hare or pheasant perhaps.

The cliff facing the village of Caching is pockmarked with caves, ancient high-rises. These man-made cave-condos are widely scattered in this region, but the identity of Mustang's early inhabitants remains a mystery. Radio carbon dating from some caves reveals they were used as far back as 800 BC for burial rites, ceremonial use or habitation; much later the caves became the living quarters of meditating monks.

After following the Kali Gandaki Valley for two days, we climb out of it, up a route hacked out of yellowish rock, poetically known as the Golden Staircase. This is the bizarre portal to the plateau: once you scale this obstacle, you enter the realm of Mustang. We pass a shepherd whose speciality appears to be vertical sheep grazing; his flock is scattered over impossible slopes, engaging in gravity-defying acts of feeding.

After an arduous day, we set up camp at the village of Samar, an oasis of poplar trees. The landscape in this region is identical to that of western Tibet and is unlike anything else in Nepal. Below, the barren beauty of desert hills, fragrant juniper shrubs, and floating high above, the ethereal snowcaps of the Himalayas, dominated by 26,500-foot Annapurna. The crystal-clear vistas redefine your sense of space. Under piercing blue skies, this awesome display of wilderness resonates right through your bones, a high-altitude tonic.

This is pampered trekking: our hardy Sherpas carry folding chairs, a mess tent and other luxuries which are not hard to get used to. To amuse ourselves, we compose limericks along the way, and recite them at evening supper. This one is devoted to hot drinks, including *dudh* (milk):

> We drink *dudh* and turn in at eight
> With our hot water bottles you know it's great
> Morning bed tea at six
> And later a hot-chocolate fix –
> And by seven there are pancakes on the plate.

Entranced by the landscape, we carry on at a steady pace. *Chortens* containing holy relics and cairns of mani stones engraved with Tibetan mantras are the markers of our passage. Along the trail only the odd mule caravan or lone Mustang cowboy with carpeted saddle and musk deer-skin saddlebags. After a while, your legs adapt and you turn into a formidable walking machine.

Dinner in the mess tent is special tonight: by the Canadian calendar it's Thanksgiving Day. A cardboard fold-out turkey is given pride of place on the dining table. This greatly mystifies the Sherpas, until Bob – with gobbling sound effects – explains that a turkey is like a humongous chicken. One concept the Sherpas can grasp: Thanksgiving is a harvest festival. They surmise that it involves drinking, and that's all they need to know. With the wind howling outside the mess tent, we devour plates of spaghetti topped with sauce and yak cheese, toast the occasion with shot glasses of *rakshi*, the local firewater, and loudly recite the latest limericks:

Valley after valley, as if in a dream
We marched on till we ran outta steam
Bob thought it was all crude
Till Gary said, 'With your *dudh*,
would you like some Bailey's Irish Cream?'

★★★★★

We trek on to Tsarang, a picturesque village with a population of four hundred. Here we camp on the rooftop of the finest house, owned by Tsewang Bista, a young nephew of the king. And how can you camp on a rooftop? Well, for one thing it's flat, and for another, it's made of rammed earth so you can dig tent pegs in.

New technology is on its way: at Tsarang's imposing Sakya-style temple I notice electrical wiring. The temple was the first to receive the light as an auspicious start when a hydro-electric power plant was inaugurated in 1990. With electricity inevitably comes video and other links, and perhaps the end of a way of life in Mustang.

★★★★★

On the sixth day of the trek excitement builds: the goal of Lo Monthang is within reach. A hike through pebble-strewn desert terrain leads up, up, up to a pass. It is composed of giant boulders, between which flutter strings of prayer flags. My heart leaps; it is as if you intrude on the landscape in the cockpit of a light plane. From this vantage point you suddenly glimpse the entire valley where Lo Monthang lies. The pass is the gateway to the kingdom! After plodding along for six days, the brain can send the message to the legs that the end is in sight, and the pounding on the knees will stop. Of course, the brain and the legs are on non-speaking terms by this point, but you can still try.

★★★★★

The town of Lo Monthang is enclosed by lofty russet mud-brick walls, the only walled Tibetan town in the Himalayas. You can make an internal circuit of the place in just fifteen minutes. It's a maze of 200-odd houses crammed together, supporting a population of nine hundred souls. Rounding a corner you might encounter a cow, a horse or a flock of goats. There seem to be as many animals as people. Animals dwell on the ground floor of housing; people occupy the upper floors; the flat roofs are festooned with yak dung or brushwood, the winter fuel source. Over the doorway hangs a 'spirit trap', designed to waylay evil forces. It consists of multicoloured strands of yarn configured in a circular pattern that looks rather like a spider's web.

The town has only one gate, at the north. Close by is the king's palace, a fortress-style white building rising four storeys. We discover that the king is due to leave town the next day so we make a hasty 'appointment' to see him. The king is open to receiving foreign guests for a brief audience, and soon we are ushered up the dim palace stairs. A Tibetan mastiff on a chain growls menacingly; above, suspended from the ceiling is its predecessor, a giant stuffed Tibetan mastiff.

Visiting the king is a surprisingly casual affair. Dignified and relaxed, he sits in a Tibetan-style tea-room with low carpeted seating, one hand twirling prayer beads, the other stroking his Lhasa apso dog. King Jigme Parbal Bista, in his sixties, is the twenty-fourth monarch in a line that stretches back to the fourteenth century. He still holds sway over his 6,000-odd subjects, presiding over water and grazing rights disputes, inheritance questions and cases of petty crime. The king breeds Tibetan horses and Lhasa apsos, and supervises the cultivation of his own fields: the royal family are country folk.

As is the custom, we each present the king with a white scarf, which is then placed back around the offerer's neck as a blessing. Like an envoy from a far-off land, trek leader Gary (a Winnipegger) presents the king with a Manitoba flag; I donate my bottle of Scotch. With one of the Sherpas acting as interpreter, Gary asks about problems with the school in Lo Monthang and maintaining the Tibetan culture. We learn about the problems of the people of

Lo Monthang, about the status of education, and about the king's expectations for the future.

Then Bob, with great crassness, asks after the king's family. From what we know, there are no heirs. But hovering in the background, serving tea, is the queen's stunning-looking niece, who is in her twenties. She wears an immaculate long Tibetan dress and could easily pass for a princess. She is tall, slim, statuesque. Out of the corner of my eye, I am following this entrancing figure, wondering about her role at the palace, and who she would be likely to marry. She serves more butter tea, we ask the king more questions, drink more tea, and then bid farewell.

The next day at dawn the king rides out of the gates of Lo Monthang, shadowed by a bodyguard with a shotgun. The king's horse is one of his finest; the carpeted saddle is exquisitely woven in glowing colours. Although there is a helipad in Lo Monthang, he prefers the two- or three-day ride into Jomosom.

I am working on the latest limerick:

We climb the stairs, take in the vista
We are meeting King Jigme Parbal Bista
Tea with the king is cool
Till Bob asks, like a fool:
'You got a family, how's your sister?'

So what is a king doing here anyway? Well, he's an anachronism, a survivor from an age when there were many more Tibetan kingdoms. Each tribe had a chieftain or king – this applied to central Tibet where religious kings ruled in early times. The powers of central Tibet commanded only that area: beyond their jurisdiction lay the tribes of the east, the Khampas, Goloks and Amdowas; to the south, the Dolpa-pas, the people of Mustang, the tribes of Ladakh and Spiti, the kingdoms of Ladakh, Zanskar, Bhutan and Sikkim. These kingdoms, with the exception of Bhutan, have been absorbed into India, China or Nepal.

In its heyday, under the Mustang kings of the fifteenth and sixteenth centuries, Lo Monthang was the fulcrum of a lucrative salt trading route: Tibetans took salt and wool south to exchange for grains from India. In the mid-nineteenth century Mustang was incorporated into the newly founded nation of Nepal. Salt in Tibet came from lakes, and eventually the trade declined due to competition from sea salt and iodised salt – mule caravans could not compete with convoys of trucks. In any case, in 1950, Tibet-Nepal trade was severely disrupted by the Chinese invasion. Since then, the tiny Tibetan Buddhist enclave of Mustang has kept its traditional ways.

Mustang's early prosperity was translated into lavish architecture and artwork, using Newari artisans. We visit the town's three temples. Composed of mudbrick, clay and wood, these ancient structures are crumbling gracefully. The one active temple of Lo Monthang, Chyodi Gompa, houses a small school for thirty youngsters who study, among other subjects, the Tibetan language. In Upper Mustang, only the monks can read and write in Tibetan – similar to the monks of Europe in the Middle Ages.

In the temple courtyard, a raucous game of volleyball is in progress with tutor-monks and novices forming the teams. Somehow I get hauled into the game, and quickly realise that there is more than technique involved here. There is altitude to contend with. After a few minutes of leaping around, I am totally winded.

Ringing the town are fields of wheat, barley and buckwheat. The harvest is in full swing, with farmers chanting rhythmically as they work. Threshing and winnowing are mostly done by hand, but some farmers use a brace of three horses to thresh buckwheat, wheeling them round in a circle – as close as you get to farm machinery here.

Lo Monthang has no newspapers, no television, no computers, no wheeled vehicles, no banks. The inhabitants still rely on ancient Tibetan medicinal practices (based on astrology and herbal cures); they practise sky burial; some still practise polyandry. But the Lo people are no strangers to the world at large. Because agriculture and animal husbandry are insufficient to support the population, extra food must be imported by mule. During the harsh winters, half the population of Lo heads off south, to Pokhara and

Kathmandu, to pursue another traditional form of generating revenue – trade.

Some trade across the Tibetan border continues: the buying of Chinese consumer goods and of Tibetan carpets and artefacts for resale to visiting trekkers. The locals are not shy when it comes to selling – they set up shop right in our camp compound. Sales are brisk, bargaining for old horse carpets, prayer beads, yak wool tuques.

Visiting trekking groups can boost the ailing economy in Mustang, but can also cause inflation. The conundrum is that with 'progress' comes loss of tradition and crumbling social structure. The Nepalese Ministry of Tourism has adopted a carefully controlled tourism model for Mustang, with the emphasis on 'eco-trekking'. There's strict enforcement of minimal impact rules – no handing out of sweets or pens to children, no burning of local firewood. Violators can lose their visiting rights. The hefty trip fee was originally earmarked to finance community and conservation projects, and temple restoration in Mustang, but little of the money finds its way here.

★★★★★

Incredibly, it was not until 1952 that the first Westerner set foot in this town, a Swiss geologist and hardy hiker named Toni Hagen. He was followed by a handful of Europeans, including Professor Guiseppe Tucci and Peter Aufschnaiter, but it was not until 1964 that French explorer Michel Peissel stayed in the kingdom long enough to study the culture. Indeed, his book, *Mustang: A Lost Tibetan Kingdom*, was the inspiration that brought me here. Lo Monthang was described by Peissel as 'the mythical fortress of a lost planet; in a lunar landscape of barren crests with jagged contours ...' I discover that Pemba, Peissel's main contact in Mustang, still lives in the centre of town. He runs the only souvenir shop in Lo Monthang; his son shows me around.

Getting to Mustang in the early 1960s was not easy. Peissel arrived at a pivotal point in Mustang's history. In 1960 Khampa guerrillas from Tibet, backed by the CIA, chose Mustang as a base to launch punishing raids on Chinese troops in western Tibet. Mustang lies in Nepal, but juts like a finger onto the Tibetan plateau, surrounded on three sides by Tibet. Khampa refugees who were given shelter in Sikkim simply disappeared; they made the trek across to Mustang. In 1966 the Khampas from Mustang annihilated a Chinese convoy that carried the PLA western commander and his entire staff: the raid yielded a treasure-trove of classified documents for the CIA.

Peissel had trouble finding caravan companions on his trip to Lo Monthang because the Nepalese feared the tall brawny Khampas, who had a reputation for being ruthless brigands. The twenty-third king of Mustang had welcomed the Khampas because he feared them as much as he feared the PLA. Peissel ran into a number of Khampa groups en route. His knowledge of Tibetan helped smooth things over, but he was still regarded with suspicion, and more than once found himself looking into the muzzle of a sub-machine gun. He eventually made friends among the Khampas and developed great respect for them.

Living in caves high on ridges, the Khampas were extremely difficult to dislodge, and their guerrilla campaign might have continued a lot longer had not circumstances – and luck – turned against them. The first blow hit in 1971, when the CIA suddenly withdrew support for the Khampas due to US rapprochement with China. Peissel wrote a book about the Khampa guerrillas called *Cavaliers of Kham*, but when it was published in 1972, the final chapter of the Khampa's story was incomplete. Fearing the wrath of China, the Nepalese acquiesced to demands that the Khampas be eliminated. Meanwhile, internal strife among Khampa leaders lead to the formation of rival groups – and treachery. Khampa resistance was snuffed out by Nepalese troops in a special operation in 1974: all the Khampas operating out of Mustang were either killed or captured. Then the Nepalese reneged on their promised package of rehabilitation aid to those Khampas who surrendered or were captured. A number of them languished in Kathmandu prisons for the next seven years.

With strict time frames stipulated on the permit, our sojourn in Lo Monthang is short – only a few days – and all too soon we're retracing our steps southwards. At Dhali La (View Pass) I linger to gaze at the now-distant walls of Lo Monthang, to drink in the vastness, the stillness and the fluttering prayer flags. Lo Monthang, with its microcosm of Tibetan society, will one day be fractured by the arrival of roads and electricity, which the people clamour for.

And then, like the fabled realm of Shangri-La, the walled town slips from view, and I set off at a brisk pace to catch up with the group.

*****

Two weeks later, sitting on a sunny terrace in Kathmandu with tea and croissants, reading the newspaper, a headline catches my attention: an unseasonably early snowfall over the Annapurna region. Several trekkers have perished, caught out on high passes. My eye falls on the word 'Mustang'. Snow has closed Mustang off; it is impenetrable. I try to imagine how the folks there will pass – or survive – the winter. The icy doors – the high passes – have closed on Mustang.

*****

On the Rocks

On my desk is a small collection of 'rocks' from the parts of the Tibetan world I've visited. There's a rock from Everest basecamp, a chorten-like clay torma (a ritual 'cake' sculpted from tsampa and yak butter) from Tsaparang, a marine-shell fossil rock from Mustang, a piece of petrified wood from Mongolia and a shard of slate, embossed with a sacred mantra, from Drepung Monastery that I bought outside Lhasa. These rocks bring back the immense landscapes – and the adventure. But there are still other hidden Himalayan kingdoms: Bhutan, Sikkim, Spiti, Zanskar, Arunachal Pradesh. I have found some doorways into the Tibetan world, but many more remain. I scheme and dream, and wait for the right opportunity. And Bhutan is still very much on my mind …

10

TIME OUT IN McLEOD

Wielding the Sword of Knowledge

I was back in the Tibetan milieu much sooner than expected. Through contacts, a volunteer teaching position came up. So I took it. The job was at Norbulingka Institute, an hour by road from McLeod. It would last three months, and I would be teaching young Tibetan refugees. I packed a couple of duffle bags and hopped a plane to Kuala Lumpur.

*****

On the Delhi leg, I get bumped up to first class and dine on poached salmon with silver cutlery and table linen, guzzle champagne and help myself to soothing aromatherapy lotions. The hovering hostess is super-polite, saying things like *Would you like a slice of lemon in your tea, Mr Buckley? Would you like a liqueur?*

I am kept really busy trying to figure out how to operate the mini TV screen that pops up out of the armrest and promises five or six films. This hi-tech gizmo has me confounded, but I don't want everybody to know that I don't normally fly this class, so I wrestle with the controls. Then I discover that the in-flight magazine carries an article I wrote on an orang-utan expert. Imagine that! A captive audience, all strapped into their seats and reading my article. Later, when I get a chance, I bag copies of the magazine from the seat pockets and rip out the relevant pages as samples of my trade for the road.

After a day of droning through the clouds, there's nothing like a ride through the Indian countryside to bring you right down to earth. And face the prospect of ending up six foot under it. I am now wide awake, wide-eyed in terror. The carnage on the road from Delhi to Dharamsala is frightening. The shocks of the minivan I'm in are shot and half the instrument panel is missing. The most essential piece of equipment – the horn – sounds like the croak of a frog in distress. The driver deftly skirts round a truck that is flipped on its side. I'm thrown off-kilter; things are rocketing towards me down the wrong side of the road, from the Canadian point of view. The driver executes heart-stopping manoeuvres around animals that suddenly pop up: ox carts, slow-moving water buffalo, even the odd camel or monkey, like an Indian version of a racing videogame.

The monsoon is in full swing – it's *pissing* down – and since the wipers work only at erratic intervals, if at all, the windscreen has been turned into an impressionist painting. Amid all this chaos and the threat of instant death, the driver's attention is focused on changing the fucking cassette to get the music right. There's a deity on the windscreen with popping lights – I can only hope that particular deity is being propitiated today, and is in the right mood. The gutters have turned to rivers of muck, and I'm still feeling woozy from the flight (*More champagne, Mr Buckley? A liqueur?*). How, you have to ask, does an Indian driver get his licence? What kind of test do they put him through? Cue up an obstacle course – two oncoming trucks, a cow, a bicycle … *Use the horn more, man! You didn't sound it enough. Shivering Shiva! You missed that old woman by a full three feet. Next time I want to see you get within a finger-width.*

A traumatic day of this, and we arrive at the gates of the most entrancing Tibetan temple complex I've yet seen. If indeed it is Tibetan, because there is something strange about it. The basic Tibetan fortress architecture is definitely there, but too much concrete, glass, steel grille-work and bluish plastic drainpipes. The main temple has classic Tibetan outlines, but set into the bevelled walls are glass cutaway sections that allow the interior to be illuminated, and which allow views of trees for those inside. Inside are modern innovations – bright lights and ceiling fans.

The setting is awesome. Norbulingka Institute lies at the end of the road in a forested valley. Behind it looms the Dhauladhar range: from the rooftop of the temple, there are breathtaking vistas in all directions. On the upper battlements above the treetops, three bright green parrots wheel around, which I take to be an auspicious sign.

The temple rooftop is actually my new home. Because of a shortage of accommodation, I wind up on the uppermost eyrie of the temple, feeling like king of the castle. The caretaker-monk shows me to my quarters. The room is comfortable, with big rounded windows, but the conditions are, well, monastic. There is sporadic electricity, but no shower. The monk indicates a large bucket. He picks up an electric rod, plunges it into the bucket and turns the power on; just wait five minutes and that's how you get the hot water to pour over yourself. As soon as he departs, I unplug the rod and put it away, out of sight. Water and electricity are a very dangerous combination, and a dead teacher is not a very useful one. I decide I can visit Norbulingka's guesthouse to take a shower.

The walls of Norbulingka enclose an entire Tibetan community of craftsmen, researchers, administrators and students. There's a guesthouse and café for tourists who come to look at the temple and the gardens. The gardens are actually the part most similar to the Norbulingka in Lhasa, the Dalai Lama's former summer palace. Norbulingka means 'jewelled garden': the site in Lhasa was once famed for its fountains and mini-lakes, its apple, peach and apricot trees, its stands of poplar trees and bamboo, flourishing roses, marigolds and hollyhocks. Norbulingka in Dharamsala features Japanese landscaped gardens with bamboo groves, small shrines and twin ponds stocked with goldfish.

There are several other Japanese touches to the complex because the creator, it turns out, is Japanese. The architect, Nakahaura, became fascinated with Tibetan style and built a Tibetan temple in Japan. That structure so impressed administrators in Dharamsala that they invited him to design this complex. The Tibetans themselves have produced few architects trained in Western ways. In Tibet, artisans like carpenters contributed to the making of a temple, rather than one overall hand. And here, at Norbulingka, Tibetan craftspeople have carried out most of the final decoration – frescos, *tankas*, wood-carving detail. The light fixtures, made with wood frames and paper, are Japanese in style, but made on-site by Tibetan craftsmen. It is a marriage of Japanese know-how and the vibrant Tibetan sense of colour and design, a style that could be called 'New Age Tibetan'.

★★★★★

The school day starts with prayers at the temple. The students perform prostrations and engage in chanting, bobbing back and forth rhythmically, and fifteen minutes of meditation.

I am teaching English at a place with the distinguished name of The Academy of Tibetan Culture. The Academy is a kind of experiment; it has been in operation for only a year. There are eighteen students, all in their twenties, mostly male, mostly from Amdo, some from the Lhasa region. There's one big difference with this school: the students walked in over the Himalayas to get to these classes. They have all escaped from Tibet.

'I didn't want to leave, but it was my karma,' Tashi tells me. It takes strength and fortitude to accomplish that – and great determination. So they are a spirited lot, even if the promised land of India has fallen far below their expectations. As I get to know them, I realise they have high ambitions: Tenzin wants to study law, Uregen is keen on computer studies. They have complex personal problems: Jamphel's sister has been imprisoned for fifteen years in Lhasa. They have lofty dreams: Youngdung wants to write books of poetry.

There's a surreal atmosphere about 'teaching' at Norbulingka. It is more like a travesty of teaching; you hope the students will somehow learn something, despite the obstacles. You never know what will happen next, and lessons never go as planned for the most bizarre of reasons. There are times when I cannot be heard over the chorus of cicadas or the torrential monsoon rains drumming down on the rooftop. Noise pours in through the window; pedagogy flies out the window. Two dogs that hang about the temple scamper through. Then, just when everything is really quiet and things are proceeding smoothly, the *chai-wallah* bursts in: pandemonium breaks loose as the students scramble for tea. The *chai-wallah*, flourishing his oversized kettle, acts as though tea were the most important thing in the world.

As if this is not bad enough, there is the daily Battle of the Light Bulbs. Down the road is an electricity station that has outages at least once a day, usually when I am trying to use a cassette player in class. The lights and ceiling fans suddenly cut out. We are sitting in the dark. Then about half an hour later the power comes on again – and blows half the light bulbs out. I carried a flashlight and stocked up on light bulbs at a local shop – they were an essential supply, like chalk. At first I thought the poor quality of the made-in-India light bulbs was to blame; later, I realised it was the huge surge of electricity that blew them out: sometimes double the normal voltage came down the line.

My teaching schedule is not heavy, only a few hours a day, but there's very little in the way of good materials, so I have to scramble. Fortunately, due to the threat of Indian piracy of Western materials, readers and grammar texts are available from the original publishers for a pittance, so I bag them. *Time* magazine becomes a source of discussion for the top group, but the messy affairs of Clinton reign for about ten embarrassing issues, which proves tedious.

We have grammar texts, we have readers, but we are missing cultural context: the books have a limited application because the students aren't familiar with Western culture and concepts, so I try to make lessons relevant by talking about life in Tibet too. I ask the students to bring in a family photo from Tibet, then paste that down on a sheet of blank paper and write about it. Youngdung brings a picture of his family at Losar (Tibetan New Year) with everybody swaddled in *chubas* and fur hats, gathered round a low table piled high with food. From these photos, I find out a lot about the quantum leap they are making from herding goats in a nomad family to studying here at Norbulingka.

Asked to write a story about a good friend, Dhondup comes up with this startling title: 'My Best Friend Was a *Dzo*'. A *dzo* is a yak-cow crossbreed. I invite Dhondup to read his composition to the class, and by the time he finishes, there are tears rolling down his face. The *dzo* was his best childhood friend. It was black, with a white face. It was unusual to have a *dzo* with such distinctive markings. Dhondup reads the story: 'We drank the same milk from his kind mother. I was too small to carry the plough. The *dzo* carried it.' The story had a very sad ending: his family sold the *dzo* to pay for Dhondup's education.

The top group presents five-minute talks, which generates lively discussion. Dickyi talks about television in Tibet – how her family used to spit on the TV whenever the Dalai Lama was denounced. Tenzin delivers a stunning talk on the reasons for the fall of Tibet – the lack of a strong army, the failure of diplomacy and failure to modernise.

There was a familiar ring to that talk. I sensed that English teaching was a hot potato at Norbulingka. The students had come to India for lessons like this; their parents had urged them to escape because they wanted them to be educated properly. There were no English classes for them in China. Like all good colonialists, the Chinese don't want their subjects to be too well educated – that could lead to deeper thinking, which in turn could lead to uprisings. They might understand CNN broadcasts!

But the staff at Norbulingka were suspicious of English for other reasons. That included the operations manager, Kim Yeshi, who saw proficiency in English as a ticket to the West, or out of the place. Kim, a thin middle-aged woman with an upturned nose and glasses, had a curious lack of warmth – she never extended her hand or offered a cup of tea. For a Westerner, an American educated in France, she should have known better. But she maintained this was the way the Tibetans had always lived, in a conservative society. She didn't want them learning about computers, watching the BBC or CNN, or learning English, in fact, because she thought these were routes to the West. If this were true, then it was the same as them being in China: they were cut off. The Dalai Lama certainly does not fit these guidelines – he has travelled widely in the West, he listens to the BBC every day and he has learned quite a bit of English.

The Tibetan language itself is of no great use in the modern world as it simply does not have the vocabulary range. Tibetan is flexible enough that English or foreign words can be imported phonetically (which is the case for a lot of geographical terms) or Tibetans can try and make up new compound words for things like 'e-mail', 'cell-phone' or 'barcode'. The Tibetan word for 'film' is *log-nyen*, meaning 'electric picture', the word for 'aeroplane' is *namdru* (ship of the sky) and in Amdo the word for 'bicycle' is *sherta* (iron horse). But new vocabulary requires consensus among the scattered groups of Tibetans to gain wide acceptance, and thus to be widely understood. There could be one term used within Tibet (deriving from Chinese) and a completely different one used in India (from English or Hindi).

Higher education in India requires proficiency in either Hindi or English. For Tibetans who want to be clued into the world at large, the key is proficiency with computers and English. Everybody was suspicious of my methods, which departed from the rote-learning model that the Tibetan instructors employed. No thinking was required, just a good memory. The Tibetan history teacher's idea of a lesson was to open a fat history book and read from it: he was doing one Tibetan king per term. The students could've done the same thing and better in the library by reading the same book. He used to stick his head in the door sometimes when I was using a board game or singing songs, convinced that the class was out of control. Once it was. I brought in a football to use for question-and-answer practice. The students were sitting in a circle: one student asked a question, then threw the ball, and the catcher had to answer. But the students got a bit enthusiastic and were in danger of taking out some light fixtures, not to mention the windows.

★★★★★

The Academy is supposed to be secular, but it is run on a monastic model with far too many irksome rules for my liking. The director, Kalsang, used to be a monk (till he got married to Kim, a Westerner – hmmm, that part wasn't traditional); the principal is a monk; the philosophy teacher is a monk; the Tibetan history teacher used to be a monk. The only ones left are Leonard and me. And

Leonard wants to become a monk. Leonard is an older American who teaches the students world history. For this job he is very well qualified: he used to be Solzhenitsyn's secretary. Among the students, one wears monk's robes; another used to be a monk; another used to be a nun.

Kim says she has computers for the students but cannot find the space to set them up. This is hokum. I try explaining that there is nothing radical about computers – even the most conservative people in the West use them. In her own office they make extensive use of computers to produce newsletters and for design work. In this same office are several Tibetans from rural areas who have no trouble, after a bit of training, using Pagemaker to produce newsletters. They are proof that the same training would easily work with the students.

The promised BBC broadcasts have not shown up because the promised TV set has not arrived. But Leonard and I score a minor victory: we start up Movie Night. We commandeer a video player and TV set from the guesthouse and set up an impromptu cinema; the students sit on wooden benches. I have a few videos along with me, Leonard has some and we can borrow more from the video rental shops in McLeod. Tuesday night at the movies becomes a high point. The biggest hit is Kevin Costner's *Dances with Wolves*, with lots of action, superb cinematography and an easy storyline. The students are intrigued by the landscape, which they say looks like parts of Tibet. They are intrigued by the way the Indians paint their horses before going into battle or hunting buffalo, and are surprised to find out buffalo look very much like yaks.

*****

I have plenty of time in the afternoons to explore the vicinity of Norbulingka. Nearby are the simple houses of Gaddi herders, who keep flocks of sheep and goats, and the odd cow. Up the hill is Dolmaling Nunnery, home to over a hundred Tibetan nuns. I stroll up there to eat at a small restaurant by the gates. Also in this direction are the metal crafters and woodworkers. One of the major aims of Norbulingka is to foster the traditional arts of Tibet such as *tanka*-making, woodwork, tailoring and appliqué work, and painting. The system is rather like a Renaissance apprenticeship: the students learn from the master, who may be engaged in a project like a custom order.

The master metalworker, in his seventies, is a rare craftsman – there are very few Tibetans left who know how to cast large-scale statues in metal. It is becoming a lost art. Together with his apprentices, the master metalworker is assembling a complex life-size Kalachakra statue with two fused bodies, multiple heads and a forest of arms.

★★★★★

A guest speaker is announced for a special lecture. All the students assemble in the temple library. The speaker is an elderly Israeli whose message is along these lines: 'Be patient in your struggle, engage in passive resistance against the Chinese. Look at us; it took us two thousand years to get Israel together, but we did it. You can be like us; you can do it all passively.'

Oh yeah, and what about all those F-16s that Israel has, and its Uzi machine guns, and its commando raids? Not to mention nuclear capabilities. The students are quite articulate in shooting this gentleman down. One asks for an example of how passive resistance might work in Lhasa. The Israeli's brilliant idea is to stage a five-minute demonstration in the Barkor, have some press photos taken and then disappear. Howls from the students. This has been attempted already – in the space of five minutes, the demonstrators have been shot or arrested, and if not, surveillance video cameras in the vicinity pick them up and they are later traced. Any press members, if indeed they were in town, would have their cameras and film confiscated and be booted out of the country. I am proud that the students are able to argue in English like this: maybe not all is lost with the teaching.

★★★★★

There's new company at the temple: a visiting monk has arrived from Taiwan. His name is Mingshin. He's supposed to teach the students Chinese. His face has a kind of waxy sheen that speaks of frail health, and yet when he speaks he does so with surprising volume and determination. He's a bit of a dark horse. When he arrives, he's wearing the grey robes of a Taiwanese monk, but he immediately switches to the red robes of a Tibetan monk. How does that work? He speaks near-fluent English, and I am looking forward to some meaningful discussion on Buddhist philosophy. But we don't get off to a great start.

On the open-air rooftop of Norbulingka café, I offer Mingshin a chair. There's a pile of foam cushions nearby, so I take one and plonk it on top of the chair.

'I'm not sitting on that,' he says disdainfully. I look at him nonplussed. I look more closely at the cushion. There's a scorpion on it. It's a small one, but a bite in the nether region would be not too pleasant a prospect.

We immediately get embroiled in a big argument over the role of women in Buddhism. Mingshin maintains that Buddhism is egalitarian and that women have equal opportunities to men: 'But how many females teachers in the Tibetan tradition do you know?' I ask him. 'And why is it considered to be a lower incarnation to be reborn as a female?'

*****

Between the goldfish ponds and the main temple at Norbulingka is a portal that features a large fresco of the Wheel of Existence. The wheel – also called the Wheel of Life – is held in the jaws of Yama, Lord of Death. It is divided into six sectors, with miniature detail painted in on activities in each.

In old Tibet lama manis (itinerant teachers) would rove around bearing this same Wheel of Existence diagram on a rolled-up *tanka*. It would be unfurled and used as a narrative device for teaching a mostly illiterate audience. The lama manis would explain the six realms. Deva Loka is the realm of the gods; Asura

Loka, realm of the demigods (demons who are in constant battle with the gods); Manushya Loka, the human realm; Pashu Loka, realm of the animals; Preta Loka, the hungry ghosts; and Naraka Loka, realm of the hot and cold hells, where the doomed and the damned live. By one interpretation, the sacred mantra *Om Mani Padme Hum* is a reminder of the six realms: *OM* – among the gods, *MA* – among the demigods, *NI* – the human realm, *PAD* – among the beasts, *ME* – hungry ghosts, *HUM* – hell-beings.

Think of this as an elaborate board-game for the next life. A spin of the giant roulette wheel and your karma determines which realm you end up in. Some interpret this not as realms reached after death, but as present reality. In this scheme of things, some live like gods (film stars, celebrities), some live ordinary lives, others live like animals, mired in greed like pigs. Others live in hells of their own making, or induced by others. And yet others are ghost-like, never able to satisfy their desires: the hungry ghosts are those who are preoccupied with things they can't have, leading a Sisyphus-like existence, permanently hungry or thirsty for the unattainable. Then, falling further still, are those in living hells – the hell of the dung heap, the hell of thorns, the forest of razors. The Wheel of Existence continues to fascinate the Westerners who come across it. Psychedelic guru Timothy Leary interpreted the Wheel as the realms that people could 'land' in when returning from an acid trip.

The fresco of the Wheel of Existence triggers a lengthy discussion on reincarnation with Mingshin. He offers his interpretation of the fresco, I offer mine and the discussion – actually an argument – proceeds from there.

Reincarnation sounds attractive as an idea; it sounds wonderful. We don't really die, we just get recycled. Trouble is, when you start getting down to the nitty-gritty, there are a few practical problems. Who gets reincarnated, and when and where? And how? And how much? I mean, what exactly is reincarnated – the brain, the body, personality, consciousness, self, soul, genes? And can that energy be transferred to living matter like plants, or only to sentient beings (those capable of consciousness)?

Buddhists maintain that what is transferred is a karmic energy package – positive energy, negative energy. Buddhism is an easygoing faith: you can be Buddhist and not believe in reincarnation, or ignore it, as Zen practitioners do. But Tibetan Buddhism demands faith in reincarnation. It actually goes one step further: it is the only branch of Buddhism that says specific lamas are evolved enough that they can channel their rebirth – the Dalai Lama being a prime instance of this.

Why is it, then, that someone could recall a past life as an Egyptian high priest, but not as a slave or a toad? Not too many can remember their past lives as animals, though Buddha himself told stories about his five hundred lives in the non-human realm. Is this system open to non-Buddhists? If you have a staunch Catholic who's expecting the company of angels, how would that person feel suddenly turning up as a grasshopper? And then having to spend the next hundred lives in the animal kingdom?

And this raises the question of extinction. What if you are designated for reincarnation as a silver fox but that species is now extinct? *Sorry, run out of those – how would you like to be a Chihuahua instead?* Must be a hell of a surprise, this reincarnation thing. Could you come back as a computer program (artificial intelligence – transfer of brains)? If you think of that kind of transfer, then a book is a form of reincarnation, or a film; it will be around a hundred years after its maker has passed away. What about sudden death, an accident? What happens to the reincarnate there?

'Every moment you are reincarnating yourself,' explains Mingshin. 'Two minutes ago, your body and mind are not the same.' Well, true enough – nobody's brain would be the same after talking to Mingshin. Mingshin is a follower of the Nyingmapa sect. He planned on going into retreat after this teaching sojourn.

'At the same monastery where Steven Seagal was enthroned?' I ask. Mingshin shoots me a brutal look. I must've hit the right *gompa*.

★★★★★

Lightning crackles, thunder rolls, electrical activity flashing through the stars. I can see it all from the temple rooftop. And then the rain moves in, pelting down with a deafening din. It's great to be inside with a good book in a downpour like this, and I have a whole Tibetan-style library to myself, with cosy low cushions, and handwoven Tibetan carpets on the floor.

I find the perfect book: *Tibet and the British Raj*, a Ph.D. thesis by Alex McKay about the interaction of the British officials with Tibetans from 1904 to 1947. I become absorbed in the story of Frank Ludlow, an Englishman teaching for the Indian Education Department. He arrived in Gyantse in October 1923 on a three-year teaching contract with the Tibetan government. The idea was to train Tibet's future administrators. It took several months to set up the school and build furniture, but even longer to persuade students to attend. The place opened in December 1923 with thirteen students: a low figure, although it eventually doubled.

Ludlow put everything he had into the project, but he ran into trouble. The British and Indian governments did not offer much help. Ludlow ran into monastic and parental obstacles: neither liked his innovations, nor the departure from Tibetan rote-learning methods. Ludlow battled on for the duration of his contract, then he was told the contract would not be renewed. Deeply disappointed, he wrote that the Tibetans 'will regret this decision one day when they are Chinese slaves once more, as they assuredly will be'. Prophetic words indeed. The Tibetan government misunderstood the importance of education.

Ludlow had one great success – he brought along footballs. The students took to the game with a passion, and had trouble keeping their tempers when playing. Even the Dalai Lama took an interest in proceedings, and enquired if it was true that Ludlow kicked the ball with his head. Ludlow ordered football strips in the Tibetan colours of yellow and maroon, and the school played against the Gyantse Trade Agency team, with Ludlow as referee. In their last game before Ludlow left, in 1926, the student team was good enough to manage a 2-2 draw against the Gyantse Trade Agency team.

Some years later, arriving in Lhasa with a new British Mission in 1936, Spencer Chapman met several old boys from the Gyantse school and found they spoke English quite well – and had a fair knowledge of football. So the British Mission set up a team called the Mission Marmots to play the Tibetans. The British were unbeaten in the first season – something to do with the fact they played with boots while their opposition ran around barefoot. The initial opposition team was from the Nepalese mission in Lhasa, and later a Tibetan team made up of robust men who served as the Dalai Lama's bodyguard. Eventually there were fourteen teams in Lhasa, and football boots were even on sale in the market. But in 1943, football playing was banned by a new conservative Regent. Monastic opposition to the passion that football generated was behind the ban, as was most opposition to modernisation. Monastic officials regarded the game as a threat to social and cultural stability.

I closed the book. It was the same at Norbulingka – nothing had changed. Here, seventy years later, in India, and in exile, opposition to simple changes was rife. The principal hated the idea of volleyball, which I had tried to get off the ground to improve the students' health. Some of them looked positively anaemic from lack of exercise. There had been some false starts. A while back, I had bought some volleyballs in Kotwali Bazaar, but the students said we would have to wait until the grass was cut. Why? Because there were still cobras out in the fields. Eventually, the grass was cut and we played – and had a great time, over the objections of the principal, who condemned the sport as a foolish waste of time. In his view, the students should be spending all their time with their noses in books learning obscure texts by heart.

Harsh reality sets in, dampening enthusiasm. The Tibetan Buddhist deity Manjushri, Lord of Wisdom, carries the Book of Knowledge in one hand, and wields the flaming Sword of Knowledge in the other. The *dorje* on the sword handle is the symbol of dealing with the forces of darkness. The Sword of Knowledge represents awareness; the sky-blue sword is supposed to cut through ignorance and misunderstanding, identified by the Buddha as prime obstacles. It is not surprising to learn that the monasteries in old Tibet were the main centres of learning; what is surprising is to learn that the Sword of Knowledge was not applied to cut through ignorance here. Monks in old Tibet clung to their ancient beliefs, verging on superstition. Ignorance of diplomacy, failure to adapt to the modern world, suspicion of new gadgets, suspicion of films – these are among the reasons that Tibet was lost.

*****

Mr Nowrojee's family has been here since Time began. That's *Time* magazine, which he sells in the family general shop, the only place in McLeod Ganj to do so. I wanted to put my name down as a regular customer for *Time*. 'How long will you be here?' enquired Mr Nowrojee sternly. I was thinking: *If I say less than three years, maybe he won't add my name to the list.* Only Mr Nowrojee could touch *Time* magazine. He seemed to spend his days cataloguing newspapers and writing subscribers' names on them.

Since Time began: the Nowrojees are Parsees, an ethnic group that moved to the Indian subcontinent from Persia about twelve hundred years ago. Mr Nowrojee was born into a prosperous Parsee family in Karachi, where he studied commerce. He moved to Dharamsala to take over his father's shop in 1938 (the shop was founded by his great-grandfather in 1860). Snowy-haired Mrs Nowrojee sits in the middle of the shop, counting rupees. Tell Mrs Nowrojee you're Canadian and she'll burble on at length about her famous nephew, Toronto writer Rohinton Mistry, who immortalised the shop in his novel *A Fine Balance*. The shop has the atmosphere of a musty museum from the 1920s, with the Nowrojees as the caretakers. Faded signs for Andrew Liver Salts, Pears Soap and Peek Frean Biscuits decorate the walls. These museum pieces belonged to an era when overheated British flocked to McLeod – to lawn tennis clubs, manicured gardens and mock-Tudor homes with cosy fireplaces.

After the departure of the British in 1947 (after a century of residence), Mr Nauzer Nowrojee was left in possession of most of the town – and left wondering what on earth to do with it. With India's independence and partition, nearby cities were cut off on the other side of the Pakistani border. Mr Nowrojee and Sons fell on hard times. Then in 1959, he heard that the Dalai Lama, having just fled Tibet, was looking for a place to stay. The Dalai Lama had been given a temporary home at the nearby resort of Mussoorie. So Mr Nowrojee wrote him a letter inviting him to stay at McLeod Ganj, an invitation that was graciously accepted. The Dalai Lama moved with his family in 1960, and formed his government in exile the same year.

Now, forty years on, Westerners flock in. Dharamsala is firmly on the tourist map: hotels are packed, cafés and souvenir shops are busy, and people are buying from Mr Nowrojee's shop. There's lots of noise and pollution, and new building going on. All the New Age glitz might not be the way Mr Nowrojee envisaged McLeod turning out, but he was right about one thing: by inviting the Tibetans, the resort of Dharamsala was revived beyond his wildest expectations (Mr Nowrojee passed away in October 2000, at the age of eighty-three, leaving his wife and sons to carry on the business).

Dharamsala may have been given a jump start, but for Tibetans, the place falls far short of their expectations. Dharamsala means 'rest house', originally a place for Hindu pilgrims, but now an apt name for Tibetan refugees who have escaped from Tibet by an arduous trek over the Himalayas. For them, McLeod Ganj must appear a very disappointing three-street town, thronged with tourists not monks, an environment of mud and mould, not desert and dryness. No large temples, and only a handful of pilgrims on hallowed walkways.

Of course there is one very special draw in Dharamsala: the Dalai Lama. Upper Dharamsala, embracing McLeod Ganj and Forsyth Ganj townships, hosts about 8,000 Tibetans, along with 6,000 Indians, and the local herders of the hills, the Gaddis.

McLeod is not sacred earth, like Tibet, and never will be: Tibetans have always believed that exile was a short-term thing. The thirteenth Dalai Lama was forced into exile twice. The first time he fled to Mongolia when the British invaded in 1903; the second time he fled to Kalimpong, in British India, when the Manchus invaded in 1910. But he did not have to wait long for his return to Tibet. By contrast, the fourteenth Dalai Lama has been based in Dharamsala for over forty years.

It's a peculiar thing: in Dharamsala, satellite receivers can pick up television broadcasts from Lhasa. This is mostly Chinese propaganda, but Tibetans in exile still watch it in hotel lobbies, mainly for reasons of nostalgia (too bad they can't broadcast the other way!). For the Tibetans, India is not home, and even though they have been resident for a long time in McLeod, they refuse to take out Indian citizenship; they use Indian resident certificates. Even those *born* in exile won't apply for Indian citizenship. But how can they retain their identity? In a land of a billion Indians, these 100,000 Tibetans in exile are a drop in the bucket.

★★★★★

The weekly visit to the Nowrojee shop became a ritual for me. Actually, I had two reasons for visiting: apart from *Time* magazine, I would purchase some fresh yak cheese, made in the Kulu Valley. The smell of that cheese conjured up all the temples in Tibet. And the smell of the people themselves, hair and face smeared with yak butter as protection from the harsh sun.

The Nowrojee's shop commands the best real estate in Dharamsala, facing the *chowk*, the main traffic circle, which is fed by eight alleyways. For people-watching, there's no finer place than the *chowk*. At dusk, half the population of McLeod seems to mill around it, leaving, arriving, or just plain obstructing. Old Tata buses, bulbous Ambassador taxis, three-wheel chariots and stray cows vacuuming food scraps all jockey for positions. Police blow whistles to direct them. On one side of the *chowk* might be burgundy-robed monks; on another, some Indian drivers sipping milk tea; on yet another, a gaggle of backpackers in tie-dyed trousers. Looking on with some amusement are idle rich Indian tourists in immaculately pressed trousers or flashy saris: the males ogling the shapes of Western women, the females ogling the fashion styles of Western women.

Then there are the cross-dressers: an American in maroon monk's robes, a Nordic blonde wearing a long Tibetan dress, an English woman wearing Pakistani clothing, the *shalwar kameez,* or a Swiss man with dirty dreadlocks. And if a bald French woman strolls by, nobody bats an eyelid: they've seen plenty of shaven-headed Tibetan nuns here. If an Israeli punk strolls past with streaks of bright red and green in her hair and pierced eyebrows and lips, they still won't bat an eyelid. They've seen women from Rajasthan whose facial features are not so much pierced as punched. Under thin headscarves, you can make out startling amounts of jewellery distributed across the face – they carry their wealth on their heads. Heavy gold rings hang off three or four punches through the earlobes, and a heavy gold chain links from one ear via a cheek-stud to form a bridge to the nose, where more heavy metal is embedded. Even so, some Westerners look decidedly odd – 'white monks' with their bare skulls far too pink. And where, I wondered, does that Dutchman get his beard braided in dual plaits below his chin?

Some candidates clearly qualified as Tibetan cross-dressers too, in the sense that you never see them this way in Tibet: a Tibetan monk at the helm of a maroon-coloured 4WD jeep with a 'Free Tibet' sticker plastered on the windscreen, or a long-haired Tibetan in jeans and cowboy boots astride a 250cc Enfield, with his girlfriend riding side-saddle, Indian-style. Then, blowing away all the costume artistes would be a sadhu, face painted silver, filthy dreadlocks down to his waist, carrying a large trident, wearing a thin loincloth, body smeared in ashes. Such apparitions – and more – might be found threading their way through the *chowk* at dusk.

★★★★★

There's one more apparition I failed to mention: a ghost by the name of Dorje Shugden. One afternoon at the *chowk*, a few dozen

Indian soldiers armed with *lathis* (bamboo batons) turn out to do battle with the followers of Dorje Shugden, should they arrive by bus and attempt to disrupt a conference on the same ghost, being conducted in McLeod.

Dorje Shugden is a wrathful spirit or protector deity, shown in *tankas* as a fearsome leering deity who rides a lion. He is actually the ghost of a disgruntled seventeenth-century abbot who came into conflict with the fifth Dalai Lama, and who, over three hundred years later, has come into conflict with the fourteenth Dalai Lama, who has advised Tibetans against the practice of propitiating the spirit of Dorje Shugden on the grounds that it fosters religious intolerance and promotes superstition.

The controversy is a delicate and complex matter. In February 1997, Lobsang Gyatso, the principal of the Buddhist School of Dialectics and a vehement opponent of the Dorje Shugden cult, was stabbed to death in McLeod, along with two of his students. The murders were thought to be linked to the Shugden cult. Exiled Tibetans are in dire straits with their entire culture in danger of disappearing, and they end up bickering over a ghost from the seventeenth century.

India can be an infuriating place. It took me three weekends to post an airmail envelope of documents in McLeod. On my first attempt, the post office was closed for two days for India's Independence Day celebrations, which seemed to drag on for three or four days as an excuse for a mini vacation. There was no notice outside hinting when the post office might re-open. The following week, I tried again. The green door was ajar, which was promising, but the staff were all sitting around sipping tea and contemplating a load of hiking shoes that a vendor had dumped in the middle of the floor. After twenty minutes of haggling for shoes, a clerk finally acknowledged those clamouring for stamps.

This time I got as far as determining the price of the package – 330 rupees – and then discovered that the highest stamp available at this location at this time was five rupees. A quick calculation revealed that there wasn't enough surface area on the envelope to accommodate the stamps, and the entire thing would have to be basted in a gallon of glue. The man behind the counter pointed to a metered-mail machine that could easily do the job of printing out a sticker for 330 rupees, but since it was electric and the power was out, I would have to come back.

On my third attempt, a Saturday, the power was on and the post office door open, so I strode in confidently and pointed at the machine. The man waggled his head. 'The machine is for parcels,' said the clerk. 'This section is closing at 1.30 p.m. You are coming back on Monday.' It was 2 p.m. and I felt like hurdling the counter and throttling the bastard, forcing him to plug the machine in and punch the buttons for 330 rupees with his nose. But a little voice in the back of my head said *Don't create an international incident.* So I abruptly left, and returned the following week to get the job done, trying my very best not to boil over when I discovered they had run out of stamps for ordinary letters.

The way to circumvent the post office was to use e-mail. Sending e-mail has its drawbacks – the person at the other end doesn't get the same thrill, the exotic stamps, the weirdly scented envelope. Nothing can replace tacky postcards sent from these far-out places. What the e-mail system can handle is lightning speed – you can punch out lots of short replies in record time. Some travellers are reluctant converts to the merits of the abrupt electronic 'attitude', the *haiku*-like telegraphic style of e-mail. I was in the Green Café in McLeod when an American woman received an e-mail in the form of a brief video clip, complete with sound-bytes. All the e-mail addicts promptly gathered round to witness this miracle. The woman was obviously new to e-mail technology, and the café manager explained what was transpiring. Amazement turned to dismay; she turned to him and asked: 'Is that it? There's no letter?' No letter, the e-mail guru confirmed. 'Lazy bastard,' she muttered, 'didn't even bother to write a letter ...'

Bhutan, however, was not hooked up to the service – yet. Months before, I'd made arrangements to visit Bhutan, but so far nothing had materialised in the way of visa or air ticket, so I was becoming worried. I had to resort to phoning a travel agent in Delhi. It is actually easier to phone Delhi than to make a local call. On street corners all over India there are little booths with cheeky signs proclaiming *STDs All Day, 24 Hours!* This is not as dangerous as it sounds – these are computer-monitored Standard Trunk Dialling phones that can reach anything on the international network. International dialling is so good that people from Delhi are known to route their calls through London and back to Delhi to get clear lines.

*****

Because it was monsoon and you couldn't walk around the hills a lot, I frequented cafés and video theatres in McLeod on weekends. It was uncanny how films only just released in the United States were already being advertised in Dharamsala. The videotapes and DVDs were mostly pirated from Bangkok. The DVDs were sharp, and the sound came across loud and clear. The videotapes were often poor quality as the cheapest ones were made with a camera mounted on a tripod in a Bangkok cinema, and you could even see people standing up to get popcorn. But you couldn't complain about the price in McLeod, 25 cents to park your bum on a wooden bench.

In McLeod's mini-screen cinemas there was no popcorn, but you could get a meal delivered to your seat. Smoking was not only allowed, it was encouraged (the sale of cigarettes being a profitable sideline). So there would be a smoky atmosphere, and water would occasionally drip in through the ceiling to remind us of the monsoon we were trying to escape from.

Video theatres bring the world – or the Hollywood and Bombay versions of it – to quiet backwaters like Dharamsala. The year 1998 proved very special; Hollywood was bringing Tibet to the silver screen. Heady times indeed for the video salons of Dharamsala: there was a choice of films about Tibet. It was magical for Tibetan audiences – they could see Tibetan and Bhutanese actors in major Hollywood productions for the very first time.

They had a choice of watching two films in which the Dalai Lama himself was portrayed, a biopic about his early life (Martin Scorsese's *Kundun*) and an adventure flick (Jean-Jacques Annaud's

Seven Years in Tibet). In fact, the Dalai Lama himself was consulted by the screenwriters of both films to check on detail. Having failed to interest the governments of the world in recognising Tibet as a nation under occupation, the Dalai Lama has turned to Hollywood for support.

Can Hollywood save Tibet? Probably not, but Hollywood has certainly raised the bar on awareness about Tibet's problems. In Dharamsala, Tibetan audiences were treated to the spectacle of Brad Pitt speaking in faltering Tibetan and a fake German accent in *Seven Years in Tibet*, Richard Gere running over Beijing rooftops in *Red Corner*, and a host of unknown Tibetan actors in *Kundun*. On film, the Tibetans were naturals – for first-time actors they did a superb job. But were they really acting? The monks in both films were real monks. As director Jean-Jacques Annaud quickly discovered, Tibetan monks make splendid actors: years of training in meditation have taught them how to focus their energies totally in the moment. They don't even require stuntmen.

Jetsun Pema, younger sister of the Dalai Lama, played her own mother in *Seven Years in Tibet*. For Jetsun Pema, who had never acted before, it was an amazing and emotion-charged experience to relive part of her past, to step back in time onto the set of a recreated Lhasa. Playing the female lead in the story, the alluring Lhakpa Tsamchoe, who grew up in Bangalore, India, says the director pretty much let her be herself. And the youth who played the young Dalai Lama, Jamyang Wangchuk, is the son of a diplomat from Bhutan, a boy used to a dignified role.

The directors of both films came up against tremendous obstacles in trying to get their films finished. It had been forty-five years since the book version of *Seven Years in Tibet* appeared and a string of directors had failed to get the opus up on the big screen. Disney's Touchstone Pictures was backing Scorsese, and Disney was threatened with the closure of a Disneyland under construction near Shanghai if the film went ahead.

Requests from both directors to film in Ladakh, the obvious choice for filming since it is actually on the Tibetan plateau, were denied due to pressure from the Chinese. The Indians were nervous about diplomatic fallout from hosting the films. So

Kundun was filmed in the desert in Morocco, and *Seven Years in Tibet* was mostly filmed in Argentina. The results, to my eye, were flawless; it was as if you were right there in the Lhasa of the 1940s. It was magical. But while computer imagery may have been used to help create a 'Virtual Lhasa', in the case of *Seven Years in Tibet*, the director himself had shot digital video footage on the sly while travelling in Tibet, and he incorporated professional 35mm footage shot by David Breashears.

Cinematic sleight-of-hand brings a lost Lhasa back to life. Film is where you can find the real Shangri-La: in another dimension, intangible, illusory. Hollywood is, after all, where the Shangri-La legend took off, if you go back to the original 1937 film version of *Lost Horizon*. But for presenting the realities of modern-day Lhasa, nothing could match *Windhorse*, which also screened in the video salons of McLeod in 1998. In a daring and very dangerous move, the American director of this low-budget 'docudrama' decided to film parts of it on location in Lhasa, defying a Chinese ban. Paul Wagner was there with his crew and actors in 1996, undercover, of course. Clandestine filming was made possible by the advent of lightweight mini-DV handy-cams which produce high-quality digital video that can later be transferred to 35mm film. The handheld video cameras enabled the crew to act as tourists, innocently filming street scenes, temples and landscapes around Lhasa. This must have made for some very complex directing problems.

I saw *Windhorse* on video at a community centre in McLeod, with a mostly Tibetan audience. It was very powerful stuff. Unlike the other films on Tibet, this was filmed in Tibetan and Mandarin, and portrayed the problems of contemporary Tibet. That gave it the cerebral edge; the Tibetans watched spellbound, with audible groans and gasps.

★★★★★

For almost two months now, I've been trying to arrange an interview with the Dalai Lama. He is overbooked, he has teachings to give, he will be going to Russia, it is not possible to see him. Then, abruptly, the word comes through – the Russian trip has been cancelled, and my interview date is set for the end of September.

The night before the interview, I am still fine-tuning questions at Khana Nirvana restaurant in McLeod. The Tibetan cook excitedly tugs me over to the balcony. The road below has been transformed into a river of candles: it's a procession commemorating the 27 September 1987 demonstration in Lhasa, and the memory of those that died. Half the population of McLeod has turned out, holding candles and singing as they circle the hill where the Dalai Lama lives. When they all assemble in the square opposite Thekchen Choeling Temple, a galaxy of candles lights up the night: a simple gesture, but one with great beauty, power and poetry.

A prisoner from a 1988 demonstration in Lhasa, a monk called Bagdro, gives a short talk at Khana Nirvana after the procession, with the assistance of a translator. Bagdro is in his late twenties. His hands tremble as he relates his story. As a novice monk, he spent five years in Lhasa studying sand mandala construction, then another year studying chanting and the Tibetan longhorn. His part in the 1988 demonstration led to three years in prison, with brutal torture to exact confessions.

In the end he confessed to everything he was required to, his role in the demonstration was deemed minor and he was set free, after which he promptly escaped from Tibet. So he came out of a dark, dank Chinese prison – hell on earth – and the next thing he knew, he was sitting at the same table with the Dalai Lama at a $400-a-plate fundraiser in Los Angeles, rubbing shoulders with Richard Gere, Harrison Ford and the glitterati, Hollywood actresses with radiant beams on their faces, daintily wiping the corners of their mouths with napkins. Extreme transitions like that could seriously warp your brain. Bagdro wrote a book on his experiences and is contemplating the making of a film. The talk is over; classical music comes on, and everybody goes back to eating pizza and tacos.

It's been an emotion-charged night. My brain is still turning over all the things I've seen and heard. At around 9.30 I head back to my hotel, Chonor House, looking forward to a quiet night before the big interview. Though on the expensive side, Chonor House is the closest hotel to the Dalai Lama's residence, which is why I've chosen it. The hotel is decorated Tibetan-style, with theme suites – the Nomad Suite, the Bird Suite. I am in the Wild Animal Suite; pandas, yaks and antelopes cavort on the walls.

Chonor House is small and cosy – you can't help bumping into fellow guests. The place is not exactly full, either. Tonight there's only a handful of guests: myself, three female guests and two CNN men. The CNN men, David and Robert, who occupy a couple of downstairs rooms, are spending a week following the Dalai Lama around. They invite everyone down to the front porch overlooking the garden for a drink. They are holding court and start name-dropping: Winnie Mandela, Castro, Mohammed Ali, the Gulf War, Baghdad, Kabul, Havana. They bring up still pictures on a laptop. Then David shows today's video footage of Robert interviewing an Indian security guard about Viagra, which he's never heard of. The women find it hysterical. I nod politely, but don't crack a smile. They look at me strangely.

I'm not impressed with their research on Tibet. When it comes to the Dalai Lama, they're clueless. They sound like they've cobbled together this thing on the plane over. The only book they have between them is the Dalai Lama's early autobiography, so they end up asking him inane questions like: *Do you dance? Do ya listen to music? What about television – you see all that stuff on TV – what do you think of those Parisian fashion models?* (short reply: *waste of time*). *What do you think of Mohammed Ali?* (curt reply: *nice footwork!*). They're a pair of highly paid CNN buffoons in search of a script. It's as though they're working on the text for *The Dalai Lama for Dummies*, or *The Complete Idiot's Guide to Tibetan Buddhism*. Let's hope their editors can make some sense out of the footage, give it some shape, because only good editing can save this one.

The Dalai Lama gets asked some pretty stupid questions. His aides could probably answer most of them, but interviewers insist on seeing the man himself. So the aides attempt the next best thing: they screen the interviewers at McLeod. People often try to ask if he can perform miracles, if he is a healer. Some even bring terminal cases in for him to bless. His routine answer is no, he is not a miracle worker. But there is one miracle: he has the pulse of a baby. You know the inconsolable grief that parents suffer over the loss of a son or a daughter. The feeling that the heart has been ripped right out of them. Magnify that feeling by a few million cruelly killed by famine or torture in Tibet, and add the loss of a homeland, the near-loss of an entire religious faith, and the ongoing incarceration and torture of thousands of fellow Tibetans. The miracle is this: it's a wonder that the Dalai Lama remains sane. Not only sane, but calm. He attributes this miracle to the four to six hours he spends in meditation each morning.

Perhaps this helps him get through taxing interviews, too. The Dalai Lama takes on all comers good-naturedly, with amazing tolerance. And he is open to wacky ideas. Surely the strangest interview ever recorded with the Dalai Lama took place in 1994 when Dutch musician and composer Chris Hinze visited Dharamsala at the tail-end of a concert tour of India. Chris Hinze recorded an interview with the Dalai Lama, and then set it to music. He extracted some spoken lines and repeated them, mixing these 'mantras' in with the deep chanting of Gyuto and Tsurphu monks, Tibetan singing bowls, Gregorian chants and Western trance rhythms, and then overlaid his own flute music. Some tracks included mantras recited by the young seventeenth Karmapa, recorded by Hinze himself when he visited Tsurphu Monastery in central Tibet in 1993. The resulting mix of music is best described as 'Tibetan Fusion'. The Dalai Lama rocks! To a hypnotic pulsing beat, the Dalai Lama delivers a message about the power of music to give people hope and the responsibility of musicians to help humanity and promote peace of mind. All this foreshadows the Tibetan Freedom Concerts, with prominent musicians in the United States taking up the Tibetan cause.

But back to CNN men: I have to suppress a smirk when I watch the raw footage, with questions like: *If the gods knew you were an incarnate, why did they give you such weak eyes, make you wear glasses?* The CNN men are fiddling with hi-tech gadgets. They play back scenes of the Dalai Lama getting up in the morning, coming out of the shower, doing exercises. We find out the Dalai Lama reads *Newsweek* in the bathroom and watches the *Larry King* show at night. Actually, come to think of it, he was once a guest on *Larry King Live*, beamed into Lhasa (in 1996, stunned Tibetan staff at Lhasa's Holiday Inn gathered to watch their exiled leader appear on the show). Maybe that's why he's giving the CNN men such unprecedented access – he's hoping for a sequel in Lhasa.

Robert casually steps out the front porch to call his mother in New York using his own satellite-linked phone. He polishes off more whisky, tells us about his sexual conquests in Vietnam. He talks to me about travel to Lhasa. But I'm on their case; they're planning to sneak in there for a few days after McLeod is over. I sense their paranoia. Would CNN be allowed into Tibet? No way! So for the fun of it, I harp on the subject, which they are now trying to weasel their way out of.

★★★★★

The next day at noon, there's a public audience with the Dalai Lama, lasting an hour. My interview is scheduled right after it. I am permitted to photograph proceedings at the public audience, alongside the CNN men, who are none too pleased about this intrusion into their exclusive domain.

'Got enough batteries?' I ask as we walk up the hill. No reply. 'You've probably got enough batteries to light up the whole of Dharamsala in a blackout,' I venture again. David looks at me weirdly, keeps walking. Robert is completely out of it; up too late last night, too many whiskys.

Indian security guards are taking no chances at the public audience: Tibetans who are Chinese operatives have recently been caught in McLeod making maps of his residence. All visitors must pass through metal detectors and submit to body searches. Monk-attendants and the Dalai Lama's personal Tibetan security men propel everybody through. In the background, Indian guards cradle machine guns.

The Dalai Lama receives guests outside his Audience Hall,

which used to be a British residence. Everybody is on edge – the security men, the monks, the visitors – but the Dalai Lama himself is not in the least nervous. He's relaxed, laughing, cracking jokes. There are three line-ups: foreigners, Indians and Tibetans. First up are the foreigners, who shake hands with the Dalai Lama. The Dalai Lama is practising what he calls a 'radical informality' – the ability to reach out to all. He wants to keep the channels open. But time-wise, he can't afford to get into any conversations with the guests. A moment of suspense: an Israeli man clasps the Dalai Lama's hand, not letting go, and starts talking about how difficult the Tibetan struggle is. Security people close in. The Dalai Lama nods, but does not speak.

Through all of this, the CNN men are videoing right on top of the Dalai Lama. He's wearing a microphone clipped to his robes. But none of this seems to bother him in the least. He's probably one of the most filmed and photographed people on the planet – he's used to it.

Next up are the Indians. They are mostly Dalits, the class previously known as Untouchables. Hinduism has not been kind to the Dalits; they prefer the egalitarian nature of Buddhism. Only one per cent of Indians are Buddhist, but one per cent of a billion is still ten million people. The Indians attempt to bow and touch the Dalai Lama's feet, or else try to touch their heads to his shoes. This bothers him – he attempts to stop them. He engages in small talk: *Are you from Bombay? Did you travel long?*

But the real talk is saved for the Tibetans, who are much more emotional. They're dressed in their finest clothes and wear white silk *khatas*. There's a complete change of tone now: the Dalai Lama talks with great animation to each Tibetan in the line-up. He hands out packages of Tibetan medicine and other small gifts. He consoles an elderly Tibetan woman who bursts into tears and has to be escorted away by monk-assistants. I recognise her from news pictures. She is Palzam, the only woman among six hunger strikers in Delhi. This feisty 68-year-old threw stones at Chinese troops in the 1987 demonstrations in Lhasa.

★★★★★

The Dalai Lama's humble residence is nicknamed 'the palace'. There's a *Lingkor*, or sacred walking circuit, around it. In his own way he is a king, and is sometimes erroneously referred to as 'God-king', with 10 to 20 million followers of Tibetan Buddhism. Though his religious following is small, his other platforms reach a huge audience. The Dalai Lama has become Buddhism's first global celebrity, and a spiritual superstar on a par with the Pope.

They are two very different superstars. Pope John Paul carries with him a litany of horrors from previous centuries – the Crusades, the burning of witches, the slaughter of indigenous peoples, heavy-handed missionary activities. The modern era is no better – the Catholic Church is associated with anti-Semitism in the Second World War, and Pope John Paul remains at loggerheads with the United Nations over population control policies. He just doesn't seem to get it.

Tibetan Buddhism bears none of this stigma. It is a religion that has traditionally turned inward, remained esoteric. The Dalai Lama talks about ethics, about non-violence, about meaningful dialogue. He's a superstar without the trappings, without the ego, even without an agenda. Unlike the Pope, he does not seek converts, he has no spiritual agenda. Apart from the Tibetan cause, his main concern is the wider platform of world peace and harmony. He cuts across the frontiers of religion, seeking dialogue with Jewish leaders, Christian leaders, inter-faith dialogue.

The Dalai Lama's Audience Hall, where interviews take place, is large and airy, with *tankas* draped on the walls. The furniture is simple – a few sofas and armchairs. Some gifts to His Holiness are on display. At the back is a silver plate with a mountain design embossed on it, given to him by Tibetans on the occasion of his Nobel Peace Prize. Curiously, the actual prize, the citation itself, is not on display. Entering the hall, I feel calm, like I've already shaken hands with the Dalai Lama a hundred times after watching all those nervous people at the public audience. And I have been in this hall before, nine years ago.

The Dalai Lama's inner well of strength, his meditation practice, serves him well. In his early sixties, at an age when most would consider retirement, he is a robust man. His mental faculties are pin-sharp, and his deep booming voice has lost none of its power. His broken English bears a Tibetan accent and is laced with some strange Indian vocabulary, like 'botheration' (adopted from the English 'oh, botheration!'). Tenzin Tethong adds to the English when it becomes muddled. We start off talking about the Tibetan world. I ask him how he views this 'forgotten realm', the Tibetan cultural sphere that stretches from Mongolia to Bhutan. He ponders a bit, then launches into a long spiel: 'My main interest is the preservation of Tibetan Buddhist culture and Buddhism. In that level, the national boundary not important. So therefore from Ladakh up to Arunachal Pradesh in the Himalayan range, then Tibet, then further north, you see, Mongolia, Inner Mongolia and in Russian Federation Republics – Kalmykia, Tuva, Buryatia … So all these thirteen, fourteen millions, same religion – that's Tibetan Buddhism. Of course, you see, in case of Mongolia, different language, different script, different race or nation, but same culture, same Tibetan Buddhist faith. So I always look at it from that angle. Then, of course, where the freedom struggle is concerned, then it's Tibet, which at the moment is under Chinese control.

'Whether people consider me as a leader or anything … that's not my botheration. My side is simply follower of Buddha Sakyamuni and Buddhist monk. So from that basis, whatever contribution I can make regarding Buddha Dharma, it is my responsibility. So that's my attitude. With that feeling, when I visit Ladakh or when I visit Sikkim – Bhutan not yet – then Arunachal Pradesh.

'Then the other field: the preservation of Tibetan Buddhist culture. There I have – not necessarily responsibility – but I have some kind of potential to help them, to serve them. And then Mongolia's case also, where their political or national affairs concerned, I have no direct or indirect connection. But then, regarding the preservation of Buddha Dharma, historically also, the Dalai Lama is very close in their mind.

'If Tibetan freedom struggle is purely politics or just freedom without connection of preservation of Buddha Dharma, then as a Buddhist monk, it may not be suitable. At present, without Tibetan freedom – at least without self-rule – Tibetan Buddha Dharma and Buddhist culture cannot survive, will not be safe. Whether intentionally or unintentionally, some sort of cultural genocide is taking place, therefore Tibetan freedom is very much linked with the Buddha Dharma, so from that viewpoint, I consider that also part of my spiritual practice.'

Prompted to follow up on Mongolia, on the bonds between Tibet and Mongolia, the Dalai Lama elaborates: 'You see, my first visit in Mongolia in 1979 – within the monastery, more freedom. Outside the monastery, there were some restrictions – people can't express freely. So in the monastery they put me on the throne, and then they make offerings. Then many of them crying. I also very much moved. Since third Dalai Lama, close relations with the Mongols developed and the thirteenth Dalai Lama visited these areas – the thirteenth Dalai Lama knows Mongolian language very well. And then, since my childhood, many good Tibetan Buddhist scholars who study in those big monasteries in Lhasa – many Mongolians became good scholars … So mentally or emotionally, you see, close with these people. And also many good texts and scriptures by these Mongolian scholars – I used to read these. When I first had the opportunity in Mongolia, I also was deeply moved and was in tears.'

The Dalai Lama held a Kalachakra Tantra Initiation in Mongolia in 1995 with an audience of 20,000. Kalachakra, meaning 'Wheel of Time', is a complex supreme tantra associated with the mystical land of Shambhala. This is one special way in which the Dalai Lama reaches out – in fact, he is the only Dalai Lama to have conferred the Kalachakra empowerment outside of Tibet at sites in Europe, America and Asia. Kalachakras have been held close to the borders of Bhutan and Nepal: although the Dalai Lama can't get into these countries, people can come and see him. He tells me the Kalachakra initiation usually attracts many people, with meditation on compassion, emptiness and visualisation. Unlike some teachings, which are very restricted – only taught in some cases twice in a lifetime – there are no limits on Kalachakra teachings. The Dalai Lama has opened up these secret initiation ceremonies to anyone that believes, and called them Kalachakras for World Peace. Think of this as the Dalai Lama's rock concert: upwards of 250,000 people can congregate for a Kalachakra initiation.

This brings us to the subject of Shambhala, the Buddhist utopia intimately linked with the Kalachakra teachings. I broach the subject of myth and geography in old Tibet: 'Shambhala is indicated in some Tibetan texts as a real place while others interpret it as a mythical place. I'm curious about the Tibetan sense of geography, which appeared to operate without maps – it mystifies me ...'

The Dalai Lama chuckles. 'Me also! Some lamas – great scholar and great practitioner of Kalachakra – wrote some texts how to reach Shambhala. I think, with great respect, I feel ... a little bit feeling of nonsense.' He laughs again.

'My position is Middle Way, like my approach regarding Tibetan issue: Shambhala certainly not exist in this small planet. But if you deny the existence of Shambhala at all, some Indian Buddhist scholars, Buddhist masters, Tibetan masters put some doubt whether this Kalachakra Tantrayana is reliable or not. I believe there should be a land, a place where the Kalachakra Tantrayana flourished – so then I feel there's somewhere – in space, I think somewhere in deep space, or perhaps there are certain ... what the Buddhist literature calls "Pure Land", one that people can't see. But then, you see, that also raises questions, again controversial.'

Wanting to switch the focus to the situation in Tibet, I pose this question: 'The year 2000 marks fifty years of Chinese occupation of Tibet – where do you go from here?'

He leans forward with a mischievous gleam in his eyes and says: 'You know a good place? If there's a place, we'll be happy to go there!' And breaks into a booming laugh. 'If there's no place to go, we'll just sit right here in Dharamsala in the same room!' Tenzin Tethong, translating into English, cracks up at these jokes. That deep laugh reverberates around the room. The Dalai Lama often claims he is a simple Buddhist monk, and other times 'a naughty Buddhist monk'. Then he concentrates on the serious side.

'My main reason to be optimistic is that China proper is changing. Today's China compared with ten, fifteen, twenty years ago, much changed already. Now the *speed* of change also seem now increasing. One example: there are some articles which are quite critical about Chinese government policy. Now these can find a publisher, but one year ago, difficult. If they have the will, easily – within a few weeks' time – things can change. Anything is possible ... I look at it another way: in the long run – how much benefit for stability and unity for the People's Republic of China? Why they follow unreasonable attitude? Or very stubborn attitude? They believe that's the only way to keep Tibet within the rule of China. And stability, less demonstrations – just, you see – *ruthlessly* control.'

He clenches a downturned fist to emphasise his point. 'Yes, it is true for the temporary situation. But if they think in long run whether this suppressive policy really changes Tibetan attitude towards Chinese government – No! In 1959, when the Chinese army put down or controlled whole Tibet, they did not expect Tibetan issue will remain almost forty years. Now today, things are not as they expected, so then their communication with outside world also increasing, so their approach is definitely changing.'

'But is it too late for Tibet? In the case of the environment, for example, the damage may be irreversible ... What do you see as the pressing environmental issues in Tibet?'

'The large scale of deforestation. This recent flood on the Yangtse creates – helps to bring about awareness – about the importance of the forest. And then, different mines, mining work. Then, unfortunately, even some local Tibetans hunting, not for survival, but for money. It's sad. I often send message when I have the opportunity. During the Cultural Revolution in the late fifties, early sixties, in some areas, because of Chinese tight control, no food – and people face starvation – and under such circumstances, OK for survival, but nowadays the economic situation is much better, so now they're only thinking money, profit, extra profit. Very sad, very sad.'

I ask about the recent films that are based on his story. I know he was invited to a special screening of *Kundun* in New York, so I ask him: 'When you saw yourself on the screen, how did you feel? Was it a strange experience?'

'I had mixed feeling – one sad, one joyous. Sad because seeing that film recalled my difficult period and sad experiences – and then joyful or happy because when that event took place – 1959 – on this planet, supporters for Tibetan issue with awareness, with sort of sincere feeling – very few in the beginning, but now today – much much greater supporters on this planet. That's a source of inspiration. For my own story, *Kundun*, Martin Scorscse, and the scriptwriter [Mclissa Mathison], and her husband [Harrison Ford], these people made this film not just thinking about money, or some other benefits or interest, but they also carried this hard work because they feel deep concern and sympathy for Tibet and me personally. They want to do something for Tibetan issue according their own profession, so I appreciate that ...'

★★★★★

Playing back the tape later, I realised that there was not a whole lot that was either new or revelatory in what the Dalai Lama had said, other than his amazing talent for stating things clearly and simply despite his language handicap – or perhaps because of it. But there was one striking new piece of information. About the Kingdom of Shambhala. He shot down the earthly geographical locations and searches by lamas as nonsense, but suggested Shambhala might exist in deep space.

Other high lamas have suggested that Shambhala is not an earthly paradise, that it is a heavenly domain, or a Buddhist Pure Land existing in a different dimension, unseen by ordinary mortals. But deep space is a different take on the question. And who knows? With advanced technology and more powerful telescopes, astronomers are still discovering new planets in far-off universes.

Some claim Shambhala is a technologically advanced society, using devices well ahead of our own inventions; its occupants get around in spacecraft. In any case, Shambhala is not small.

Shambhala's eight petal-shaped sectors are supposed to support 120 million people apiece, making 960 million inhabitants in all. Which makes it a rather large place to be hidden away in the Himalayas, considering it would equal the entire population of India.

*****

The practices of Tibetan Buddhism are obscure, arcane, esoteric. Down the hill from the Dalai Lama's residence is a temple devoted to rather peculiar functions. Nechung, in Gangchen Kyishong, is the temple of the state oracle. It was on the cryptic advice of the state oracle that the Dalai Lama left the Potala in 1959 and fled into exile. The state oracle wisely fled to India at the same time, but only six of the original 115 monks attached to Nechung in Lhasa managed to escape. It was not until 1984 that the temple of the state oracle was fully reconstructed in Dharamsala, but in the meantime the oracle had died. In 1987, a new state oracle was discovered and took up residence at Nechung.

Tibetan Buddhism is the only kind of Buddhism that employs oracles, possibly a throwback to Bon shamanism. The Dalai Lama consults three or four oracles, one a woman. Like the ancient Greek oracle at Delphi, these mediums speak in riddles, offering advice and rendering prophecies. While the oracle trance-dances, thrashing his sword above his head, the Dalai Lama and members of his cabinet pose questions. The answers are delivered in high-pitched Tibetan, often in poetic stanzas. What a wild cabinet meeting!

Qualifications for the oracle's job: ability to mumble cryptically, schizoid leanings, ability to dance around with huge weight on the head, ability to engage in vivid dreams and recall them. The state oracle is a medium who conveys messages to the Dalai Lama from Dorje Drakten, a protector-deity. Ceremonies where the state oracle goes into a trance are secret: the oracle is dressed in a traditional brocade costume and a heavy headdress of precious metals. On his chest is a circular mirror; he also wears a harness that supports flags and banners.

The entire outfit weighs more than seventy pounds, and when not in a trance, the medium can hardly walk in it. The headdress itself weighs in at over thirty pounds (in former times, it used to weigh double that) and is normally too heavy to be worn without support. However, when in a trance, the oracle's strength increases considerably, and attendants quickly strap on the headdress. During the trance, the oracle is said to dance around as if the headdress were made of feathers.

11

AN EYE-OPENER

The Shangri-La Syndrome

I digress. When I speak of eye-openers, I digress, head off at a tangent, zone out, build castles in the air, trip the light fantastic, conjure up imaginary worlds. Let me tell you the tale of Lama Lobsang Rampa, the ultimate New Age guru.

In 1956, British publisher Secker and Warburg came out with a book titled *The Third Eye*. It proved to be the publishing event of the year, a runaway bestseller. Purporting to be the autobiography of a Tibetan lama and doctor called T. Lobsang Rampa, the book detailed the painful opening of the Third Eye, the wisdom eye, the power to see things clearly.

Rampa claimed he was initiated at Chakpori Medical College in Lhasa at the tender age of eight: to put it bluntly, a hole was drilled in his forehead to enable him to see auras, which in turn enabled him to divine the intentions of those around him. However, in traditional Tibetan medicine, surgery is never used, so this seemed a bit far-fetched. Trepanation – drilling holes in the head – was an ancient Egyptian and Sumerian speciality. Rampa also described 'temple cats', who attacked those trying to steal jewels from shrines, a concept also of Egyptian origin. In *The Third Eye*, Rampa wrote about monks flying around on giant kites and sightings of yetis. Most remarkably, Rampa claimed he was hired by the thirteenth Dalai Lama to hide behind a screen and read the auras of the members of a visiting Chinese delegation to determine if their intentions were honest or treacherous (Rampa determined that the auras were full of hate).

In January 1958, when *The Third Eye* was at the height of its success, the *Daily Mail* revealed that Doctor Rampa was in fact not a Tibetan monk, but the unemployed son of a plumber from Devonshire by the name of Cyril Henry Hoskins. The *Daily Mail* further claimed he was married to a registered nurse. Further investigation revealed that the extent of Hoskins' medical background was that he'd once been employed in a company making surgical fittings – actually, making corsets. In fact, he originally submitted two manuscripts to publishers, one on Tibet, the other on corsets. And his experience of other-worldly phenomena seems to have been limited to a stint when he was employed as an accident photographer.

Bald, bearded Hoskins evidently had a fertile imagination: he spent a lot of time in the British Library in London, boning up on Lhasa. After the *Daily Mail* story broke, Rampa was hounded by reporters from rival newspapers. With his wife and cats in tow, he promptly decamped to a seaside resort near Dublin. Rampa claimed the move was necessary because of seriously failing health, the same reason that he refused to give interviews to reporters. He also claimed to have developed a mental block in speaking Tibetan. He refused all contact with Tibetans, probably something to do with the fact he couldn't speak a word of the language.

One writer who did manage to get through to his residence outside Dublin was Eric Newby, later to make his mark as a travel writer. Newby was told by Fred Warburg, the publisher of *The Third Eye*, to go to Dublin and get a statement from Rampa about his book. Newby found the lama, who had adopted the name Dr Kuan-so, was very reluctant to talk in person – he was handed audiotaped messages. Newby was insistent on seeing the lama, and eventually, through the lama's wife, the plump matronly Madame K., was allowed a brief face-to-face. And what a face it was: Rampa was one weird-looking dude. Newby describes the lama as having a long nose, luminous, powerful eyes, a beard, a completely bald head and a high-domed forehead with a slight dent in it. By promising to show the lama in a more favourable light than the hatchet job of the *Daily Mail*, a photographer from the *Daily Express* actually managed to take some pictures. When these were being developed, the photographer said he was shocked to discover a kind of phosphorescent halo around the head. Maybe there was something to this aura business after all.

Hoskins – or his alter-ego Rampa – struck a goldmine with

The Third Eye. It became a bestseller in Europe and the United States, and was translated into a dozen languages. Rampa followed up with another book, *Doctor from Lhasa*. He acquired a cult following. He received an enormous amount of fan mail from readers. He counselled his new-found followers in spiritual matters. He milked his fans, indulging in spin-off marketing, shamelessly selling meditation robes, incense, touchstones, audiotapes with meditation discourses, you name it. From being an unemployed layabout, Hoskins had metamorphosed into a very rich guru, held in high esteem by scores of readers. The publishers were laughing all the way to the bank.

Despite his success, the three-eyed lama was evidently rankled by his detractors. His behaviour as a writer would have been perfectly acceptable if he labelled his works 'fiction', but Rampa stuck like Velcro to his identity as a real lama, probably because this is what gave the books their credibility and authority (if written by an ordinary Englishman, the sales figures certainly would not have been the same). To confound the sceptics, Rampa penned a third book *The Rampa Story*, published in 1960 in which he tried to weasel his way out of monstrous contradictions. In this book, he made the startling claim that he was a Tibetan lama who had transmigrated – shifted souls – into the body of an Englishman after his own body had been rendered useless through illness and debilitation. In other words, he was the spirit of a Tibetan lama who had possessed Hoskins' body, and Hoskins had been snuffed out.

In *The Rampa Story*, he claimed he had left Tibet in 1927. After lengthy voyages as a Tibetan monk and doctor through wartime China, he was captured by the Japanese, tortured, and sent to Hiroshima. When the atom bomb was dropped on Hiroshima in 1945, Rampa seized this opportunity to escape (*are you still with us?*). He made it to the Russian coast, and then to Moscow, and set off across Europe to deliver a stolen Mercedes. When encountering various Mafia types with knives or broken bottles, he simply dispatched them with his knowledge of martial arts, learned from the great masters of the East.

Then he went to America, and finally back to Tibet, which he found occupied by the Communists and not to his liking – monks and nuns were being killed and tortured. So while in a deep meditative trance in Lhasa, Rampa succeeded in travelling by astral projection to London, England. Here, in the summer of 1949 (astral travel allowed him to journey back and forth in time), he had taken over the body of an unemployed Englishman. The Englishman was sick of being unemployed and was only too willing to give up his body, but forewarned the good lama about the extreme mental unease of being unemployed. But no problem for the lama. Racking his brains about how to make a living, the Rampa-inhabited-Hoskins-body hit on the brilliant idea of writing a book, which was, of course, *The Third Eye*.

More howlers were to follow. It was revealed that the initial 'T' in his full name (T. Lobsang Rampa) stood for 'Tuesday'. And how exactly had Rampa acquired this English first name? Was that the day that the Tibetan lama had taken over Hoskins' body? Was it the day he had a hole drilled in his forehead? Wisely, Lama Rampa's publishers chose to ignore the full name in the interests of higher sales figures.

Rampa continued to insist that all the accounts he wrote were true. He might have succeeded longer had he not had his name attached to a book titled *My Visit to Venus*, in which he describes how he travelled to the red planet, which was inhabited by an advanced race. The book was cobbled together by a publisher from articles Rampa wrote for a UFO magazine. The tome is out of print and rare – apparently Rampa himself had second thoughts about releasing it and tried to prevent its publication. Astral voyages to Tibet were one thing; interplanetary voyages were quite another. Even hardcore Rampa followers had their doubts about this one.

Meanwhile, Rampa – or Dr Rampa, or Lama Rampa, Dr Kuan-so, Hoskins, whoever – continued to crank out the books. There are nineteen of them in total, with sales in the millions. *Living with the Lama* was supposedly dictated to Rampa telepathically by his cat, Mrs Fifi Greywhiskers (*Bejasus! Where can I get my hands on a cat like that?*). Earlier on in his writing career, around 1960, Hoskins and his wife had fled Ireland for the Land of the Red

Indians (Canada), where he is rumoured to have founded an ashram outside Toronto. Here the trail grows cold. Rampa died in Calgary, Canada, in 1981: his wife continued to write books under his name.

The Third Eye has, to date, been reprinted more than thirty times, and it is one of the most widely read books ever written about Tibet. Rampa's (posthumous) fan clubs continue to flourish in cyberspace. To this day, librarians and booksellers are mystified about where to file Lama Rampa's books: under religion, mysticism, occult, paranormal, thriller, fantasy, science fiction or autobiography? The best solution yet seen: New Age.

Here's a peculiar connection: Rampa's oddball brand of metaphysics seemed to have a lot in common with Theosophy, a kind of New Age forerunner. It's more than possible that Rampa cannibalised material from the Theosophists and regurgitated it. Rampa was not the first to claim an astral voyage to Tibet. Not by a long shot. Back in the 1880s, the Russian spiritualist Madame Blavatsky had danced the astral fandango timewarp. The key founder of the Theosophical Society, she claims to have visited Tibet, if not in person, then in spirit, for a period of seven years. She claimed that the Mahatmas, keepers of the ancient wisdom of the lost continent of Atlantis, lived in Tibet, where they congregated to escape increasing levels of magnetism produced by civilisation. The secrets of this lineage were archived in Tibetan monasteries. How did Blavatsky know all this? Well, she communicated with them telepathically. Through them via 'automatic writing' she produced *The Secret Doctrine* (1888), which is a monumental work of gibberish, running to five volumes. Madame Blavatsky was somewhat monumental herself: in later years, she became obscenely overweight. She faced a lot of public ridicule and was variously maligned as an impostor and a fraud, but her brand of mysticism continued to flourish.

The British invasion of Tibet in 1903–1904 sparked a new round of revelations from Tibet, with output on mysticism spurred by the demands of English editors. One big difference: these writers had actually set foot in Tibet. One striking similarity: they still churned out the same waffle. Expedition leader Francis

Younghusband himself claims he underwent a revelatory experience on his last night in Lhasa. Having survived the rigours of the Tibetan campaign, Younghusband was almost killed after being hit by a motor car in 1911, in Belgium. Whether as a result of the near-death experience of the motor accident, or the Lhasa revelatory experience – or a combination of both – he ended up founding several oddball societies in England including the World Congress of Faiths. He also wrote a book called *The Living Universe*, in which highly evolved asexual aliens inhabit the far-off planet of Altair. It was not, apparently, intended as fiction.

Younghusband's societies went nowhere, but Madame Blavatsky's Theosophical movement was influential in Europe and the United States. Whether charlatan or genius, Blavatsky wielded considerable clout in mystical circles. Among her followers was the French mystical writer and explorer Alexandra David-Néel and Russian visionary Nicholas Roerich. Roerich travelled far and wide on the Tibetan plateau in search of the Tibetan utopia of Shambhala, and of another Buddhist paradise known as Agharti. On a 1924 expedition through Mongolia and Tibet, a lama had told him that Shambhala was a great city at the heart of Agharti: Roerich was convinced that this place was linked to all nations of the world by subterranean tunnels. The Potala Palace was, in this scheme of things, linked by tunnels directly to Shambhala. Taking up Blavatsky's theme, Shambhala was depicted as the spiritual powerhouse of the world, with adepts forming an inner circle that secretly guided human evolution.

It's embarrassing but true, that Theosophical Society notions about Shambhala, leftovers from Atlantis, Aryans who once ruled the earth (and who had evolved from Atlanteans), and the underground tunnels, were highly attractive to the Nazis. Particularly engrossing was the prospect of an underground society of pure Aryans: Hitler is said to have believed in a race of supermen living underground. The Tibetan plateau was viewed as a repository of racial purity, long cut off from the influences of the outside world. In one of the weirder chapters in the dark, twisting history of Tibet, a special SS mission was dispatched to Lhasa in 1938.

Spielberg's film *Raiders of the Lost Ark* shows the Nazis hell-bent on a quest to unlock the secrets of powerful ancient relics, like the Ark of the Covenant. Seems that this is not far off the mark. Hitler, who was right off his rocker, dabbled in the occult, and relied heavily on astrology for auspicious timing when making decisions. Herr Himmler was the founder of the Ahnenerbe, or 'Ancestral Heritage' office of the SS. This bizarre institution carried out archaeological digs at various sites in Europe, trying to give scholarly credence to German racial superiority.

Tibet seems to have exerted a special fascination for the Nazis. The most famous Tibet explorer of the era, Sven Hedin from Sweden, was a fervent Nazi. A picture showed him shaking hands with Hitler after Hedin delivered the opening speech at the 1936 Olympic Games in Berlin. Also photographed shaking hands with Hitler was mountaineer Heinrich Harrer. Harrer later argued that he joined the Nazi party because he needed the sponsorship to get to the Himalayas on a climbing expedition, but in the same breath he described his SS membership as the biggest mistake of his life. At any rate, Harrer failed to come clean about this when he could easily have done so in his post-war book, *Seven Years in Tibet.*

The patron behind the 1938 expedition to Tibet was none other than Herr Himmler and the Ahnenerbe. Expedition leader Dr Ernst Schäfer and his five-man crew of 'scientists' and filmmakers bumbled their way into Tibet and reached Lhasa in January 1939, stayed a few months and left just a month before the outbreak of war between Britain and Germany. Naturally, the Germans were not popular with the British residents in Lhasa, nor were they particularly popular with the Tibetans: the Germans soon ran into trouble by arguing with mule drivers and slaughtering wildlife. In Lhasa they were stoned for taking unauthorised pictures during a religious festival.

Expedition motives were complex. There was definitely an element of spying: Schäfer made detailed maps of Tibet, which would come in handy if Tibet turned out to be a good site to launch attacks on British India. A bit of light ethnic research:

measuring up Tibetan heads to check for the origins of the Aryan race. There were rumours of large gold deposits in Tibet – always worth checking into. And who knows, maybe the expedition was looking for all those underground tunnels that lead to the power-base of Shambhala. And finally, there was a film to make – Ahnenerbe filmmakers shot a documentary called *Mysterious Tibet*, which was eventually released in 1943, complete with swastika images and propaganda about race (the film is still screened occasionally, minus the swastikas and Third Reich symbols, which were banned in Germany after the Second World War).

The German mission to Lhasa also came to establish relations with Tibetan nobles, to tell them that Germany was the most powerful nation on earth, and to swap swastikas with them. This made for good photo opportunities: there are pictures of Schäfer and other expedition members having tea with high-ranking Tibetans; in the background, hanging on the walls, are Nazi swastika banners. The swastika is actually an ancient Vedic symbol of longevity, peace and good luck. In Tibetan, the symbol is known as *yungtrung*. Early versions of the *yungtrung* were Bon, and were left-facing; however, Tibetan Buddhists changed the direction to right-facing (the same as the Nazi swastika). This auspicious symbol is often used on a tapestry in front of the throne of a high lama, but Tibetans today are reluctant to use the *yungtrung* in a Western setting, knowing what terrible meaning the Nazis have imbued into the symbol.

The Nazi party stole the swastika symbol around 1920: they set it on an angle with a white background, and gave it a very bad name, linked with genocide, death and destruction. The Nazis even stole the word 'swastika'. *Sva-as-tika* is actually a Sanskrit term: *sva-as* meaning 'thus it is', 'forever like it' – and *tika* meaning 'mark' (the dot worn on the forehead in Hindu custom), so the whole thing transliterates to 'the mark of immortality', or 'foreverness mark'.

That very positive connotation was reflected in early editions of Theosophy texts, which included the swastika in the seal of the society. In fact, Madame Blavatsky was one of the first Westerners to adopt the swastika symbol (understandably, the Theosophy

Society no longer employs this symbol as a logo). In India and Asia, Hitler has had no impact: the ancient Vedic swastika appears on a variety of products – matchboxes, soap and Pokemon cards – and the anticlockwise swastika is today used as the symbol of Falun Gong, the quasi-New Age sect in China.

Going back to the Theosophists as forerunners of Western New Agers, in the 1920s, wealthy Theosophist Dr Evans-Wentz journeyed from America to India, where he commissioned a translation of the text *Bardo Thödol*, better known as *The Tibetan Book of the Dead*. Dr Evans-Wentz added his own rambling Theosophical-type commentary, together with liberal footnotes. Improvising upon his handiwork and taking up the torch in the 1960s, was psychedelic guru Timothy Leary, who used the Evans-Wentz translation as the basis of his book *The Psychedelic Experience*, claiming the Tibetan manual was really a guide to tripping on LSD.

By this time, the obscure *Bardo Thödol* (unknown to most Tibetans since it was an esoteric Nyingmapa text recited as last rites) had been transformed into a kind of New Age Bible. By the time The Beatles took up the chant in the 1966 album *Revolver* with the track 'Tomorrow Never Knows' (*turn off your mind, relax and float downstream – it is not dying, it is not dying ...*) the arcane text was in danger of going mainstream. Snippets were being chanted, mantra-like, over the radio by John Lennon.

By the mid-1960s there was no need for anyone to consult Tibetan-lama-impersonators like Rampa, or take advice from Timothy Leary on esoteric Tibetan texts. There were suddenly hundreds of real live Tibetan lamas around. Before 1960, Tibetan Buddhism was an esoteric faith that jealously guarded its secrets. On the heels of the Lhasa Uprising in 1959 and the dramatic escape of the Dalai Lama, half the high lamas had fled Tibet to India and Nepal, and Tibetan Buddhism became accessible to the world at large for the first time. Key lineage holders – the Sakya Trizin and the Karmapa – escaped to India. Tibetan high lamas travelled abroad to establish new centres; Westerners flocked to India to study under the lineage masters, and continue to do so.

Like the civilisation of ancient Egypt, the mystery of the

pyramids and ancient burial rites of the Pharaohs, Tibet has somehow struck a chord with the New Age set. Most religions hate New Agers because they throw their belief systems for a loop (as in Madonna MTV operettas), but Tibetan Buddhism welcomes them. It needs them. Early in the piece – in the 1960s – Tibetan Buddhism was in danger of disappearing altogether, of being wiped out in Tibet. The faith needed all the converts and sympathisers it could muster. Perhaps the elements of Bon within Tibetan Buddhism – the built in elements of magic and sorcery – attract New Agers. The stuff about yogis meditating on beds of ice, clothed only in cotton; levitation; trance runners; astral projection.

It is said that Buddhism readily adapts itself to every culture it encounters. Of course, New Agers have customised Tibetan beliefs to suit. Look what they did to angels: they turned them into personal guardian angels. So what have New Agers done to Buddhism? Made it more instant. White Buddhism, a brand of instant karma. Gone-too-far-west-Zane-Grey Buddhism.

Some very strange permutations of Tibetan Buddhism have taken place in the West. Exiled Tibetan Kagyu Lama Chogyam Trungpa was dubbed the 'cocktail lama' due to his scandalous predilection for women and wine, and his highly unconventional personality. He established training centres and retreat communities in Scotland, where he promulgated his 'crazy wisdom' visionary approach, and adopted counter-culture values of free sex and psychedelic drugs. In 1970 he shocked even his students by marrying a young aristocratic English woman and flying off to North America. He gained a large cult following in the United States, establishing a series of dharma centres under the banner of Shambhala International. The eccentric Chogyam Trungpa increasingly acquired regal trappings – and dress – connected with the mythical kingdom of Shambhala. He surrounded himself with an inner circle of courtiers and bodyguards. He died in 1987, aged forty-eight, of an alcohol-related disease.

The Tibetan Book of the Dead, meanwhile, refuses to die. It just gets more and more translated. I recently saw in a catalogue that you could get a compact edition of Chogyam Trungpa's translation of *The Tibetan Book of the Dead* together with a 'Tibetan Dead Hot Sauce Pack'. Or you could buy a recording of Trungpa's translation, read by Richard Gere, the world's second-best-known Tibetan Buddhist celebrity.

Buddhism is cool. Look at 'Zen', a modern buzz-word. Look at book titles: it all started with *Zen in the Art of Archery*, which led to *Zen and the Art of Motorcycle Maintenance*. There are now so many *Zen and the Art of ...* book titles that Robert Pirsig could have started up a publishing empire comparable to the Dummies series. Zen and the Art of Skin Maintenance: Hydra Zen is a brand of skin moisturiser from Lancôme. Cool and Zen is the name of a super-soft paper tissue that brings out 'the true nature of skin, giving you the chance to lead a new existence'. *Dakinis* in bikinis: Disco Zen is a fashion line, a juxtaposition of bikinis and kimonos; Zen Sport by Danskin is a line of spandex tank-tops and waist-cut trousers. Zen in a bottle: Black Zen is tea-based fragrance from Bulgari that is supposed to embody 'the Zen concept of thinglessness'. Buddhism is about being awake, about waking up. So how about the Zen alarm clock? The clock is set in a triangular hardwood case, and makes a gentle Tibetan-bell-like chime at the appointed hour. The face has no numbers – it displays a soothing sand garden pattern or a Hokusai wave design.

*****

All of the above might explain how I came to be locked in heated discussion with an intense man from California over the origin of a set of exercises called 'The Five Tibetans'. He is trying to tell me that this yogic-like practice derived from Tibet centuries ago, and I am trying to tell him it came from America quite recently. The American yoga instructor who devised the exercises, based on energising the *chakras*, wanted something that sounded ancient and catchy, so he simply added the word 'Tibetans'. The exercises themselves are of Himalayan origin, more likely northern India or Nepal. Just as silly is the concept of Tibetan Power Yoga, which is most likely not Tibetan at all.

The café we're sitting in lies in the heart of McLeod Ganj, the New Age capital of India. Westerners flock in. Like 'The Five Tibetans', a lot of the New Age offerings have little or nothing to do with Tibetan Buddhism, but appeal to spiritual shoppers anyway. McLeod offers a mystical New Age smorgasbord – a pot-pourri of courses: *Holding the Wind, Channeling, Biorhythm, Magnetic Healing, Polarity Massage, Rebirthing, Palm Reading, Face Reading.* You have to wonder if you go to one of these courses whether someone will come at you with acupuncture needles, a TV remote control device, or a big magnet. I conjectured about other courses: *Releasing the Wind, Feeling the Power, Coming to Grips with Your Inner Slippery Self, Sorting Out Your Past Lives, Finding Your Inner Idiot, Compassion for Dummies, Tantra for the Serenely Challenged.* And there's a lot of potential for 'how-to' books. *How to Strike it Rich by Reading Auras, The Idiot-savant's Guide to Tantra. Karma Clearing – how to erase past-life records that can block you.*

People in McLeod are walking around carrying books like *An Astral Body*, or *Meditations for Women Who Do Too Much*. Actually, the last one belonged to a middle-aged European woman I met, who was taken with the wonder of it all. She's done a Reiki course and a ten-day meditation retreat and speaks in glowing terms of her personal transformation. It has obviously relaxed her to the point where her judgement is impaired. We walk past an Indian presiding over a tangle of umbrella spokes.

'It's magic what he does – miraculous – he's *reincarnating* umbrellas,' she whispers with stars in her eyes.

And so it goes. In cafés, you would overhear snippets like: *Oh, your friend has cancer? No problem – get him to go and see the rinpoche. He'll take care of it.* Or: *The guru is going into complete silence in April – I have to take the course before then.* McLeod is full of spiritual junkies: it is the New Age navel of India, and whether he likes it or not, the Dalai Lama is a king figure to all these New Agers, as much a leading light or icon as he is to the Tibetans. The Dalai Lama himself has decried any such behaviour as silly, saying he should not be worshipped as a Living Buddha. But he can't escape the connections.

*****

Worship of the Dalai Lama is one of the main obstacles to the introduction of democratic values in the community in exile: Tibetans simply cannot bring themselves to disagree with what the Dalai Lama says. He sticks to his plan of asking for autonomy in Tibet, leaving defence and foreign policy to the Chinese – but most Tibetans want independence.

'Let me put it this way,' said Jamyang Norbu, quaffing his Thunderbolt Lager. Jamyang is a staunch proponent of *rangzen*, Tibetan independence. 'If the Dalai Lama were to say tomorrow that he wanted full independence for Tibet, the Tibetans would have absolutely no hesitation in joining him. They would back him up a hundred per cent. But when he calls for autonomy in Tibet, they flounder – they are not sure about that – but they go along with what he says anyway.'

This is where followers get confused: disagreeing with the Dalai Lama is taken as a mark of disrespect. Jamyang shows me an essay he wrote about this phenomenon. The essay is titled *The Opening of the Political Eye*. The title is a take-off on the first book on Buddhism written by the Dalai Lama, called *The Opening of the Wisdom Eye*, originally written in Tibetan in 1963 and published in English in 1972 by the Theosophical Society.

Something clearly got warped in translation, or perhaps it was a deliberate ploy on the publisher's part to attract attention, in a Rampa-ish vein. The book could have been titled *The Essence of Dharma* or *The Essence of Wisdom*: the introductory preface says it is a 'clear Wisdom Eye-opener', a concise, scholarly approach to explaining the essence of the dharma. A decade later, the book was re-issued by Wisdom Publications under the title *Opening the Eye of New Awareness*.

But back to *The Political Eye*. 'It's just not open,' says Jamyang. 'Tibetans don't give a toss about democracy.' The Dalai Lama tried to introduce democratic reforms, but nobody took him seriously. He says he doesn't want to be a politician, he wants to devote himself to his religious role. He says that if he were to return to Tibet, he would hand over the running of the place to his ministers – he has little interest in politics. But the Tibetans won't let him step down from the political role. This leads in turn to another problem: dependency. Because of great dependency on the Dalai Lama as a figurehead, the Tibetans would be lost without him.

Jamyang is bull-necked middle-aged man with a drooping moustache. He's an iconoclast who has little patience for New Agers and others who distort the Tibetan culture or cause, or warp it for their own purposes. There is even a term coined for this phenomenon. It's called the 'Shangri-La Syndrome', denoting Westerners who seek answers to a variety of personal questions by means of the Tibetan cause. Jamyang calls the phenomenon a kind of 'New Age colonialism' – Westerners who embrace the Tibetan cause as long as it suits their own agenda. They avoid the reality of the situation and offer cosmetic help. Ironically, most Tibetans have never heard of a place called Shangri-La: they know only of its prototype, the mythical kingdom of Shambhala. Regrettably, the powerful legend of Shangri-La has clouded Western thinking on Tibet itself to the point where the region is viewed as an unreal place. A steady stream of writers have embroidered this vision, compounding the problem.

Lobsang Rampa would be a prime early example of the Shangri-La Syndrome; he was unemployed, and Tibet's problems solved his problems. Tibetan Buddhism has become a spiritual playground for Westerners, Jamyang says, a religious Disneyland.

★★★★★

At Amnye Machen Institute, an entire wall is plastered with a complete set of US Defence aerial maps of Tibet. This is one of Jamyang's most ambitious projects: to drag Tibetans headlong into the modern world by producing the first cartography from a

Tibetan perspective using computers. And to take on the Chinese, who interpret maps from an occupation point of view. The Tibetans refer to Greater Tibet, which is a much wider area embracing former Kham to the east and Amdo to the north-east. The Chinese refer to the much-reduced area they call the Tibet Autonomous Region (TAR), created in 1965. There is nothing autonomous about the region at all; large chunks of Kham and Amdo were carved off and donated to the neighbouring Chinese provinces of Gansu, Qinghai, Sichuan and Yunnan. And the Tibetans are not the only ones upset by Chinese cartography: India, Vietnam and half a dozen other neighbouring nations are up in arms about Chinese interpretations.

Jamyang sounds off about the battle of the cartographers and shows me a bank of computers he has acquired for use in map layouts, book layouts and other graphic design. He's had a lot of trouble finding sponsors to purchase computers. Sponsors imagine Tibetans hunched over looms weaving carpets, not sitting at computer terminals. Back in Tibet, monks are still inking woodblocks to run off sacred texts, and artisans are chipping mantras into stone; here in Dharamsala, they are creating CD-ROMs with Tibetan text. Jamyang is training staff to produce CD-ROMs in Pagemaker and Quark. Making the leap from woodblocks to Pagemaker: Jamyang says the Tibetan language lends itself quite easily to the computer screen. Any Western keyboard can be configured to take the elegant Tibetan alphabet, which is more than you can say about Chinese characters. But computer work in Tibetan is mostly used in re-printing ancient religious texts, not for translating modern works, says Jamyang.

Jamyang is best known as a polemic essayist, but he also makes forays into fiction. In fact, he was following up on the missing years of Sherlock Holmes, writing a book titled *The Mandala of Sherlock Holmes*. Conan Doyle, evidently sick of writing about Holmes and Watson, decided to kill his famous character off. In 1893, locked in battle with arch-enemy Professor Moriarty, Sherlock Holmes was written off, plunging over an abyss to a watery grave in the Swiss Alps. But later, due to popular demand (and a five-figure sum paid by a magazine), Conan Doyle resurrected Sherlock Holmes, who told Watson, 'I travelled for two years in Tibet, therefore, and amused myself by visiting Lhassa, and spending some days with the head lama.' It's odd that Conan Doyle did not write about this interlude himself, given that he had a deep interest in the occult and wrote a two-volume *History of Spiritualism*.

So what was Sherlock Holmes doing up there on the Tibetan plateau exactly? Well, according to Jamyang, he was involved in sorting out intrigue over the manipulation of the Dalai Lamas by their guardians. The ninth to the twelfth Dalai Lamas all died young under suspicious circumstances and were rumoured to have been poisoned. Real power was wielded by the Regent. Would the young thirteenth Dalai Lama survive assassination attempts by the Chinese delegation and live to rule over an independent Tibet? Sherlock Holmes was on a mission to save him. The climactic battle between the forces of good and evil, which takes place at the Ice Temple of Shambhala, is written up in a chapter called 'The Opening of the Wisdom Eye'.

McLeod's foggy streets under monsoonal conditions could easily double for a pea-souper in Holmes' London. And that's the damp reason the British were probably attracted to McLeod in the first place.

★★★★★

Once a year in Dharamsala, TCV Day takes place. That's when the students from the Tibetan Children's Villages around Dharamsala all get together at an open-air stadium to stage a parade, a display of callisthenics and to perform Tibetan opera. Thousands of children are marshalled and choreographed to form human chains, resulting in messages (in English) which read LONG LIVE HIS HOLINESS, or WE SALUTE OUR MARTYRS, as viewed from the section where dignitaries are seated, foremost among them being the Dalai Lama.

This year the dignitaries and the Tibetan audience witness a piece of choreography that has never been on the programme before: the Dance of the Twenty-one Taras. Tara, the protectress of Tibet, is said to have twenty-one manifestations: wrathful, serene, wise and so on. The medieval 'Hymn of the Twenty-one Praises to Tara' is well known to Tibetans: it is chanted in Tibetan monasteries and nunneries. The dance, however, is of very recent origin – it was devised in Hawaii, and is performed by women from the States. Bored with just reciting the songs in seated meditation, a woman in Hawaii devised a dance version. She then shared this with other women, and presto, the choreography ensued, with each manifestation performed by a single dancer.

At TCV Day something must've got lost in translation, or maybe the music is not amplified enough. The dancers, in long billowing dresses, form a large circle. Then, like marionettes, each performs a version of Tara. The thing drags on much too long. In any case, the whole point of the dance is somewhat lost on the audience. Among the Tibetans, you come up against a major problem: the only ones who perform sacred dance among Tibetans are lamas. Sacred dance is an all-male prerogative. Perhaps the female version might be misconstrued as having erotic overtones, which would be unbecoming for nuns. It's true that other Buddhist cultures, like the Cambodians, have sacred dances performed by females, which are erotic. The choreographers of the Tara Dance apparently horrified the keepers of Dolmaling Nunnery when they volunteered to teach the nuns.

★★★★★

My time at Norbulingka Institute is drawing to a close and my replacement, Lesley, has arrived to take over teaching duties. I am feeling jaded, worn out with battling over petty matters with the administration; she is fresh and idealistic. And though I hint at the obstacles, I don't want to take away that energy. I haven't got the heart, either, to tell her about the occasional visit by scorpions at the guesthouse, which is where she will be staying. Maybe she will find out in the shower one day.

Changing of the guard: the time has come for me to say goodbye to the students and staff. They arrange an impromptu farewell dinner: everybody from the principal down gives speeches, which makes me pretty uncomfortable because I don't like the formal setting. But suddenly the speeches are over, and the principal departs. Tashi stands up and starts singing a *cappella*. Everybody is clapping along. Let the games begin! There is a raucous round of musical chairs, during which two chairs are destroyed, and we introduce the Limbo Dance, which everybody quickly catches on to. More singing, more dancing, more breaking of chairs. It turns into a pretty wild night.

The next day I load my duffle bags into a taxi for the final trip up to McLeod. The principal comes forward and places a *khata* round my neck and shakes hands. The students come up one by one and add *khatas* until I have a whole neck-load. Wreathed in *khatas*, I slip into the taxi and bid farewell. It's a wrenching moment, but I know I will see these students again.

★★★★★

There's one last stop in McLeod. An invitation to the premiere of a BBC documentary proves irresistible. It is called *Shadow Circus*, profiling CIA involvement back in the 1960s. A lot of the material has been de-classified, which means that the reporter is able to interview key CIA agents in the United States, as well as long-retired Khampa guerrillas, living in abject poverty in Nepal. The Americans called it 'Operation Circus', with codenames taken from clowns. Remarkable footage taken by the Khampas themselves shows an attack on a Chinese truck convoy. Spliced in is rare footage, somehow unearthed in archives in Moscow, showing the Chinese arriving in Lhasa in 1951 on camels. But the most remarkable thing about the documentary is that it has been made by a Tibetan. Tenzing Sonam and his Indian wife, Ritu Sarin, have produced several documentaries for the BBC on Tibetan subjects. After the premiere, I talk to him. Yes, he says, you can count the number of Tibetan filmmakers on the fingers of one hand.

★★★★★

I am going to make my break: to move along to the other end of the Himalayas to Bhutan. Through a travel agency, I arrange a ride in a minivan to Delhi, sharing with another passenger, a woman. I don't meet the mystery woman till the morning of the departure.

Shssssh! she cautions, apparently meditating on the sunrise and the mountain views. The minivan winds down the hill with the dramatic sunrise. When we finally exit from the mountains, she breaks out of her reverie and starts to speak. And doesn't shut up for the next two hours. I am riding with one of the Taras who came to perform in Dharamsala. Her name is Marcia. She speaks about the super energy level that comes from being on a whirlwind tour with the other Taras, visiting a dozen holy sites in India and Nepal. So much energy is crackling around that she can't handle it, and decides to take a short break from the group to find herself again, to commune with the mountains. I get an earful of babble about meeting an oracle, about meeting an incarnate lama, about being initiated at some arcane ceremony. At the end of which Marcia confides in a whispery voice: 'You know, I think I'm a Buddhist.'

'Oh my stars! Really?' I respond.

She shoots me one of those 'Which-planet-are-YOU-from?' looks. What kind of cretin are you? She strikes me as the sort who frequents New Age bookshops, browsing for hours at the shelves on Goddesses or Angels.

I discover that this woman doesn't trust everything entirely to eastern philosophy. She carries a massive bag of medicines obtained from her local chemist back in California. Every so often, she reaches into the bag and takes some pills. It seems she takes pills even if she feels fine, just to make sure, a kind of medical roulette. Some pills are vitamins, others for malaria, for dysentery – the list goes on. And the huge suitcase in the back is, I discover, full of bottled mineral water, which she brought in from the States.

★★★★★

AN EYE-OPENER

Back at Delhi airport a security guard refuses to let me through the door. 'You don't have a ticket,' he says. 'It's waiting for me at the Druk Air counter,' I tell him. 'Sorry, no ticket, no entry,' he says, waving his machine gun in my face to emphasise the point. This is all part of overenthusiastic anti-terrorist security measures. I wave like a windmill to attract the attention of the counter clerk at Druk Air. No luck. I shout. Eventually, he notices and makes his way over: 'Ah yes, Mr Buckley – your ticket is here.' Because my application was a special deal, waiving the customary US$200-a-day tariff for tourists, it was also a low priority to process. After six months of paperwork, faxes and cajoling, I have a ticket. Which also means I have a visa waiting on arrival in Bhutan.

12

IN DRAGON COUNTRY

Under the spell of Bhutan

Out of the porthole looms a navigation landmark that I've seen before from the air: Mount Everest. The flight from Delhi is aboard the world's smallest national carrier, skirting the Himalayan giants before plunging into one of the world's most reclusive destinations, the tiny kingdom of Bhutan. The entire Bhutanese air fleet consists of two BAe-146 jets, both blessed by lamas. They need the benediction; Paro runway rates as one of the globe's trickiest. The plane banks sharply above mountains and drops into a valley of rice paddies, skimming over a hilltop temple and landing abruptly on the short tarmac.

Right away, from the traditional-style buildings at the airport, you know you've arrived somewhere extraordinary. It's a modern runway, yet distinctly Bhutanese. A row of prayer flags is flapping in the breeze. Do these act like a wind sock for pilots? I am grinning from ear to ear – *I've made it!* Stopping to snap a few pictures, I disembark and get the precious Bhutan stamp in my passport. But they stamp in two weeks instead of the four weeks I want.

Prayer flags flapping in the breeze. Bhutanese-style terminal building. Must write that down. I'm supposed to be the brochure writer on this scouting trip. Shelley waves. Shelley is the tour consultant who orchestrated the reams of paperwork that got me into Bhutan. She's been invited to Bhutan to check out the lie of the land for birdwatchers, culture vultures and trekkers, and I've managed to get myself invited along too. Right now, Shelley is in a very dark mood. They sent her air ticket to Delhi. She had to argue her way onto the plane in Kathmandu. On top of all that, they lost her luggage. Two planes in the entire fleet and they lost her luggage! She was the last to get on the plane in Kathmandu; she had second thoughts about the luggage going down the conveyor belt – you know, that awful feeling when you wonder if you'll ever see those bags again. Her luggage ended up on the wrong flight, probably bound for Delhi, because the next flight booked on that counter was going there. She has only the clothes she's wearing.

There's a car waiting, courtesy of our host travel agent from Thimphu. It's a two-hour drive from Paro to Thimphu. Bhutan unfolds by the roadside: a land of wooden chalets set in dense pine forests. It looks like chunks of the Rockies or the Swiss Alps. It drifts by the window, dream-like. The capital, Thimphu, has no traffic lights, just a few policemen who perform graceful t'ai chi-like movements with white gloves. Not that there's much traffic to direct in this town of 45,000 anyway. In an age where Asian capitals have let their traffic run amok, Thimphu appears to be remarkably quiet, slow and sane. After the pollution and frenzied streets of New Delhi, this is nirvana for motorists.

We drive straight through town and out the other end (*That was it? That was the capital?*) headed for the exclusive 'suburb' of Motithang, where several of the royal family hang out. The hotel lies in the forested hills overlooking Thimphu, a large cottage made entirely of wood, with huge ornate fireplaces and high ceilings. In the foyer, greeting us, is a stuffed bear, standing on its hind legs and holding a tray of fresh-cut flowers.

It's the men who wear the robes in Bhutan; a knee-length robe called the *gho* is mandatory for males. The *gho* is a kilt-like garment, and some of the patterns are tartan-like. This is complemented by a pair of knee-length socks, often argyle, leaving you to wonder whether a regiment of Scots in kilts got lost here earlier in the century. The big question is: when Prince Charles showed up in Bhutan, what did he wear to dinner? A kilt? Because knee-length socks are in full view, they become something of a fashion statement in Bhutan. Men strut around in brazen hosiery, like Henry VIII. The women wear a graceful ankle-length gown (the *kira*), fastened at the shoulders with twin silver brooches. A fine can be levied for not wearing traditional dress in public, although exceptions are made if playing football or indulging in other non-robe-conducive activities. Army personnel and the king's regiment of royal bodyguards wear standard khaki trousers, probably because no enemy would take them seriously in robes.

Tashi, our assigned guide, tells us that the finest quality hosiery comes from New York. He ought to know – he used to smuggle argyle socks from New York, along with fibreglass archery bows until he got busted with a load of contraband socks at the Indian border. Rumour has it that the Bhutanese got a rude shock when they turned up for an international archery competition and found that technology had left them far behind with their wooden bows, and that fibreglass bows were much more powerful. Now the savvy Bhutanese use imported fibreglass bows in local competitions.

The top of the *gho* can be shuffled off, exposing message T-shirts, as we found out in a tiny bar we stumbled across in the back alleys of Thimphu. Three men who worked in the auto trade were sipping beer at the tables, *ghos* at half-mast, revealing T-shirts, flashy argyle socks and Reebok trainers. Before long we were drinking beer together. You come to a reclusive place like Bhutan expecting to have trouble communicating, but those educated in Thimphu speak excellent English and are keen to practise if chance should throw a native speaker their way.

Aspects of Bhutanese culture immediately reminded me of traditional lifestyles in Mongolia, and spoke of the cohesiveness of Tibetan-based culture. The men in both countries wear robes, the favourite sport is archery, and Mongolia's horse-head fiddle is a dead ringer for Bhutan's dragon-headed lute, the *damnyen*. And both nations issue their own whimsical stamps.

★★★★★

In the interests of producing better brochurese, I get to see a fair bit of the kingdom, and to ask a lot of questions. I imagine myself peppering the prose with phrases like 'the Last Shangri-La' and 'the Hidden Kingdom'. But I'm already having trouble with the adjectives. I've crossed out 'exotic' and replaced it with 'quixotic', for reasons that will soon become apparent. And I have discovered that a number of doors are closed to outsiders. Mainly the doors to temples. Some say this is because of fear of art theft; others say that foreigners do not wear the right clothing. The fashion police are at it again. At temples a new dress code comes in: in addition to wearing their finest *ghos* or *kiras*, men must wear a ceremonial scarf and women must wear a shawl. The more you delve into Bhutan, the more you realise things are not quite what they seem. Bliss in Shangri-La comes at a price: conformity.

We're off to see the takin. Strange to see a creature for the very first time. How to describe it? A cross between musk ox, bison, moose and deer. This large-bodied herbivore with a bulbous nose stands about three feet tall at the shoulder; its thick neck is short, so sometimes it strains to reach grazing areas, and other times it simply kneels on its front legs to dine on choicer grass. Even though it's a herbivore, the takin can be dangerous, and has been known to charge. Tashi feeds one of them thorn bushes through a wire fence. The beast munches the thorns with relish. Tashi is tall, wiry and reed-thin; his gangly form is emphasised by his *gho* and argyle socks. Put these two together – Tashi feeding the takin – and you have the makings of storybook fantasy. If a griffin or a dodo popped up at this point, I wouldn't have been in the least surprised.

The takin is protected – it is the national mascot. In fact, the hunting of wildlife is banned in Bhutan (although the king, who originated the ban, is reputed to have bagged his fair share in the course of royal shooting forays). Rare Himalayan fauna and flora are protected here in a scheme unprecedented in Asia, which qualifies as the world's most polluted and environmentally degraded area. Bhutan is all clean and green: an impressive 60 per cent of the country is forested by law, and some 20 per cent of the land area is set aside as reserves or national parks (by contrast, India's *total* forest cover has dwindled to 19 per cent of land area). The export of all logs and unfinished timber to India has been banned; no hunting is permitted in Bhutan, and the wildlife is fully protected. You can see why UN development planners love being posted here – things actually seem to work in Bhutan.

*****

To my great surprise, when we go to refuel at the pump, the petrol station building is constructed Bhutanese-style, with overhanging wooden eaves. The effect is startling: this is the first time I've seen ancient Tibetan-style architecture put to any modern use. An ancient-modern tension is created; I find myself staring in wonder at a petrol station. Tashi explains that by law all buildings, including apartment blocks, schools and hospitals, must be crafted in traditional style, with paintings of mythical animals or lucky symbols gracing exterior walls. Sometimes you even see snow lions painted on taxis. I saw a bus stop shelter that was constructed Bhutanese style with a twist: large prayer wheels were attached to it, so the commuter could spin them and send prayers heavenward while waiting for the bus.

This is better than Alice falling down the hole in Wonderland. A land with king, queens, ministers and monks, all in robes, and castles (*dzongs*), which serve as administrative complexes. Regulations about everything from wildlife to satellite dishes are promulgated by *khaso* (royal decree). The lost architecture of Tibet is preserved, but in a slightly different guise: since Bhutan experiences tropical monsoons, the flat roofs of Tibet are not practical here. The roofs are sloping. A distinctive triple-roof design can only be employed in a monastic or royal building. Architecture soars to new heights at majestic Tashichho Dzong, the seat of the national assembly, located on the outskirts of Thimphu. Most of the buildings are of recent origin, but they could be mistaken for structures that are centuries old.

Across central Bhutan, castles dominate main towns. Most of these fortress-monasteries were built in the seventeenth century, after the country was united by Shabdrung Ngawang Namgyal, a great religious leader from Tibet. The political system he created, a kind of feudal theocracy, lasted till 1907, and the *dzongs* still function today as district government headquarters. *Dzongs* are so central to Bhutanese life that the native tongue is called Dzongkha, the language of the *dzongs*.

The kingdom of Bhutan is roughly the size of Switzerland and seeks to be as neutral. In fact, so neutral is Bhutan that it sat through both world wars with most of its citizenry blissfully unaware of what was transpiring. The Bhutanese were, however, aware of the British invasion of Tibet in 1903–1904. Because of Bhutanese assistance in this venture, the British supported the establishment of a new monarchy in Bhutan in 1907, the Wangchuck Dynasty (the reincarnate lineage of the Shabdrung, by more than coincidence, seems to have later been snuffed out because of trouble with the monarchy). In 1910 the Bhutanese signed an agreement with the British, enjoying the status of a sovereign kingdom; in 1948, the second Wangchuck monarch signed a friendship and cooperation treaty with newly independent India.

By a stroke of genius, the third Wangchuck monarch landed Bhutan a seat in the United Nations in 1971, thus protecting the kingdom from a takeover by India, which had its eyes on it, and from the designs of China, which claims territory in Bhutan. Bhutan relies on the Indian army to patrol its northern borders and keep Chinese troops at bay. And Bhutan relies on the United Nations to monitor its environmental and other programmes, and provide aid. Relations between Bhutan and China are frosty; with Nepal, non-existent, so the kingdom is heavily dependent on India as a trading partner, though there is some trade with Bangladesh.

★★★★★

There's nothing traditional about television sets in Bhutan, unless you count entombing the tube in a wooden case carved Bhutanese-style. But Bhutanese domestic programming follows traditional guidelines: only one or two hours a day, broadcast in Dzongkha, with programmes either news-related or educational about the environment or health. Technology tangles with tradition. Technology tangos with tradition. Doing the techno tango. Just how far can you take this concept? Can you make mobile phones look 'traditional'? Can you make cars look centuries old? But think about this: monks in the Dark Ages spent years creating handwritten manuscripts, so why couldn't monks apply the same patience to creating Web pages?

Television broadcasting in Bhutan has a curious genesis. In a nation committed to preserving traditional values, the telly is seen as a powerful and evil influence, exposing Bhutanese youth to jeans, miniskirts and tank-tops (MTV), assorted flesh (Indian films), and some very strange ideas (*The Simpsons*). Richer folk in Thimphu have long had access to television via satellite dish, picking up Indian programming, but the dishes were not legal and could be confiscated until the World Cup final took place in 1998. The king permitted football-crazy residents to watch the final and dishes sprouted everywhere. The king himself is an avid fan. He used to play goalie, until he realised that none of his subjects dared score against him. The World Cup proved to be the point of no return: domestic programming was introduced the following year.

Another source of home entertainment in Thimphu is video. Shops that rent out videos from Bombay and Hollywood advertise their business with small posters. Business is brisk, with recent bootlegged tapes making their way in from Bangkok, courtesy of the Druk Air link to that city. In the iconography sweepstakes in Thimphu, a surprise contender is Leonardo Di Caprio. Leo wrapped in a kiss with Kate, Leo on the bow of the Titanic shouting *I'm the king of the world!* It's a toss-up between Leo and the king in some parts of the capital – the Leo poster is everywhere. And think about this: *Titanic* grossed more in 1998 than the entire kingdom of Bhutan did that year.

In a restaurant, I did a double take. What at first appeared to be a portrait of the king turned out to be a Bruce Lee poster from the film *Enter the Dragon*. But then it struck me that the king rather resembled Bruce Lee. And they're both heavily associated with dragons – the dragon warrior and the dragon king.

Unwittingly, I'd brought along the perfect gift for my travel-agent hosts: two videos from Canada, which I had shown at Norbulingka. One was the film, *The Bear*, a survival story told from the bear's point of view; the other was *Fly Away Home*, starring

Canada geese. My hosts were amazed how the animals in these films could be coached into being such flawless actors.

*****

By an odd coincidence, the first Tibetan-language film to premiere at the kingdom's grand total of three cinemas – and also on Bhutanese TV – is about the World Cup final of 1998. The film is *The Cup*, directed by Bhutan's only known film director, Khyentse Norbu.

The Cup is based on the true story of football-crazy monks at Chokling Monastery in north-west India, who fall over themselves trying to rent a TV set and satellite dish to watch the World Cup final. Most of the 'actors' play themselves. The Tibetan refugee shown in the film arrived two weeks before shooting began: he lost his brother and sister when they fell into an ice crevasse attempting to escape from Tibet over the Himalayas. The monastery abbot is played by the real abbot. In a dialogue with Geko (the head monk), the abbot is puzzled about why two great nations would fight over a ball. When he finds out the reward for all this is a cup, he is even more incredulous. He ponders, 'A cup … Hmmmm,' as he sips butter tea with a trace of a smile on his face.

Khyentse Norbu gets across the message that monks have their own passions and aggressions, just like everybody else. And they happen to love watching and playing football. This sets up tension between austere monastic rules and the thrills that go with viewing the World Cup. In its own irreverent fashion, the film raises the absurd question: which force is more powerful, religion or football?

Khyentse Norbu has no formal film training. He learned the ropes as special consultant on the set of Bernardo Bertolucci's *Little Buddha*, which was mostly filmed at Paro Dzong in Bhutan. The rest he gleaned from watching countless films. *The Cup* was shot on a shoestring budget – the monk-actors were not paid. The story is striking for its simplicity, wryness, honesty and candour. In 1999, 37-year-old Khyentse Norbu took his two lead actors to Cannes, where the film was a surprise hit (well, the subject was still fresh in the minds of the French, winners of the 1998 World Cup). He didn't receive any awards, but said that just getting there was an award in itself. This is the first director from Bhutan or Tibet ever to show up at Cannes. And he showed up in robes, because Khyentse Norbu is a rinpoche.

I later caught up with Khyentse Norbu for an interview. He was born in Bhutan and educated both there and in Sikkim. At the age of seven he was recognised as a reincarnate lama in a non-sectarian Tibetan lineage dating back to the nineteenth century. He is heir to a monastic seat in eastern Tibet, but has only briefly visited, because he finds it difficult to function under the Chinese regime. He travels on a Bhutanese passport, embossed with a double *dorje* design on the cover. He spends a few months a year in India; the rest of the time he is globetrotting, teaching at meditation centres worldwide, and still finds time to go into meditation retreats himself.

Of the handful of Tibetan filmmakers, Khyentse Norbu is highly unusual because of his revered status among Tibetans as a teacher. You have to put this in context: is it right for a rinpoche to make films? In old Tibet, definitely not. As with most modern advances (and new-fangled European ideas, such as football itself), anything to do with films was viewed with great suspicion by conservative clergy. In pre-1950 Tibet, modern advances and technology were seen as threats to spiritual life and traditional values.

If it seems like a contradiction to have a high Tibetan lama indulge in filmmaking, Khyentse Norbu doesn't see it that way. He has been asked many times how a Buddhist monk can be interested in making films. He answers that he can't see why not. He says, 'I think the problem is that many Westerners categorise Buddhism as a religion, which it really isn't. It's a study of life. Think of a scientist. Can a scientist be a filmmaker? There's no contradiction.' Of making a film, he elaborates that it is 'better to understand the power of this influence than be its victim ... Making a good film, I suppose, is a bit like doing good Buddhist practice. It all begins with an awareness of how we're conditioned.' Filmmaking becomes an extension of his teachings: by writing and directing a film like this, he says, he can reach far more people than by building temples. 'Films tell us a lot about who we are,' he says.

Khyentse Norbu sees film as dealing with another level of reality. And here he probes a concept that lies at the very heart of Buddhism – the concept that the realm of the senses is illusory. Buddhism speaks of two levels of reality, the conventional, functional level of self and phenomena, and the ultimate reality of the empty nature of things, in which self and phenomena lack any inherent existence. Film is at the junction of both levels of reality; it appears to be real, but it is not. The filmmaker is a magician: films are a type of sleight of hand on celluloid. The lights go down, and the audience surrenders to the make-believe. Film is an orchestrated illusion: it tricks the eye and the brain into believing that it is real. But it exists in a different dimension, intangible.

The Cup far exceeded Khyentse Norbu's expectations, prompting thoughts of making another, and giving him the credibility to pursue such a project – if he ever finds the time from retreats and teaching commitments to make another film. And just how provocative can Khyentse Norbu get? Well, he has a few ideas kicking around. One is a film about ... condoms. 'It's about birth control, about a village man who suddenly discovers condoms,' he says wryly. A film directed by a Buddhist monk about the pleasures of sensual life – almost erotic – might surprise a lot of people. But Khyentse Rinpoche takes it in his stride. The film would be shot in a village in Bhutan.

★★★★★

Meanwhile, back in Thimphu: after leaning on quite a few people and being obnoxiously persistent, I've wangled a visa extension, boosting my legal stay in Bhutan to a month. I keep kicking myself to make sure I'm awake and this is not a dream. It is the realisation of a dream. Bhutan has been the toughest place on my 'wish list' to get into.

Before 1962, the only way into Bhutan was on foot or with pack animals. The fall of Tibet to Communist China, consolidated in 1959, was a wake-up call for the Bhutanese: the third king started to modernise. In the 1960s, the first roads were built in the kingdom by India.

The coronation of the fourth – and present – king, Jigme Singye Wangchuck, in 1974, permitted a trickle of privileged Western visitors to enter Bhutan. But getting into the kingdom is not an easy prospect. Intent on preserving its culture and language, the Bhutanese government allows only entry to those on group tours, and levies a hefty $200-a-day tariff on each visitor, an amount that covers most land-based expenses, and keeps backpackers away. Bhutan sees only about 7,000 visitors a year, which suits Bhutanese officialdom just fine; they don't have the infrastructure to deal with larger numbers, and they see a great influx of tourists as a threat to their traditional values. Who needs a whole lot of foreigners barging into monasteries and firing off pictures?

Here's a nation with a difference: the king professes to be very concerned about the 'spiritual wellbeing' of his subjects. Something to think about: they don't count how many TV sets or radios or bicycles you have. They want to know if you're spiritually tuned up. The king's big thing is Gross National Happiness, which includes free health care and school education, and access to electricity and clean water. And the king is introducing telephones and Internet access. Maybe his title will be extended to: His Majesty, Light of Cyber Age. This is a place where folk still believe the earth is flat, not round with satellites in orbit around it. In the rural areas, they consult the local astrologer when making decisions on auspicious dates for travel or when to get married. The astrologer uses quite a different version of cyberspace. In joining the international community online, Bhutan is performing a remarkable technological leapfrog from medieval values right into cyberspace.

Life is disarmingly simple in Bhutan. Consider these vital statistics. Area: 18,150 square miles. Population: don't know, maybe 700,000. Number of radio stations: one. Number of colour magazines: one (Druk Air's in-flight magazine, *Tashi Delek*, whose title means 'welcome'). Number of newspapers: one. Embassies: two, plus one consulate.

Kuensel, the weekly newspaper, running to about sixteen pages, is printed in English, Dzongkha and Nepalese. The gravest concern in Bhutan right now, I discover from reading editorials, is the proposed introduction of a personal income tax scheme for the first time in the history of the kingdom. Though the tariff is modest, it is treated with great suspicion by Bhutanese folk.

★★★★★

The Dalai Lama has never been invited to visit Bhutan. An odd situation, you might think, especially as the main faith of Bhutan is Tibetan Buddhist. This may have a lot to do with the Dalai Lama's older brother, Gyalo Thondup, who stands accused of dangerous intervention in Bhutan. Gyalo Thondup, whose Chinese wife was the daughter of a high Kuomintang official, presented a double threat to the Chinese: from militant Tibetans and militant Taiwanese. Gyalo Thondup was connected with overseeing funds from the CIA and masterminding the Khampa guerrilla campaign from Mustang (depending on which sources you consult, he is also charged with misappropriating CIA money and trying to undermine the guerrilla campaign).

The Tibetan government in exile is very reluctant to talk about Bhutan. Relations soured between Tibetan refugees and the Bhutanese in the early 1970s. It appears that the Tibetan mistress of Jigme Dorje Wangchuck (the third king of Bhutan), attempted to usurp the role of the king's legal son and heir by placing her own (illegitimate) son on the throne. Reaction was swift: after the Tibetan mistress fled to India, all the Tibetans in Bhutan were rounded up and given the third degree. Some, like the Dalai Lama's adviser, were thrown in jail and the key was thrown away. Inexplicably, the Tibetan mistress was treated to royal honours by the Indian authorities.

Jigme Dorje Wangchuck died in June 1972 while on safari in Nairobi, Kenya, apparently of a heart attack. He was only in his forties. His son Jigme Singye Wangchuck ascended the throne in 1974 at the age of eighteen, at the time, the youngest monarch in Asia.

In a Thimphu curio shop, I spot a small Dalai Lama picture on the wall. The owner is Tibetan. He tells me there are three to four thousand Tibetans left in Bhutan, mostly living in special camps. You'll see them in the markets, he says. You can identify the women by their gowns and striped aprons – they don't wear *kiras*. And though by wearing Tibetan dress they break Bhutanese law, the garments are close enough that the Bhutanese are prepared to turn a blind eye.

★★★★★

It's not so much what you can see in Bhutan that surprises, it's what you don't see. There's no rubbish in the streets. There are no crowds of people like in India. People in Thimphu are remarkably friendly, polite and good-humoured for city dwellers. There are few beggars. There are no big billboards for Sony or Coca-Cola scarring the landscape. There are no plastic bags in use – these have simply been banned from the kingdom. No chemical fertilisers are employed. And driving out of Thimphu, what you see is magnificent forests and greenery, a great tonic after India.

Our 'scouting group' – myself, Shelley, Tashi and driver – head east of Thimphu by car. We're driving along the country's only east-west road, towards the town of Jakar in the Bumthang region, to catch the annual festival there. A little way out of Thimphu, we crest Dochu La, marked by a cluster of prayer flags. The pass offers a Himalayan horizon – a great string of snowcaps, including Gangkar Punsum, Bhutan's highest unclimbed peak. Idyllic pastoral snippets float by: most of Bhutan's population is engaged in subsistence farming, combining crops, livestock and forestry. Ubiquitous in these rural regions are wooden two-storey farmhouses with red chillies drying on shingle rooftops. And ubiquitous in rural regions are marijuana plants, which cloak the hillsides. Cows and pigs apparently fatten up by munching the leaves, so no wonder Bhutan looks dreamy – you're probably eating marijuana-saturated beef or pork.

At breakfast in our wayside inn, the driver and Tashi dig into *ema datsi* – chillies cooked in a cheese sauce and poured on rice, the staple Bhutanese dish. A kind of Bhutanese pizza, if you like, with a fierce after-burn. Bhutanese culture is distinct; it draws from India and Tibet, and yet ends up being neither of these. It is Bhutanese. So the Bhutanese don't eat *tsampa*: their staple is rice, which is more in keeping with India. The chillies are definitely Indian. Here's a twist: the Bhutanese eat *momos* (meat dumplings), which are Tibetan in origin, but they fill them with chillies.

The inn at Tongsa has what they call in brochurese 'old world charm' (there's no bath, toilets are outside). It's a family-run place, and the family kitchen is also our dining salon, decorated with hanging copper pots, a tea-churn, low tables and carpeted seats. Out of the windows are views of majestic Tongsa Dzong, one of Bhutan's largest monastic fortresses. Its spectacular perch on a mountainside was put to good use in the eighteenth century, when criminals were manacled, shoved into canvas bags and heaved off the balcony to plummet hundreds of feet into the river below. If he survived that fall, the criminal's penance was considered done. The more you delve into Bhutan, the more you realise that things are not quite as they appear.

It's not on the cards for us to gain entry to Tongsa Dzong, but just up the street is some local action, a round of long-range darts. The number one sport of Bhutan is archery, but a runner-up is this sport, using larger-than-normal darts that are launched like mini javelins. To me, this is mounting evidence that a regiment of Scots was indeed lost in Bhutan earlier in the century. Dart contestants take up positions at opposite ends of the village green: the target is a (barely visible) stake of wood. Crazy Bhutanese spectators dance around each target as the darts are hurled. These artful dodgers perform an exuberant jig if the thrower succeeds in the thousand-to-one odds of actually hitting the wooden stake.

With hands up in the air and elbows at right angles, the jig looks suspiciously like a Scottish highland dance.

*****

The Bhutanese follow a form of Tibetan tantric Buddhism: monastery or *dzong* courtyards are venues for annual religious dance festivals, which rank as prime touring attractions. Though religious by nature, these dance festivals, we discover, are also an excuse for the locals to get together, picnic and party, and indulge in archery competitions and long-range darts. And gambling. And to get sozzled on *chang* or beer.

To ward off evil forces and ensure auspicious happenings, lamas perform a series of masked or costume dances, among them, the Black Hat Dance and the Dance of the Terrifying Deities. Intermission means picnicking, where locals, dressed in their finest, get down to the serious business of consuming plates of chillies and cheese with their bare hands, and washing it all down with Bumthang Beer.

I accept only a little *ema datsi*, concentrating on the rice and avoiding the fiery chillies. Fortunately there are more familiar foods, excellent cheese and apple juice, produced with Swiss-backed technology in Bumthang. A man with a jester mask circulates, bopping women on the head with a large wooden phallus and cracking lewd jokes. All this elicits hearty guffaws from the picnickers. The Jakar Festival is notoriously phallocentric: this is all in aid of fertility blessings.

After stuffing ourselves we stagger back for the next round of dance, The Day of Judgement. This sobering number is actually more of a medieval passion play: dancers with wild animal masks chase a poor huntsman, a sort of Everyman figure. The dancers wear skirts of looped silk scarves and elaborate shoulder decorations; their masks are the same as those seen carved under the eaves of *dzongs* – griffins, eagles, blue lions, dragons and tigers – representing spirits of the underworld. Technically the huntsman is in a post-death limbo zone; the dancers chase him up a tree to bring him in for judgement. His life's deeds are contained in two bags of small stones, white for good, black for bad. Weighing up the pros and cons is the Lord of the Dead, seated on a throne, wearing a large mask embroidered with skulls, and holding a sword and a mirror. The spirits of the underworld look on. The jester tries to intercede on behalf of the hapless man on trial, but to no avail. At the end of play, the suspect goes to hell, I think, and all the Bhutanese rush over to the Lord of the Dead for a blessing. The man behind the mask is a real lama, and a highly revered one, judging from the amount of pushing and shoving going on. Tashi tells us there's a naked masked dance around a bonfire at night, but this is taboo for foreigners to watch.

★★★★★

Curiouser and curiouser! We first saw the huge phalluses painted on the walls of whitewashed farmhouses. These renditions are a shocking sight in a nation that is so prudish about any public displays of sexuality, like kissing. But in Tongsa another fascinating detail caught my attention: a crossed sword and penis, both made of wood, hanging from the eave of a building. And another. And another. It prompted this terrible pun: *the penis is mightier than the sword*. Actually, that's not far off the mark. Drukpa Kunley, the mad monk, used his penis to subdue evil spirits. Floating in both stylised and anatomically correct form, his penis adorns barns and farmhouses all over the country.

We make it to the tiny temple of Chime Lakhang on the most auspicious day of the year. There's a steady line of Bhutanese in their finest *ghos* and silken *kiras* hiking up to the hilltop location. Tashi reckoned we wouldn't get into the grounds, but not only did we get in, we were allowed to take photographs.

Chime Lakhang was built in 1499, and is dedicated to the Divine Madman, Drukpa Kunley, who lived from 1455 to 1529. Born in Tibet, Drukpa Kunley was trained as a monk, but veered away from traditional Buddhism in a rather shocking manner. He was an oversexed libertine. He drank a lot, he swore, he broke wind like a dragon. And he developed some highly unorthodox methods of exorcising demons.

Drukpa Kunley's mission in Bhutan was to destroy or enslave troublesome demons, even transform them into benign protector-deities. People in sixteenth-century Bhutan lived under the spell of animist superstition: it was Drukpa Kunley's duty – and pleasure – to battle the demons that cowed the Bhutanese. Sometimes he took on demons by using his penis as a battle weapon. And sometimes he exorcised demons from women using his penis. He was a portly man with a beard and a leer, who travelled everywhere with his dog Shachi. He wrote reams of pornographic verse – his songs had lyrics like: 'My meditation practice is girls and wine, I do whatever I feel like, strolling the Void.'

And so Drukpa Kunley wandered around Bhutan, fathering children and happily blending sacred and profane: he is once said to have tied a blessing string around his penis. He had children by nuns, who claimed they broke no vows because they had made love to a mad saint.

Drukpa Kunley's favourite pastime – archery – has been adopted as the national sport by the Bhutanese. At Chime Lakhang, pilgrims are blessed with his old bow and arrow, or hit on the head with an ivory phallus, then a wooden one, symbolic of Drukpa Kunley's prowess. They sip holy water and offer gifts of butter, wine, incense and small ngultrum notes (the currency of Bhutan). School children come to pray for good grades on exams. Women who have trouble conceiving visit for a special blessing – this is Bhutan's top pilgrimage spot for those eager to conceive.

A group of Americans – mostly women – arrive. They barely acknowledge our presence: they are completely absorbed in their visit. I notice two of the women are blessed with the phalluses at the inner sanctum of the temple. That can only mean one thing: they must have come for the fertility blessing. So a fertility tour for women who have trouble conceiving; that's a very original angle. Wonder how the brochure copy reads: *Having trouble getting knocked up? Get the blessing of the sacred penis of Drukpa Kunley. It's what Bhutanese women have sworn by for centuries …*

I later found out how Tovya Wager, an American tour operator, came to Chime Lakhang and the Jakar Festival in 1996 to seek a fertility blessing. At the time she was forty-six years old: within several months of the blessing she became pregnant. When she returned with her ten-month-old daughter, she brought along a few couples who, as it happens, were very interested in the special blessing. She advertised the trip as 'Fertility Blessing: Spiritual Bhutan'.

★★★★★

Back in Thimphu there are more celebrations, this time marking the king's forty-third birthday, at a downtown arena. The king himself is not present; we passed him leaving town in a convoy of Landcruisers. Kicking off the show is the Royal Army band – bagpipers in full regalia, with bright Tibetan boots, *ghos* and snow-leopard skins draped over their shoulders. They wear centuries-old iron helmets. Children in school uniform follow in a parade, bearing banners with *Long Live Our King!* and other slogans. There are displays of callisthenics and traditional dance, and much pomp and ceremony.

The king's face does not appear to be the same from one photo to the next. Comparing two photos, I notice one has been touched up – zits on face removed and receding hairline blurred. So someone has the job of retouching portraiture of the monarch. Job description: *royal visage enhancer.* There's plenty of work: photos of the king hang everywhere in Bhutan, in houses, shops and hotels.

Picture this: in a discreet private ceremony in 1979, King Jigme Wangchuck married four gorgeous daughters of a Bhutanese nobleman. You have to wonder how this was arranged; the king drops by on a visit one day, and says *Stunning! I'll take all four!* He had 'twins' the next year, a prince and a princess by different mothers. And the same in 1981. In a public ceremony at Punakha Dzong in 1988, when he remarried the four sisters in a formal public ceremony, there were eight (out of ten) royal progeny present, miraculously divided into equal numbers of princes and princesses. His Majesty is a touchy subject: every enquiry I have made about him has been met with total silence. Certainly nobody dares joke about him: the penalty for this, as in Thailand, is probably a lengthy jail sentence.

Because of the birthday holiday, the national flag, which features a dragon, flutters from all buildings in the capital. You're in dragon country here. Bhutan was so-named by the British. The origin of the English name is uncertain, although it may derive from Sanskrit, meaning 'land at the edge of Tibet'. It is also known as Drukyul (the Dragon Kingdom) because when a founding warrior first arrived on this soil from Tibet, there was a clap of thunder, a sign that the celestial dragon had spoken. King Jigme Wangchuck holds the title of Druk Gyalpo (Precious King of the Thunder Dragon); male and female turquoise thunder dragons entwine on the royal crest. The kingdom has taken the dragon concept to extremes, with the dragon logo appearing on everything from bank notes to cans of mango juice. At the Druk Hotel, you can even order a cocktail by the name of Fiery Dragon, based on its reddish colouring (though I reckon they should rename it Furry Dragon, based on what it does to your tongue).

Isolated as it is, Bhutan has some surprisingly Western ways. Basic education is free, the literacy rate is high, and English is the medium of instruction in schools. Bhutan is one of the very few South Asian countries to achieve the feat of universal primary education, which explains how, during the celebration, a boy is able to ask me with near-perfect diction: 'May I know your name, sir?' (*Michael*) 'And where is your village?' (*Vancouver*). 'Do they eat rice in your village?' (*Yes, lots*). 'What is the biggest problem in your village?' (*Leaky condominiums*).

'And what about Bhutan?' I ask him. 'What's the biggest problem in Bhutan?' 'Well,' he says matter-of-factly, 'we have terrorists in the south.' Which is true: Bhutan has what is politely referred to as 'the Southern Problem'. Bhutan must be the only country in South Asia that doesn't have a population problem (a sparse 15 people per square mile), but it does have major people problems. In particular, clashes with Nepalese settlers.

Nepalese immigrants were encouraged by the colonial British to work the lowland (southern) farms of Bhutan, but they did not integrate with the Bhutanese, nor learn the language. In 1988 a census revealed that Nepalese immigrants were threatening to turn the Bhutanese into a minority in their own country. Mindful of what transpired in the neighbouring kingdom of Sikkim (where a flood of Nepalese immigrants helped precipitate the deposition of Sikkim's ruler) the Bhutanese reaction was swift. The same year of the census, compulsory dress and conduct codes were brought in, Nepalese language was downgraded and immigration laws were tightened.

The population is thought to be divided into 50 per cent Drukpas (the original inhabitants), 35 per cent Lhotshampas (ethnic Nepalese) and 15 per cent other tribal groups. The king is not at all keen on a multi-ethnic Bhutan; he stresses a policy of 'One Nation, One People', by which he means the majority Drukpa ethnic group.

In the early 1990s, thousands of Nepalese were booted out, creating large refugee camps on the Nepalese border. Refugees recited stories of atrocities committed by the Bhutanese army and police, and spoke of whole villages razed to the ground. A pro-Nepalese militant group began targeting government officials and burning down schools, shocking in a country where most violent deaths only occurred from bear attacks. A group of armed insurgents attacked a truck and forced the driver to take off his *gho*, an apparent reaction to the introduction of new dress codes (those in the south claim the *gho* and the *kira* are too hot for tropical conditions). To add to these woes, tribal insurgents from Assam have spilled over Bhutan's southern borders to escape Indian army searches.

But in Thimphu we are far removed from the Southern Problem. We dance the night away at a disco downtown. It is actually a small bar where a dancefloor is improvised, as long as the authorities turn a blind eye. And keeping an eye on things is an undercover policeman who is a dead giveaway because he's the only one in the room wearing a *gho* and argyle socks. Since we are not exactly in public, the *gho* is not required dress here. The *gho* was not designed with disco in mind; the undercover man looks quite bizarre dancing to the strains of *I'm a Barbie girl in a Barbie world* …

★★★★★

Bhutan cleaves into three distinct geographic bands: southern lowlands, central area and northern highlands. It stretches from the frigid Himalayan snowcaps to the heat of the Indian plains, ranging from a dizzy 24,000 feet right down to a lowly 900 feet. The southern area is off-limits to tourists, and I've cut a swathe through central Bhutan, so that leaves the northern alpine region to explore. And there's only one way to go – on foot, with pack animals.

The first trek we cue up leads from Thimphu to Paro, a convenient end-point because Shelley will fly out from there. I will hang around in Bhutan for a few more weeks. Tsering is our guide, a strong hiker with a good command of English. Like Mustang, the whole show is carried around on horseback. Bhutanese nomads must think foreigners are a bunch of softies: hot tea is served to us in our tents at sunrise, and hotwater bottles are delivered before retiring to a cosy air mattress at night. Dinners are elaborate four-course affairs served in a mess tent.

The trek is short, only three days, but strenuous. It showcases terrific alpine scenery. The only other trekkers in sight are a school group, in a state of high excitement as they explore their own backwoods. We camp near the same temple located at a pass, and share the same campfire.

★★★★★

The National Museum in Paro is housed in a gothic-looking tower with walls several feet thick, and once served as part of the town's defences. The museum covers ethnography, costumes, fauna and flora, but the most striking part for me was the stamp display. The stamps are gimmicky: there is a 3-D series of

Bhutanese dance masks, a floral series imbued with real scents, a large holographic stamp issued to mark the twenty-fifth anniversary of man's first step on the moon. There are stamps that show Goofy and Donald Duck. There are silk stamps – miniature religious banners printed on silk – and a stamp in the shape of a miniature gramophone record that plays the national anthem.

A number of these stamps are obviously destined never to be glued to an envelope. They are intended to generate foreign exchange, a marketing ploy used by small nations like Monaco, San Marino and Mongolia. But the stamps have another rationale behind them; they establish Bhutan as a sovereign state in the minds of the world, and feature facets of Bhutanese culture. They are 'little ambassadors' for Bhutan, spreading goodwill for the kingdom.

The big question in my mind, as I strolled through this museum, was what would've happened if, like Bhutan, Tibet had remained independent? How well would it have fared with self-government? It was the same question that I'd asked myself in Mongolia, and it yielded similar answers. If Bhutan was any indication, Tibet would have done well, very well. Far better than it is doing under Chinese occupation (where, according to the Chinese, the economy runs at a loss, requiring huge subsidies).

A free Tibet would, like Bhutan, receive lots of foreign aid to develop its education system and healthcare facilities. It would attract NGOs. Tibet would develop a solid tourist industry, based on trekking and sacred festivals, like Bhutan. Tibet has a pristine environment as its trump card, and like Bhutan and Mongolia, it is very sparsely populated. Bird watchers would throng here; animal lovers would come for glimpses of the Tibetan wild ass and the rare Tibetan antelope. Westerners would come to study at its great monastic universities. Traditional building would expand greatly: new accommodation would be built in Tibetan style, new temples would be consecrated. Tibetan pilots sporting Ray-Bans would fly routes from Nepal, winging over Everest as the Bhutanese airline does. Like Bhutan, a Tibetan-run airline would produce its own in-flight magazine. Tibet would print its own stamps with Buddhist themes or Walt Disney characters, like Bhutan and Mongolia do – collectors would scramble for them. Spiritual seekers would be drawn to Tibet's peaceful mountains and fresh air, to its great masters and its festivals.

Talking of great masters, fresh air and peaceful mountains, Tashi took me on a hike to Tiger's Lair, several hours from Paro. It is so called because Tibetan mystic Padmasambhava landed there after crossing the Himalayas on a flying tigress. The year was AD 747: Padmasambhava's mission was to teach tantric Buddhism. The exquisite monastery of Taktsang Lakhang, perched impossibly on the cliff face, was built in his memory. It is thought to be one of the oldest *gompas* in Bhutan.

'In April this year it burned to the ground,' said Tashi. 'Nobody knows the cause of the fire, but we think it was deliberately lit to hide the work of thieves, stealing statues.'

'Will they build it again?'

'They have to. Taktsang is the symbol of Bhutan. It is one of the great holy places.'

Whether set deliberately or not, fire is a great problem in Bhutan due to the large amount of wood used in structures. Most of Paro village itself is new because of a devastating fire that whipped through in the mid-1980s.

★★★★★

On a much longer jaunt – a week of strenuous hiking – I set off from Paro northward, to see the sacred peak of Chomolhari, and to witness the rough-and-tumble lifestyle of nomadic yak herders. My guide is Tsering again, wearing his bright red Chicago Bulls cap (Do the Chicago Bulls have Himalayan distributors?) and a luminous yellow jacket, and carrying a big Bowie knife sheathed on his belt. Our horse handler is a real character, constantly chewing betel nut. The cook spends all his free time chasing local women up and down the valleys.

Soon we are hiking through pristine forest, with glacial-blue rivers to cross. The scene could've been lifted straight out of the

Canadian Rockies, except for one detail: a man having a bath. In the distance, Tsering points out a pit dug into the ground and lined with stone. It is filled with water from the nearby river, which would normally be freezing, but that temperature has been altered by heating up large stones on an open fire and placing them in the bath. The man is soaking up the morning sun, lounging around in the ingenious stone bath and taking in the fabulous views. We wave as we pass, greeting him in Bhutanese fashion by saying '*Kuzu Zampo!*'

Take me higher: sluggishness and fatigue set in when entering the 13,000-foot elevation zone. But any altitude-induced hardship from trekking vanishes when you see ethereal vistas like the snowcapped peak of Chomolhari. The hills are carpeted in rhododendrons which bloom in the spring along with the rare blue poppy.

Into this idyllic setting, inject some adrenaline. Suddenly, round a corner, a huge yak comes thundering down the trail. In a split second, I bound uphill and hide behind a treetrunk. Tsering has jumped down off the trail. It is a scene that you imagine could only happen in a Tintin comic. Just as we emerge from our hiding places, a second yak comes thundering through, followed by two breathless handlers who stop only long enough to profusely apologise for almost having killed us, and then set off at a blistering pace to catch up with their charges. Tsering explains that the yaks are not too happy about going to market in Paro because they have an inkling that market means slaughter; they hit the bull's-eye on that one.

More domestic animal drama: at our campfire that night we are joined by a man and his two sons who are looking for their horses. From what I can glean, this is a problem equivalent to the loss of a relative. Animals represent wealth, which in this case has walked away. The men have been hiking for three days on their quest.

Round the campfire, Tsering tells stories about the Abominable Snowman or *migoi*, and of the elusive snow leopard. Moving along to higher altitude the next day, we set off on a detour to find this cat. Fat chance of glimpsing one, considering the beast's legendary stealth and superb camouflage. Unless, of course, you are a herder. Our herder-guide says he's seen them, but in places he prefers not to see them – like chasing his baby yaks.

We do, however, encounter lots of unruly grunting yaks, and we sneak up on a herd of blue sheep. Snow leopards regard blue sheep as a kind of roving fluffy buffet. Looking at these animals through binoculars, I wonder how on earth they got the name blue sheep, since they are neither blue nor sheep – they are brown and white, and they more closely resemble mountain goats.

We get to see the likely lair of a snow leopard, the caves where they hang out. And we get to see some snow. At lunch, we huddle round an impromptu fire in the shell of a derelict building. Finally, I ask Tsering if he's ever seen a snow leopard. No, comes the answer. There's one thing he neglects to mention, which might explain why. It's something I discover later: snow leopards are mostly active at dusk and dawn. The rest of the time they spend lazing around on rocky crevices. Or sleeping.

13

HEADING FOR THE HILLS

In the troubled heart of Sikkim

I finally got to see some snow leopards – around the corner in Darjeeling. I travelled by car from Thimphu to Phuntsoling, crossing the border from Bhutan to India. Then off through the tea estates, cardamom plantations and villages, skirting Tibetan monasteries, to finally reach Darjeeling. Darjeeling Zoo is small, but remarkable because it specialises in Himalayan fauna. Among the rarer species are the red panda and the snow leopard, and there is a unique snow leopard breeding programme in operation.

I watch spellbound as a cub romps with its mother in an enclosure. The snow leopard occupies the top of the food chain on the Tibetan plateau. You'd expect a cat like this to make blood-curdling roars; instead, it makes plaintive mewing noises. This mottled greyish-white cat is incredibly agile. Its huge bushy tail lifts off the ground when sprinting to help maintain balance, and its cushioned feet are excellent shock absorbers. The cub twists and turns, leaps over logs, springs straight up in the air. The purpose of these agile movements is, however, all lost. It is genetically programmed to bring down its favourite prey, the blue sheep. But this cat, bred in captivity, will never get to chase blue sheep. Numbers of the elusive cat have dwindled to a few thousand on the Tibetan plateau. It is hunted for its pelt and for use in traditional Chinese medicine; its natural habitat is being encroached on by the clearing of forests for crops and grazing. The snow leopard will become as mythical as the snow lion. I am looking at a creature that is nearly extinct.

★★★★★

Out of the guesthouse window, floating over the top of Darjeeling's bazaar, is the Kangchenjunga Massif. The view is uninterrupted as Kangchenjunga, the world's third-highest peak, is only forty-five miles away. At certain times – dawn, dusk, by moonlight – the ethereal vista seems to gain power, making the spirit soar. And all this seen from a room that goes for $10 a day, including hot shower. This is a small family-run guesthouse, my favourite kind of lodging. You get to know the family this way, and grandmother makes a great security guard; she knows who is who. Downstairs is a cosy dining room, windows steamed up from the hearty food, where it's easy to meet other travellers, and there are several shelves of novels that can be borrowed.

I've come to Darjeeling because it is the gateway, both in terms of permits and transport, to the former kingdom of Sikkim. A few years earlier, entering Sikkim meant reams of paperwork in Calcutta or Delhi. Now it only requires visits to two offices in Darjeeling. My destinations in this region all revolve around Sikkim: Darjeeling and Kalimpong both once belonged to Sikkim, and I want to reach Pelling and Yuksum in western Sikkim, as well as Rumtek and Gangtok in the east. A glance at the map will show the strategic importance of the Sikkim region: it is sandwiched between Nepal, Bhutan, India and Tibet, and at various times in its history, all of them, plus the British, have occupied parts of Sikkim.

The cool mountain air is what attracted the British to Darjeeling. At an elevation of 7,000 feet, the area provides an escape from the heat of the sizzling plains, and associated illnesses, like malaria. The British first moved in around 1835, leasing land from the Maharajah of Sikkim to set up a sanatorium. It was then discovered that Darjeeling's climate and conditions were ideal for tea planting. Tea bushes thrived when introduced by the East India Company, so in 1857, the British blithely annexed the Darjeeling region and turned it into the summer seat of the Bengal government.

The British flocked to Darjeeling to recuperate, relax, play polo and send their children to the finest schools. By 1900 Darjeeling had the refinements of schools, a Gymkhana club, theatres, botanical gardens and a hospital. And its own toy train – the Darjeeling Himalayan Railway – a narrow-gauge engineering wonder, with a miniature steam engine winding up from Siliguri through ravines, switchbacks and great loops. Darjeeling had grown into an important administrative and political centre, dubbed the 'queen of the hill stations'.

Today, tea and tourism battle it out as the top income earners in Darjeeling, and rich Indian tourists come for their first glimpse of snow. While run-down colonial churches and hotels survive in Darjeeling, the biggest legacy of the British may be the schools, which form an important part of the town's economy.

Some of Darjeeling's early schools were highly unusual. In 1874 the British opened Bhutia Boarding School to provide education for Sikkimese and Tibetan lads resident in the region. But there was another less publicised reason. The British wanted to train Bhotias and Lepchas as explorer-assistants – interpreters, surveyors and geographers. The purpose of this was, ultimately, to explore the unknown terrain of Tibet using instruments hidden in prayer wheels, using rosary beads to calculate distance. The school met with limited success in this endeavour, but the Bengali headmaster, Sarat Chandra Das, became one of the greatest trailblazers in the exploration of Tibet. Disguised as a pilgrim, this British secret agent forged his way through to Lhasa in 1866. When the British invaded Tibet in 1903, they used geographic information derived from Chandra Das and the other Indian-trained 'pundits'.

Serving as an interpreter with the British expeditionary forces of 1903 was David Macdonald, son of a Scots tea planter and his Sikkimese Lepcha wife. Macdonald studied English and Tibetan in Darjeeling; by 1903 he had mastered an incredible seven of the north-east frontier languages. He went on to become the British Trade Agent in Gyantse from 1905 to 1925.

Today, you won't find a more diverse mix of students anywhere else in the Himalayas. In the streets of Darjeeling you see Nepali, Sikkimese, Bhutanese and Tibetan schoolchildren in groups wearing grey sweaters, red blazers or otherwise colour-coded according to the school they attend. The students come from rich families, sent by their parents from all over the region to study at colleges with stern gothic exteriors like St Joseph's (run by Jesuits) or Loretto Convent (run by sisters from Ireland). The school trade suffered during the 1980s and 1990s when Nepalese settlers, who comprise the biggest ethnic group, initiated a nationalist movement for a mythical Gorkhaland, with sometimes violent results.

It's odd to think that the Jesuits have succeeded in schooling the Tibetans to high standards, while the Tibetans have failed to establish such schools themselves. In the early 1960s, Canadian Jesuits from Darjeeling were invited to establish schooling in Bhutan, with an English-language curriculum. The best of the Tibetan administration in McLeod Ganj were educated at St Joseph's in Darjeeling (you can tell when they swear and say *Jesus!*). Jamyang Norbu was educated here. The third king of Bhutan was educated here. So was the fourth king, briefly, before he left for England.

★★★★★

Darjeeling must rank as one of the most pleasant places in India to take a stroll. In urban India, you have to understand, pedestrians fall into the absolute lowest caste, denied even the basic right to a pavement. This is the case in lower Darjeeling, which has seen a population explosion, with slum-like conditions. But upper Darjeeling has a walking street – the Mall – and a square – Chowrasta – off-limits to motorised traffic. The area is lined with shops, street stalls, old British shopfronts and hotel buildings, giving it the atmosphere of an English village. Except that the people bear almond-eyed Mongolian features – Gurkhas, Bhotias and Tibetans, and the original tribespeople, the smaller-bodied Lepchas.

I stroll around Observatory Hill, where, commanding the best views, are rambling English mansions that would not look terribly out of place in Brighton. The fancier ones have been converted for use as hotels or as exclusive residences for Indian administrators. I saunter back to Chowrasta Square, where I while away the afternoon by browsing at Oxford Books. Remember what 'browsing' meant before computers came along? There's an entire shelf devoted to Anglo-Indian writers, including Booker Prize winners Salman Rushdie and Arundhati Roy, and contemporary authors Vikram Seth, Anita Desai, Gita Mehta and Upamanyu Chatterjee. The stupendous stable of subcontinental writing would've amazed the colonial British who couldn't have foreseen what far-reaching effects their education system might have.

Walking along the Mall, I spot a street banner advertising a cybercafé. Later that evening, I trot off to investigate. It's a private business operating from the Red Rose Hotel, with two computers hooked up to a server in Calcutta. The owner of the operation, Hemant, is in the tourist communication business, offering fax, IDD calls, and now e-mail. He's been open barely a week, and I'm one of the first customers. It's a cosy office with a phone booth and photocopier. The thick aroma of incense pervades the air from offerings at two small shrines, one to Ganesh, the elephant-headed god (consulted before undertaking any new venture), the other to Lakshmi (goddess of wealth).

In the course of an hour I handle fifteen pieces of e-mail, an exercise that costs less than the price of sending a single fax to North America. Net-wallahs – purveyors of Internet communication technology – are beginning to surface in the damnedest places.

I'm laptopless because I want to escape from computers. But I have an even greater dread of the Indian post office. Time was, a few years back, you had to rifle through piles of mail at some horribly crowded corner called poste restante, and if you unearthed a dog-eared letter that was actually addressed to you, you would triumphantly jump up and down and crow: 'I've got a letter!' This is because poste restante is hopeless – half the time the letter is filed under your first name or your middle initial, or it goes to Lower Slobovia when it should have gone to Upper Pretoria. Or the clerk has sent it back to the sender the day before you arrive. But now you can pull it all out of cyberspace, plug right into a web-based e-mail address and come up with superbly organised letters, all arrayed in boxes and files.

E-mail, however, is a paradox for the traveller – you can be on the other side of the planet, and still be a few keystrokes away. You don't have to panic if you lose all those precious addresses as they're all safely embedded in the e-mail system. Here's the really odd part: cybercafé e-mail provides a novel brand of traveller angst – the anxiety to log on, the fear of losing it in cyberspace. Quite aside from the anxiety generated by the erratic behaviour of computers in Indian cybercafés (and the erratic behaviour of the servers), there's a certain sub-group of travellers who constantly check their e-mail: they're still plugged into the world they left behind. They rush in, backpack still on their shoulders, and log on. *Tune in, log on, zone out*, the mantra of the digital traveller. It's like watching television: once a week, OK; but two or three times a day, and you're turning into an e-mail addict, a digital junkie.

Worse still, some were uploading pages about their travels to a website back home, so all the folks could track them electronically. Techno-nomads is how they describe themselves. E-mail is so efficient that travellers are now counting on it to keep track of fellow nomads. Ever tried to find someone in India, a nation of a billion people?

I couldn't help overhearing some of these digital junkies when they chattered excitedly at a terminal. A couple came in, opened their Yahoo! e-mail account, and groaned when they saw eighty e-mails banked up (although secretly, they were probably quite pleased, if you measure your social worth by the volume of e-mail messages accumulated). *Look, for heaven's sakes, Paul's had a car crash. Oh my God, and Alison's had the baby, oh it's a girl! Look at that – a picture of the baby … Wow, and get this: Dave's divorcing Gail …*

★★★★★

Darjeeling, says the local tourist literature, 'is a place to steep yourself'. What they meant was drink in the views of Kangchenjunga and so on, but for a tea freak like myself, 'steep yourself' means many cups of tea, and possibly some hot baths. Or both together. Tea estates carpet the hills around Darjeeling, and the place offers the elixir in all its Anglo-Indian forms, except that is, for teabags.

There's a certain ritual involved in tea: more than a drink, it's a state of mind – what some call 'Tea Mind'. Drinking tea is all about serenity and slowing down, chatting to people, taking your time. So I took some time out to observe the rituals. I started at street level in Darjeeling and worked my way up the tea scale. I sampled sickly-sweet milk tea from an Indian street stall selling sweets and loose cigarettes – it caters to petty cravings. The tea is served in a glass, and if you don't drink it fast enough a skin forms on the surface, which turns your stomach. The tea is all brewed up in a big kettle – the leaves, the milk, the sugar – and then filtered into a cup. An intriguing variation at street stalls is ginger tea, which is *chai* with raw ginger and cardamom added to spice it up.

At Glenary's, a British-style bakery and confectionery shop, there are steaming pots of tea, and serve-yourself trays that you fill up with coconut cookies, jam tarts, apple pie or vegetable-filled pastries. A very dangerous thing for me to do – my eyes are much bigger than my stomach. Out the bay window, there are views of mighty Kangchenjunga.

Affording even better views is the nearby Planters' Club, where seventy-seven tea estates are managed from. But no tea is served at this snooty club – perhaps the growers are sick of the stuff and prefer to get sozzled on gin. On the front balcony an old Maxim gun is parked. Donated by a British regiment, it is immaculately polished. I do not have much time to take in the details – I am being chased around the premises by some official who demands to know my purpose in visiting. The airy dining hall is not the kind of place I could eat or drink anything; the ceiling is ringed with stuffed animal heads – tiger, blue sheep, bear, antelope. It looks like an animal morgue.

The Windamere Hotel at 4 p.m., time for high tea. On the noticeboards outside the reception office are pictures of annual Christmas festivities at the hotel with Santa Claus (a tea grower), Sikh bagpipers in tartans, plum pudding, the whole works. Here, in a cosy tea parlour, the British Empire lives on as a turbaned waiter serves up a silver tray of tea and sandwiches.

This is the kind of place you imagine British administrators with handlebar moustaches and tweed jackets lounging in, or prim women, their hair up in buns, with parasols and gowns and petticoats, swishing through. The liveried tea server would murmur *Yes Sahib! Yes Memsahib!* and the British would all *oooh* and *aaah* at the cucumber sandwiches, the lemon cheese tarts (*Mustn't have another one!*), curry puffs and cinnamon buns. And then everyone would discuss the horrid details of the latest Indian revolt in the south.

Later came a very different breed – the alpinists. The early British expeditions to both Kangchenjunga and Everest were mounted from Darjeeling. In those days Darjeeling served as the main gateway to Tibet. Expeditions moved north through Sikkim, crossed high passes and proceeded to Gyantse. Darjeeling's most famous climber, however, was of Tibetan blood. Though he claimed to be a Sherpa, Tenzing Norgay, conqueror of Everest, was actually born and grew up in the Kharta Valley, on the eastern approach to the mountain. He may even have met George Mallory, who spent a day in his home village of Moyun while exploring the eastern approaches to the peak in August 1921 (Tenzing would've been seven years old at the time if that historic meeting took place).

This intriguing material came to light in a book, *Snow in the Kingdom*, by mountaineer Ed Webster. Written with the full sanction of Norgay's family, the book reveals that he obscured his origins and claimed to be a Sherpa because of political obstacles. His impoverished family migrated to a village on the Nepalese side of Everest in the early 1920s, and Tenzing moved to Darjeeling from Nepal in 1932. But it was only after he reached the top of Everest in 1953 with Edmund Hillary that the Indian government offered him a passport, personally guaranteed by Prime Minister Nehru. Tenzing in fact had no nationality – and no passport – and was in a jam about acting on an invitation from London to go to the United Kingdom for a victory celebration. That year – 1953 – Tenzing became Chief Instructor at the

Himalayan Mountaineering Institute. The HMI, on a hilltop in Darjeeling, today functions as part museum, part inspiration and is instruction-based. Tenzing died in Darjeeling in 1986: a grand statue of him standing victoriously atop Everest's summit was unveiled outside the HMI in 1997 by his climbing partner, Sir Edmund Hillary.

All the hype on Everest has meant that Kangchenjunga, the third-highest peak on the planet, has remained neglected and obscure. My teatime companions are Canadian climbers Pat and Baiba Morrow, who are in the process of doing a grand circuit around Kangchenjunga, as well as an attempt on the peak of Siniolchu.

My own approach to Kangchenjunga is considerably less ambitious. I'm happy to just zoom in on Kangchenjunga as winter is closing in, and I have no desire to eat more snowflakes than I did in Bhutan. At the office where I get my permit in Darjeeling, they are stoking the old British wood-burning fireplace. And so I ride a crowded jeep up to Naya Bazaar, and cross into Sikkim, the twenty-second state of India.

Sikkim seems to have no soul. Flashes of former brilliance can be found in its villages – Gezing, Pemayangtse, Tashiding – with the occasional active monastery where prayer flags flutter gracefully on long poles. I forge through to Yuksum, the village at the start of the trek to Kangchenjunga basecamp. Kangchenjunga beckons, but I will have to return another time. I make a beeline for Gangtok, the former capital of the kingdom of Sikkim.

★★★★★

Things are never what you expect. In my head, I carry a picture of Gangtok as a tiny hill station. But there's obviously been an explosion of concrete and a fair bit of high-rise building too. One part, however, seems to be little changed: the park and walking region near the Chogyal's palace. The palace itself is off-limits: trying to sneak onto the grounds, I was chased down by an Indian soldier and hustled out the gates. I found another way of 'seeing' the grounds: I hiked uphill to a TV tower that looked over the palace area. From this perch, through binoculars, I could make out the 20-room European-style villa-palace and, near it, the imposing Tibetan-style two-storey royal chapel, with its distinctive yellow roof. It is to this chapel that the last direct heir to the Sikkimese throne, Prince Wangchuck, comes to meditate. It was in the same chapel that the Chogyal of Sikkim was crowned in 1965.

The story of the fall of Sikkim has all the elements of a fairytale – one that went seriously wrong. Palden Thondup Namgyal was the crown prince of Sikkim: his Tibetan wife had died in 1957, leaving three children. Enter Hope Cooke, an awkward American debutante, fond of miniskirts and heavy mascara, who claimed to be studying Tibetology. They met at the Windamere Hotel in Darjeeling in 1959. He was forty and she was twenty-three when they were married in Gangtok in 1963, a match that was by no means popular and, in Sikkimese court circles, considered faintly ridiculous. The aristocratic families of Bhutan, Sikkim, Mustang and Tibet rarely married outsiders, so imagine the shock when the ruler of Sikkim married an American. The same year – 1963 – the prince's father died. In 1965, Palden Thondup Namgyal ascended the throne as the Chogyal, with Hope Cooke crowned as the Gyalmo of Sikkim.

That may sound like the fulfilment of a fantasy for Hope Cooke, but she had set her sights higher: she was obsessed with becoming a real oriental queen of an independent nation. 'Chogyal' and 'Gyalmo' are ancient Tibetan titles, roughly meaning 'ruler'. Since 1947 Sikkim had been a protectorate of the newly independent India, shorn of the latitude of sovereignty that it enjoyed under British rule. The Indians referred to the Maharaja of Sikkim, not the Chogyal. A dogfight over titles ensued: a fashion show organised by Hope Cooke in New York adapting Sikkimese material and designs to Western modes was boycotted by Indian diplomats because the invitations went out in the names of Their Majesties the King and Queen of Sikkim. With Hope Cooke's guidance, the trappings of royalty were dusted off and revamped, and history was rewritten in Sikkim's schoolbooks to establish the kingdom's validity as a sovereign nation. The Chogyal pressed Delhi for increased independence: this was playing with fire because Delhi viewed Sikkim as vital to its defence against the Chinese forces occupying Tibet, who were now clashing with Indian border troops.

More irksome to the Indians was Hope Cooke's generation of an enormous amount of publicity for Sikkim; because of her, the region came under the international press spotlight. Western newspapers fell over each other to wax lyrical at the 1965 coronation, effusing over the kingdom's 'improbable magic', the '400 species of wild orchid', and 'the ancient mystique of Sikkim', which was now 'radiant with Hope'. Yet Hope Cooke remained distant from the people of Sikkim: she never converted to Buddhism and she made frequent trips to Europe and America with the couple's two children. Her shopping sprees were legendary; American friends carted off Tibetan silver and *tankas* to sell in a New York boutique. Hope Cooke eventually left the king, returned to New York with her children, and filed for divorce. In 1974, when the fourth king of Bhutan was crowned in an elaborate ceremony in Thimphu with a number of important guests invited, the Chogyal turned up dressed in his finest robes and fur-hatted crown, but without Hope Cooke, whose glaring absence was feebly explained by her having to arrange their children's schooling in the United States.

In the end, Hope Cooke helped bring down the Sikkimese dynasty. The Indians took advantage of the unrest created by the odd marriage: they set up a referendum to decide Sikkim's fate, and in 1975 annexed the place by force.

Picking up the tale in 1980 is the publication of Hope Cooke's autobiography, *Time Change*. The jacket blurb describes this book as 'an intimate self-portrait of a girl growing into a woman ... and growing in awareness of the dangerous political realities of a small country caught between two powers.' Hope Cooke comes of age – and a 330-year-old kingdom bites the dust. That's quite a spectacular coming-of-age. Although the jacket describes Hope Cooke as a 'gifted writer' with 'a sharp eye and an uncommon ear for atmosphere and intrigue', only a ghost-writer could've saved this book. Hopie – as she calls herself – is far too fond of trivial distracting detail, like what outfit she was wearing at a particular time, or what kind of food was being served. At one point she writes of her husband, the Chogyal: 'He is really simple, not ratty sophisticated, and likes natural people, even though sometimes I see him looking at my nicotined, bandaged fingers, wondering how he's going to make a lady out of me.' Hope hit on an important fact: she lacked grace and sophistication, key requisites of royalty. But the Chogyal was evidently blind to this, even after she took up drinking (which she in turn blamed on the Chogyal's womanising).

What happened in Sikkim is exactly the scenario that the Bhutanese fear – invasion by an ethnic group that does not assimilate, and takeover by India. The British had tried to 'water down' Sikkim's culture by introducing large numbers of Nepalese farmers, who were, naturally, not interested in Sikkimese royalty, nor in Tibetan Buddhism. The Indians simply came along and used this to their advantage. The Chogyal of Sikkim died in New York in 1982, supposedly of throat cancer, more likely of a broken heart. He had lost his wife, his children and his kingdom.

*****

By chance one morning in Gangtok, I got talking to a travel agent who, upon discovering my great interest in Tibet, marched me down the road to a large hall. Crammed inside was the entire Tibetan community of Gangtok, some four hundred souls. It was like a lost tribe. Cups of tea were being poured and passed around. So was milky *chang*. The focal point was a big altar with two pictures on it, one of the Dalai Lama, the other of the missing young Panchen Lama. The same 10 December celebration was taking place in Tibetan communities around the world. It was a dual celebration commemorating Human Rights Day (and the fiftieth anniversary of the Universal Declaration of Human Rights) and the 1989 award of the Nobel Peace Prize to the Dalai

Lama. A statement from the Dalai Lama on the anniversary of the UDHR was read out.

These proceedings are all the stranger when you consider that the United Nations has done absolutely nothing for the Tibetans. The United Nations promulgated a couple of sternly worded resolutions in the 1960s, and the Chinese would skulk a bit, and then they'd turn around and blithely carry on with the killing. In 1970, after the PRC took up a seat as a permanent member of the UN Security Council with full veto powers, they could shoot down any resolution on Tibet before it even got off the ground. And the Chinese have consistently exerted pressure on UN officials to exclude the Dalai Lama from any UN event (including, ludicrously enough, peace conferences).

In Tibet, simply being in *possession* of a copy of the Universal Declaration of Human Rights in Tibetan is cause for a lengthy prison sentence. But the Tibetans are not intimidated. At this gathering, they sang songs of protest. It was truly awesome to see eight-year-olds in Tibetan costume belting out a song about Tibet, a place they'd never been to. And I kept thinking of all the liberties that we take for granted in the West, and how the carefree Tibetans had lost everything yet they could still remain cheerful through all that.

It was dark by the time they let me out of there, flushed in the face and somewhat bloated from too much food, tea and *chang*. I reeled around, wondering what had hit me, where I was, and what on earth I'd set out to do that day.

★★★★★

A few hours by bus from Gangtok is Rumtek Monastery, which was established as the seat-in-exile of the sixteenth Karmapa, leader of the Karma Kagyu sect of Tibetan Buddhism. Like many high lamas, the sixteenth Karmapa fled his traditional seat in Tibet, Tsurphu Monastery, after the 1959 uprising. Judging from the size of Rumtek, the sixteenth Karmapa was planning on a long stay in exile – the grounds are expansive; the temples and lodging for the monks are equal to anything in Tibet. The Karma Kagyu became probably the most successful sect in exile. The sect wields enormous influence in Ladakh, Bhutan, Arunachal Pradesh and parts of Nepal. The main faith in Bhutan derives from the Kagyu sect: the sixteenth Karmapa was a frequent visitor to Bhutan. By the time of his death in the United States in 1981, the sect had become extremely wealthy with assets valued at over a billion dollars, and had acquired a large following of Westerners.

In pictures and iconography, the sixteenth Karmapa appears to be hanging onto his hat. That's because it is the fabled Flying Crown – if he didn't clutch it at all times, it would fly away, or so the legend goes. The celestial Flying Crown rests somewhere within Rumtek, and may remain there because of a dispute over the recognition of the seventeenth Karmapa.

The problem was that the sixteenth Karmapa failed to leave any of the traditional signals or instructions concerning his rebirth. Four regents had been entrusted with managing his considerable assets and finding his reincarnate. Frustration with a ten-year search evidently led to 'forging' of Karmapa-like instructions by the regents. In 1992, one regent was mysteriously killed in a car crash. At the funeral rites at Rumtek, the three surviving regents came up with contradictory stories on the search for the reincarnate when questioned by followers. Situ Rinpoche claimed to have found instructions from the sixteenth Karmapa hidden in an amulet he'd given him. This lead to the discovery of a boy from eastern Tibet, who headed to Tsurphu Monastery. This candidate was also recognised by the Dalai Lama. Shamar Rinpoche was unconvinced; he was still seeking a rival candidate, also in Tibet. As the rituals for the dead regent continued at Rumtek, rioting broke out between rival groups of monks.

In 1992, Situ Rinpoche's candidate was installed with great pomp and ceremony at Tsurphu, the first incarnate to be recognised by the Chinese since 1959, and unusual because for once the Chinese and the Dalai Lama had agreed on a specific choice. In Tibet, reincarnates were all right, it now seemed, as long as they toed the socialist line and were controlled by Beijing. The boy was paraded by the Chinese as evidence of its enlightened religious policies. That meant the boy could visit Beijing, but not Sikkim.

Meanwhile, a rival Karmapa candidate managed to leave Tibet for India: how is not exactly clear. Rumtek Monastery is occupied by followers of Situ Rinpoche. This is evident from the large pictures of the Tsurphu boy on the altars. The followers of the rival candidate were ejected. Some live at a house several miles from Rumtek.

★★★★★

Down the road from Gangtok, in Kalimpong, I meet the rival Karmapa candidate, living in a large house, with one room converted into a throne hall. He is not allowed to visit Rumtek; he has, however, visited Bhutan, where the sixteenth Karmapa had a particularly strong link. Thaye Dorje, a teenager also from Tibet, is a soft-spoken young man with glasses. He is watching CNN when I arrive, and breaks off to welcome a group of Westerners who are effusive in their praise of him.

Who is the real Karmapa? Will he ever take up residence at Rumtek? The dispute is described by Tibetan scholar Tsering Shakya as a 'sort of medieval tragicomedy'. A possible solution is to declare both candidates as authentic manifestations, as the Dalai Lama has suggested, but the basic problem remains that there can only be one throneholder. Two people can't sit in the same chair.

★★★★★

In the 1950s, Kalimpong was called a 'nest of spies' by Nehru. The Chinese variously called it the command centre of British imperialism, and later a centre of Kuomintang activity. The town even attracted the attention of Mao Zedong, who described it as a hotbed of Tibetan exile activity.

The town started life as an obscure outpost, flared into a blaze of glory between 1900 and 1950, and then plummeted into obscurity again. It used to belong to Sikkim, but in 1706 it was seized by the Bhutanese, who ruled for 159 years. The Bhutanese royal family still maintain a residence in Kalimpong, and there is a Bhutanese-style temple in town. In 1865, Kalimpong fell into British hands. It was only after 1903, when the trade route to Tibet opened up from India, that Kalimpong shot to prominence as a key spot along the route that led through Sikkim over the Jelap Pass up to the Tibetan plateau.

In its heyday, Kalimpong employed more than 10,000 men sorting mounds of dirty white, grey and black wool from Tibet into neat, compact bales for the onward journey to America or England. Mule caravans from Tibet brought yak tails, borax, musk, Tibetan curios, Chinese rice and Kuomintang silver (and later, when he fled Tibet by this route, the Dalai Lama's gold). Muleteers enjoyed a ten-day rest in Kalimpong, so cottage industries sprang up to cater to their needs, from feed for the mules to exotic entertainment for the masters (mainly drinking and gambling). Going back the other way, into Tibet, were caravans loaded with cement, kerosene and Indian manufactured goods.

I drop into the Himalayan Hotel. On the walls here are photos signed by queens of Bhutan and by Alexandra David-Néel. Back in the 1930s and 1940s, the hotel was a popular meeting place for those travelling to and from Tibet. It was at this inn that Heinrich Harrer wrote the first draft of *Seven Years in Tibet*. Maybe he took the title from the original owner of the inn, David Macdonald, who wrote a book called *Twenty Years in Tibet*. Macdonald set up the hotel, basically an extension of his family house, back in the 1930s. Macdonald, himself of mixed Sikkimese-Scottish descent, married a Nepalese woman and had a large family. One son, John, was involved with the 1920s British Everest expeditions as an interpreter and naturalist. The three older daughters, Annie Perry, Vicky Williams and Vera Macdonald, ran the Himalayan Hotel. They described themselves as a 'Himalayan cocktail'. The hotel is still in the hands of the Macdonald family, run by David Macdonald's grandson, Tim, together with his Indian wife Nilam.

Chatting in the homely lounge area, Nilam insists that I pay a visit to George.

This turns out to be a most remarkable encounter. Meet George Tsarong, a living link to pre-1950 Tibet. He's in pretty good shape, considering he's seventy-eight years old and still smokes. He is tall and thin, and has a dignified air about him: the Tsarongs were Lhasan nobility, the aristocrats of Tibet. In the 1930s, he was given the English name George at St Joseph's College, Darjeeling, by teachers who found his Tibetan name, Dundul Namgyal, too difficult to pronounce.

George lights up a cigarette and then shows me a book he self-published in India. It is a treasure-trove of photography. He took the photos surreptitiously in Tibet, since monks frowned on photography as disrespectful. George developed the black and white films himself, but all colour films had to be sent to Kodak Bombay in India. Developing took a few agonising months as film travelled down on horseback from Lhasa to Bombay and back again. Some of the precious film was lost in the process. Only a handful of people could claim to have photographed the Tibet of the 1930s, 1940s and early 1950s: this is a rare record of independent Tibet. Some of the photos were taken by George's father; the majority were taken by himself. Some photos were culled from grainy 16mm film that George shot with a Kodak camera. In 1959, his father died in a Chinese prison: he had crossed back from India to Tibet to help the Dalai Lama escape.

'That picture was taken by my father,' says George. We are looking at a photo of an Austin A-7, with a number plate *Tibet No.2*, the same one that lies rusting away at the Norbulingka Palace in Lhasa. I've never seen a picture of this car intact. There are two Tibetans standing next to it. The year is 1932.

'The man on the right is Kunphel La, a close associate of the thirteenth Dalai Lama,' relates George. 'Kunphel La and my father were both in charge of Drapchi Mint. Kunphel La used the Austin to drive from Norbulingka to the mint. That day they were invited along to the British Mission for lunch, so they drove.'

What a time capsule! George and his father represented the forces of modernisation, which ultimately failed in Tibet. His father, who used to be commander-in-chief of the Tibetan army, tried to modernise the force in the early 1920s. The progressive thirteenth Dalai Lama approved of the plan, but the conservative clergy, who raised their own private armies, were jealous and felt threatened. So they sank it.

George was adept at learning about modern devices, and took great interest in cars and cameras. He used to go down to Calcutta for supplies and bring them back to Lhasa, which was fine under the progressive Reting Rinpoche, the Regent of Tibet, who owned several motorcycles himself. But in 1943, the fifth Reting Regent was involved in political intrigue and sexual scandal and was thrown into a dank dungeon where he perished.

A new ultra-conservative regent, Tak Drak, took over. He brought in a blanket ban that forbade the use of motorcycles, bicycles, the playing of football, the wearing of felt hats and the use of certain leather products (modern boots, shoes, foreign-made saddles). This closed the door on modernisation: bad timing because the Chinese would invade in 1950. George himself was caught in the ban: he'd just imported a 250cc BSA motorcycle from India. He never used it and the motorcycle went into storage. Eventually he gave it to a relative who was returning to India.

Going through the photos I find one of Peter Aufschnaiter, who was companion to Heinrich Harrer. The Tsarong family is the one that welcomed Heinrich Harrer and Peter Aufschnaiter in Lhasa – no accident, since they were all into foreign things and modernisation. George's father is portrayed in the film, *Seven Years in Tibet*. George's son and grandson both act in *Kundun*. His grandson plays the mature Dalai Lama, in his early twenties, while his son plays the Regent.

Peter Aufschnaiter was working under George on a new hydro-electric scheme, about three miles east of Lhasa. The project was abandoned with the invasion of the Chinese. George had pictures of the first Chinese arriving in Lhasa – not the way you might imagine. They were soldiers with machine guns, but they were on horses or camels. There was a picture of a lone jeep, which, George said, was carried in parts on animal-back and assembled the day the troops reached Lhasa.

Poring over George's book, I arrive at a page that my eye, at first, can't decipher. Perhaps because it seems preposterous: the chassis of a car, being taken over Nathu La, the pass leading from Sikkim into Tibet, in 1954. 'Taken over' means shouldered by porters carrying the whole thing on wooden poles. The car was swaddled in cloth to protect it, and there were about fifteen porters humping the thing over the pass at 14,300 feet. Men carrying car instead of car carrying men.

'The car was a Humber. It was a gift for His Holiness,' says George, 'but I don't remember who presented it.'

What about the engine, the wheels? Would it not have been easier to leave the wheels on and push it over the pass? George tells me that the chassis, engine, gearbox and axles were all carried by manpower, and that the wheels and small parts were packed on mule transport.

After the Chinese arrived in Lhasa in 1951, wheels started appearing in greater numbers. George remembers many bicycles were imported from India – he imported two hundred himself. In the early 1950s, George bought a Land Rover in Calcutta, hoping to introduce modern transport into Tibet. He disassembled it, packed it into boxes and loaded it on camels.

'Got it all to Lhasa, re-assembled it and then put the key in,' he says, grinning broadly. 'The engine started first time.'

Epilogue

ESCAPE FROM TIBET

A magical Black Hat, a missing lama,
and some very red faces ...

The curse of writing guidebooks, you quickly learn, is that absolutely nothing stays the same. Buddhists have a word for this phenomenon: *anicca*, the impermanence of all things. Telephone numbers mutate, buses switch routes, restaurant standards suddenly plummet. The things you thought were bedrock – immutable – can change swiftly too. Coral reefs get eaten away, forests burn down, buildings are swallowed by mudslides. Sometimes whole towns vanish from the map. Impossible politics happen: the Berlin Wall falls, the USSR collapses, Nelson Mandela is set free.

So the minute I saw the face on the front page of the newspaper, I knew one of those momentous changes had occurred. I was cycling past a newspaper display box in downtown Vancouver when I locked onto the face and wheeled around. I'd seen that steely gaze before on the face of the young seventeenth Karmapa, Ugyen Trinley Dorje, up close and in person four years earlier, at Tsurphu Monastery outside Lhasa. Only this time, thousands of miles away, I was reading about how the Karmapa had miraculously escaped to India from right under the noses of his Chinese guardians.

It is the oldest trick in the Tibetan Buddhist book: the retreat as a disappearing act. And at the dawn of the new millennium, it was used with dramatic effect by the Karmapa. The 15-year-old youth was growing increasingly restless about his monastic education. He had been denied access to his spiritual mentors: the Chinese had reneged on promises to allow these lamas to visit Tibet and refused to allow the Karmapa to visit India. Worse still, he was clearly being groomed as a patriotic alternative to the Dalai Lama. It was simply a matter of time before he would be called upon to denounce the Dalai Lama publicly.

When I say the oldest trick in the Tibetan Buddhist book, consider this incredible piece of deception from the seventeenth century. In 1648 the fifth Dalai Lama completed construction of the White Palace, phase one of the Potala in Lhasa. But the Great Fifth knew he would not live to see the completion of phase two, construction of the lofty Red Palace. So, worried that this work would be discontinued, he instructed his chief advisor to conceal his death. The advisor pretended that the Great Fifth had gone into a long retreat, and found a monk who resembled the deceased to act as a double. The Red Palace was completed in 1694, twelve years after the fifth Dalai Lama's death.

The stakes for the seventeenth Karmapa to attempt an escape from the Chinese were very high: any mistake would be costly for the highest profile religious figure living in Tibet. Meticulous planning was essential. In late December, 1999, the Karmapa informed his Chinese minders that he was going into solitary retreat in his private quarters for a week, and would not entertain any visitors. Nothing unusual or greatly suspect about that. But parked outside the monastery was a Mitsubishi SUV, requisitioned by a senior Tsurphu monk for a fundraising trip. And distracting the attention of everyone inside – including Chinese overseers – was a newly acquired television set.

Late on the night of 28 December, with monks and minders engrossed in the new television, the Karmapa changed into civilian dress, slipped out a back window at Tsurphu, jumped into the waiting SUV and stole off into the night. At Tsurphu, meanwhile, his teacher and cook kept up the charade of attending to him while 'on retreat'.

The Karmapa's real retreat was from Tibet: he and his four trusted companions proceeded on a circuitous route across Tibet in the SUV, travelling day and night, dodging military checkpoints along the way. Fortunately, during winter there was little military presence and several posts were unmanned. Approaching a dangerous checkpoint by night, the Karmapa and two others got out of the SUV and skirted the area on foot, scraping their hands and legs on thorn scrub in the darkness. To their immense relief, the SUV driver eventually showed up: he had driven past the checkpoint in darkness.

And then the SUV simply drove across the unmanned Nepalese border right into the kingdom of Mustang. Here, they abandoned the SUV and switched to horseback. Hiring fine horses from the Mustang region, they rode hard from Lo Monthang for a few days to reach Kagbeni, and then forged on to a helicopter rendezvous site at Manang, on the Annapurna Circuit. From Nepal, they telephoned Tsurphu to find out what was happening: when a stranger answered, they hung up (the fates of the teacher and the cook at Tsurphu are unknown). Flying into the Pokhara vicinity, the Karmapa and his entourage took a taxi to the Indian border, bribing their way past Nepalese border guards.

From here, train and taxis took them through north-west India to Dharamsala. The Karmapa arrived, exhausted, on the morning of 5 January 2000. An hour later, the Karmapa was greeted in an audience with the Dalai Lama. It was a moment of astonishment and delight, the meeting of two bodhisattvas, and the end of an amazing journey.

The Karmapa's escape echoed the flight of the Dalai Lama from Tibet forty years earlier. The Dalai Lama is the one person in the world that the Chinese did not want the Karmapa to meet. The Chinese insisted the Karmapa left the motherland on a shopping trip, to get his hands on a Black Hat, certain musical instruments and other ceremonial items belonging to his predecessor, the sixteenth Karmapa, who was based at Rumtek in Sikkim. The Chinese call a reincarnate lama 'Soul Boy' (*lingtong* in Chinese). Nothing to do with the *Blues Brothers*, but the seventeenth Karmapa certainly had a bad case of the blues. You can almost imagine the headlines in China: *Soul Boy Steps out of Motherland on Black Hat Shopping Expedition.*

The Black Hat they talk about is sacred. The rightful owner must keep one hand on the hat while wearing it, as it is reputed to have the ability to fly away by itself. That's because, according to legend, the Black Hat is woven from the hair of countless *dakinis*, celestial female deities, or 'sky walkers'. Also known as the Flying Crown, the first mentions of it date back to the twelfth century;

the present hat dates from a few centuries later and was smuggled out of Tibet to Rumtek. Controversy rages as to whose head the crown will grace, since there is a rival Karmapa candidate in India, but both young Karmapa appointees seem impervious to the conflict. There's a lot more than a hat at stake here: worldwide Kagyu sect assets are estimated to be worth over US$1.2 billion. Who is the real Karmapa? Will he ever take up residence at Rumtek? Will he wear the sacred Black Hat? Will it fly off his head? Whatever the case, Ugyen Trinley Dorje is not out on a religious relic shopping spree: he's highly unlikely to go back to Tibet.

Times have changed dramatically since Heinrich Harrer's account of his amazing escape in *Seven Years in Tibet*, tracing his flight from a British internment camp in India to the safe haven of neutral Tibet in the early 1940s. Since 1959 the escape route has been in the opposite direction, away from Chinese oppression. In the sad saga of Tibet, the Karmapa's miraculous escape was a cause for great jubilation among the Tibetans, and the cause of acute embarrassment among the Chinese. The Chinese occupy Tibet by brute force, but they cannot lay claim to the territory of the heart.

Abbreviations

PAP – The dreaded People's Armed Police, a paramilitary group.

PLA – People's Liberation Army, the national army of China.

PRC – People's Republic of China, created when the Communists came to power on 1 October 1949; aka the Middle Kingdom.

PSB – Public Security Bureau, omnipresent division of the Chinese police.

TAR – Tibet Autonomous Region, created in 1965 by the Chinese by carving off central Tibet from Greater Tibet. There is nothing autonomous about it.

UDHR – Universal Declaration of Human Rights, formulated in 1948.

Glossary

Bodhisattva – One who compassionately refrains from entering nirvana in order to save others; one who is on the way to becoming a Buddha.

Bon – Pre-Buddhist religion of Tibet, involving shamanist practices and sorcery.

Chang – Fermented barley beer, a potent milky liquid.

Chorten – Inverted bell-shaped shrine containing relics, or the ashes or embalmed body of a high lama (*stupa* in Sanskrit).

Chuba – Cloak-like outer garment, usually made of sheepskin, also used like a sleeping bag by Tibetan nomads.

Dakini – A voluptuous female deity or 'sky dancer' who personifies the wisdom of enlightenment.

Dalai Lama – One in a series of incarnate lamas dating to the fourteenth century; head of the Geluk sect of Tibetan Buddhism, recognised as manifestations of the bodhisattva Avolokitesvara; supreme rulers of central Tibet since the seventeenth century; the current Dalai Lama, Tenzin Gyatso, is fourteenth in the lineage.

Dharma – The word of the Buddha and his teachings, also called 'Buddha Dharma'.

Dorje – 'Thunderbolt', a sceptre-like ritual object, made of brass, used against the powers of darkness.

Dzong – Castle or fort, usually grafted onto a high ridge.

Gompa – Active monastery.

Gonkhang – Protector chapel at a monastery, and site of special initiation and other ceremonies.

Kalachakra – The 'Wheel of Time', a complex supreme tantra associated with the mystical land of Shambhala.

Karmapa – Leader of the Karma Kagyu sect – an incarnate lama lineage dating back to the twelfth century.

Khata – White greeting scarf, made of cotton or silk, presented on ceremonial occasions or offered at monasteries.

Kora – Clockwise circuit of a sacred temple, lake or mountain.

Lakhang – Chapel or inner sanctuary.

315

Lama – Master spiritual teacher or guru.

Losar – Tibetan New Year, usually celebrated around February.

Mandala – Mystical circle, often enclosing a square, representing the Buddhist cosmos – used as a meditational aid.

Mani stone – Stone tablet inscribed with mantras, often included as part of a mani-wall, composed of many such stones.

Mantra – Sacred syllables repeated many times as part of spiritual practice, such as *om mani padme hum*.

Momo – Tibetan meat dumpling.

Monlam – The Great Prayer Festival, around the time of Losar.

Nestorians – A breakaway Christian group, dating from the fifth century AD.

Nirvana – Release from the cycle of mortal existence and rebirths.

Panchen Lama – Head lama of Tashilhunpo Monastery in Shigatse in a reincarnate lineage, recognised as a manifestation of Amitabha Buddha. The selection of the eleventh Panchen Lama is currently disputed.

Prayer flag – Small flag printed with sacred prayers, activated by the power of the wind.

Prayer wheel – Large fixed wheel or small handheld wheel containing mantras, activated by the spinning of the wheel.

Prostrator – Pilgrim who measures the distance to a sacred destination with the length of his or her body, flung prone along the ground.

Rangzen – Tibetan for 'independence movement'.

Rinpoche – 'Precious one', a reincarnate lama, also known when young as a *tulku*.

Sadhu – Wandering Indian ascetic, dedicated to the pursuit of the sacred; depends on handouts from locals to survive

Saka Dawa – Day of Buddha's enlightenment, celebrated around June.

Shambhala – Buddhist 'Pure Land', a Tibetan utopia where disease and ageing are unknown, said to be located deep in the mountains to the north of the Himalayas.

Stupa – See *chorten*.

Sutra – Sacred text, written or spoken teachings of the Buddha.

Szechuan – Older spelling for the Chinese province of Sichuan.

Tanka – Painted portable scroll, usually depicting a deity, on fine cotton or silk; can be used as a teaching aid.

Tantra – The 'web of life', or Vajrayana, is the form of Buddhism most often associated with Tibet. It employs radical steps to seek enlightenment within a single lifetime.

Tenjur – Sacred text, part of the Tibetan Buddhist canon that contains commentary on Buddha's discourses.

Torma – Ritual 'cake' sculpted from *tsampa* and yak butter.

Tsampa – Ground barley flour, a Tibetan staple food.

Yak – Hairy high-altitude cattle, 'cow with a skirt'.

Yabyum – Tantric sexual pose of deity and consort, symbolising fusion of opposites, often misconstrued by Westerners.

the hotel on the roof of the world

five years in Tibet

alec le sueur

summersdale *travel*

The Hotel on the Roof of the World

Five Years in Tibet

by Alec Le Sueur

Few foreigners have been lucky enough to set foot on Tibetan soil – Alec Le Sueur spent five extraordinary years there, working for an international hotel chain. Against the breathtaking beauty of the Himalayas he unfolds a highly amusing and politically enlightening account of his experiences.

Fly infestations at state banquets, hopeful mountaineers, unexpected deliveries of live snakes, a predominance of yaks and everything yak-related, the unbelievable Miss Tibet competition, insurmountable communication problems and a dead guest are just some of the entertainments to be found at the 'Fawlty Towers' of Lhasa.

Daily challenges are increased by the fragile political situation. Le Sueur, the only foreigner since the days of Heinrich Harrer to spend so long in Tibet, examines its intriguing cultural background, thus providing a fascinating insight into a country that is virtually impenetrable to today's traveller.

For a current catalogue and a full listing of
Summersdale travel books, visit our website:

www.summersdale.com